Ecology, Meaning, and Religion

Ecology, Meaning, and Religion

ROY A. RAPPAPORT

University of Michigan

NORTH ATLANTIC BOOKS
RICHMOND, CALIFORNIA

Ecology, Meaning, and Religion
Copyright © 1979 by Roy A. Rappaport

ISBN 0-913028-54-1

Publisher's Current Address:

North Atlantic Books
635 Amador Street
Richmond, California 94805

Distribution for Resale:

Book People
2940 Seventh Street
Berkeley, California 94710

Ingram Book Company
347 Reedwood Drive
Nashville, Tennessee 37217

The text is set in ten-point Garamond 3
on Mergenthaler Linocomp equipment

Cover: George Mattingly

This book is for

Gregory Bateson
and
Theophile Kahn

Contents

Preface

Like all essays these must speak for themselves, so I shall be brief in sending them on their way.

The first two were written a good many years ago. The second is reprinted unchanged, but for the first I have prepared a "new" final section, based upon an unpublished article also written in 1961. My reasons for expanding an essay almost two decades old with an equally ancient argument are twofold. First, the constraints of original publication were such as to require so drastic a condensation of an argument concerning the ecological bases of differences in social stratification in Polynesia that it became almost incomprehensible, but, made clearer in the present expansion, it may still be of interest to some students. Second, the propriety of the distinction between populations and social orders upon which that argument rests remains a matter of debate in anthropology. Because it has been the object of rather sharp criticism within the last several years, it seemed to me useful to present it in the comparative ethnographic context in which it was originally conceived.

Of the remaining essays, one—"On Cognized Models"—has been written especially for this collection, and the others are all rather recent. I have felt free to revise them because I do not regard them, in either their original or present forms, to be so much finished works as thoughts in progress. Sections IV, X, and XI of "Ecology, Adaptation, and the Ills of Functionalism" are new, and so are many other passages in that essay and the others. These revisions represent second thoughts and elaborations, but I have also edited extensively to reduce the repetitiveness otherwise inevitable in publishing together articles on related subjects originally appearing separately for different audiences. I have, however, chosen not to eliminate all redundancy. To do so would have made some complex arguments even more difficult to follow and would have imposed hardship upon those readers who may want to read some, but not all, of the essays or who, in any event, will not read the volume through at one time. Moreover, reiteration is not devoid of advantages of its own: the appearance of particular points or arguments in more than one essay cannot help but make explicit the themes that articulate them all.

Those who read the collection as a whole will surely become aware of the general direction in which it moves. The first and second essays could be construed as exercises in a rather strict ecology. The concerns of "The Obvious Aspects of Ritual," the penultimate essay—with the understandings entailed by ritual's form—could hardly be "less ecological," at least on the face of it. The intervening essays, however, constitute an attempt to elucidate some of the connections between them. "On Cognized Models" is centrally concerned with the relationship between the "meaningful," which is culturally constructed, and the "lawful," which is naturally constituted. "Adaptive Structure and Its Disorders" represents an attempt to elucidate structural features of systems in which meaningful and material processes are ordered, to discuss the relationship of those structural features to adaptation, and to argue that maladaptation can be regarded as structural anomaly, or disorderings of such structures. The last essay, "Sanctity and Lies in Evolution," brings themes developed in "The Obvious Aspects of Ritual" to bear upon questions of adaptation and evolution raised earlier in the volume.

Although the collection as a whole moves in a certain direction and although this movement is roughly chronological, it should be clear that I have not, in developing the interests expressed in the later essays, disavowed the concerns of the earlier ones. In my view the incapacities of the ecological approach developed in the first and second essays are not so much a product of flaws as of limitations. There is, simply, a great deal that cannot be explained or interpreted by reference to ecological principles. It was, in fact, a profound sense of the inability of any ecological formulation to account for the meanings inherent in ritual's structure that led me to the mode of formal analysis that operates in "The Obvious Aspects of Ritual." But limitations, after all, are not themselves errors nor do they produce errors unless they are ignored or overridden, and to say that an approach is limited is not to distinguish it from any other systematic attempt to enlarge understanding, except in particulars. If no particular form of interpretation or explanation can provide all of the understanding we may hope for, and if the limitations of each are different, we must consider the possibility that relationships between or among at least some differing modes are complementary rather than alternative or competitive. This issue is approached in the last sections of "Ecology, Adaptation, and the Ills of Functionalism."

*   *   *

To acknowledge all those who have influenced these essays or who have in one way or another made it possible for me to write them would include most of the people to whom I have ever spoken. Moreover, to express gratitude to each of those from whom I have learned things reflected in the pages that follow might also seem to inflate claims of significance for what I take to be a modest and tentative work. My appreciation to those from whom I have learned is no less deep and real for remaining general in its expression.

It is proper, however, to thank the institutions that have supported me or extended hospitality to me while I wrote these essays, in either the original or present versions. They include my own institution, the University of Michigan; the Department of Anthropology of the University of Cambridge; the Wenner-Gren Foundation; the American Council of Learned Societies; the Guggenheim Foundation; and the East-West Center in Honolulu.

I also owe special thanks to Richard Grossinger, the anthropologist and publisher who invited me to gather these essays together, and to several colleagues: Frithjof Bergmann, Ray Kelly, Robert Levy, Ellen Messer, Sherry Ortner, and Aram Yengoyan, each of whom read one or more of the essays rewritten for this volume, offering suggestions for their improvement. I have, in the main, followed their advice, but wish to exonerate them from all responsibility for the collection's flaws and shortcomings. Karen Shedlowe deciphered my handwriting brilliantly and improved my prose as she, with saintly patience, typed the manuscript. Ann, Amelia, and Gina Rappaport have, as always, been enormously supportive.

Finally, I mean the volume as a whole to express my gratitude to the two great teachers to whom it is dedicated.

ROY A. RAPPAPORT

Aspects of Man's Influence

upon Island Ecosystems:

Alteration and Control

I

This paper will first be concerned with components of prehuman Pacific island ecosystems, and with the cultural and noncultural elements likely to have been introduced by human agency in pre-European times. Then, some of the possible alterations in these ecosystems subsequent to and resulting from human introductions will be discussed and suggestions will be made concerning possible implications for human social organization of man's participation in the various kinds of ecosystem.

For the sake of convenience, we shall refer to the prehuman ecosystems as the "pristine ecosystems." Their reconstruction is no easy task. Many essential data have not yet been provided by paleoecological investigations, and the inferences that may be made from existing island ecosystems are limited. In those ecosystems in which man has had a place, pristine conditions have presumably been obscured by man himself as well as by continuing physiographic and climatological processes, and the few islands without permanent populations may, by their nature, have special characteristics and therefore cannot be used uncritically as models for reconstructions of prehuman ecosystems in general. Nevertheless, some tentative characterizations of the pristine ecosystems can be made. Zimmerman (1965) has outlined for us in some detail the

This essay was originally presented at the tenth Pacific Science Congress in Honolulu in 1961 by A. P. Vayda and Roy A. Rappaport. H. E. Maude commented on it. It was revised by Rappaport alone, incorporating some of Maude's comments, and was first published in F. R. Fosberg, ed., *Man's Place in the Island Ecosystem* (Honolulu: Bishop Museum Press, 1963).

characteristics of the pristine terrestrial ecosystems of high islands. It would be well to review some of these characteristics briefly.

Owing to the difficulty of transportation across open sea, these systems were generally characterized by the presence of few genera. The relative number of genera in the various situations was roughly in inverse proportion to the distance from the large land masses of Australia and Melanesia, the points of origin for most of the forms, although some plants and animals did arrive in various islands from other directions. Members of many large taxonomic groupings were able to arrive only rarely if at all; thus, for instance, very few terrestrial vertebrates became established in, and mammals were totally absent from, large portions of the island world. The forms which did establish themselves, however, frequently did so in the absence of those biotic and edaphic features which had kept them in check in their earlier habitats, and often found "ecological vacuums" in their new homes. These two factors made for rapid, sometimes explosive, population expansion. Indeed, conditions on the high islands, which are characterized by great meteorological and physical variety within restricted space, encouraged rapid and prolific speciation. (Thus, in Hawaii, 1,200 or more species of land snails in nine families have arisen from possibly no more than twenty-four ancestral stocks.) Many of the adaptations associated with this speciation were extreme and narrow, however, and were possible only in the absence of forms better able to exploit the same sets of resources. Thus, as new immigrants arrived there was frequent replacement of forms, and it is unlikely that equilibria were ever approached.

While the biotic elements in the pristine high islands were taxonomically restricted, those on the low islands were even more so. The indigenous vegetation of uninhabited Rose Atoll, for instance, included only three vascular species in as many genera (Sachet 1954: 15). While this example is extreme, similar data may be found concerning larger inhabited islands. Hatheway (1955: 2) studied the vegetation of Canton Island some twenty years after the arrival of relatively permanent residents. Of the approximately 160 vascular plant species present at the time of his study, he regarded only 14 species in as many genera to be indigenous. On the same island, Van Zwaluwenberg (1955: 11) found only 93 species of insects, not all of which were indigenous (Degener and Gillaspy 1955: 48). On Kapingamarangi, an island peopled a relatively long time ago, Niering (1956: 4) found 98 vascular plant species, 58 of which had been introduced by man.

Several factors combine to make the terrestrial biota of the atoll among the world's most retricted. Fosberg has suggested that in addition to the factor most pertinent in high islands, that of difficulty of transportation across open water, the relatively short period of time during which dry land has been exposed on coral atolls is of primary importance. He points also to the lack of topographic or altitudinal diversity which was crucial in the processes of speciation in the high islands, and, finally, to special edaphic conditions such as high salinity and calcareousness prevailing on atolls (Fosberg 1953: 5).

It is possible, however, that despite the lack of diversity in the low island biota, equilibria were more closely approximated on atolls than on the high islands, for conditions were so special that the introduction of most new forms was in large measure prohibited. Those floral elements which did become dominant were highly adapted for both water-borne dispersal and for survival under the forbidding conditions offered by the atoll. Consequently they were almost invulnerable to displacement by other forms. It is interesting to note that none of the 150 floral species recently brought to Canton by man has shown any tendency to invade the still undisturbed areas of the island, which continue to be dominated by indigenous forms (Hatheway 1955: 2).

Reef-lagoon biota, found in association with both coral atolls and high islands, may be regarded as belonging to distinct ecosystems which contrast strikingly with those of dry land. Considerable stability and great taxonomic variety in reef-lagoon ecosystems is indicated by some recent investigations, such as Hiatt and Strasburg's study (1960) of 233 of the approximately 600 species of fish judged to be present in Marshall Islands reef communities. The 233 species belonged to 127 genera and 56 families, and it should not be forgotten that the biota included many organisms in addition to fish. Odum and Odum (1955), who studied the reef community of Eniwetok Atoll in the Marshall Islands, also discuss the variety and richness of reef-lagoon ecosystems. Moreover, they point out that the Eniwetok reef-lagoon system seemed to sustain itself; the primary producers were members of the community and apparently there was little derived from exotic plankton. To Odum and Odum this seemed a "true climax community" with little or no variation in living biomass. Similarly, Hiatt and Strasburg (1960: 66) refer to reef ecosystems as "steady state equilibria," self-adjusted and apparently fluctuating in composition very little, if at all, from year to year. The stability of these reef-lagoon systems, despite the exploitation to which they have been subjected for considerable time, gives some grounds for supposing that the difference between observed and pristine conditions is probably much less in reef-lagoon than in terrestrial ecosystems.

II

Pacific island ecosystems were eventually entered by human populations, together with their associated mutuals, parasites, and commensals.

Information concerning the biotic associations arriving at the various islands is scanty, but it is clear that a simple reconstruction of an early Pacific cultigen inventory would only mark the range of *possible* introductions into any particular island. While the range of Pacific cultigens was limited, it was broad enough to ensure that no human group transported the full inventory, and the range of organisms associated with either the humans or the domesticates and cultigens in relationships of commensalism or parasitism was even broader. It must be assumed, therefore, that each island in the Pacific received a set of organisms that differed to a greater or lesser degree from the sets introduced into other islands.

The migrating human populations should be seen as units comparable to other animal populations being introduced into the island ecosystems. A population, human or not, may be defined as an aggregate of organisms that belong to the same species, occupy a common habitat, and have in common certain distinctive means whereby they exploit one or more niches in one or more ecosystems. Needless to say, human populations rely most heavily upon extrabiological (that is, cultural) means in exploiting niches in ecosystems; but there is no advantage, for ecological inquiry, in treating cultures as entities to be separated from the culture carriers. Particular means may be regarded as attributes of particular populations, particular cultural means as properties of particular human populations.*

Considerable diversity must have obtained among human founding populations in the Pacific islands. Even in such restricted areas of the island world as Polynesia, the circumstances of settlement were such that we cannot assume common human traits, both biological and cultural, to have been brought equally to all islands. A multiplicity of points of embarkation is indicated by linguistics and stratigraphic archaeology (Emory 1961; Goodenough 1957; Grace 1961; Green 1961). Furthermore, immigrant groups, which often seem to have comprised only a few people (Vayda 1959), no doubt represented chance samples of their ancestral populations. They brought with them neither the whole gene pools nor the entire cultures of those populations (Goodenough 1957).

Continuing investigations should elucidate some of the variations, particularly in technology, which pertained among human founding populations. Questions concerning differences in tool inventories will, to some extent, be answered by stratigraphic archaeology. But while it is already evident that there were marked differences among the forms of tools even in the inventories of groups as closely related historically as the Polynesian populations, the functional differences among these forms

---

*For a discussion of the implications of populations as units of analysis in ecological formulations in anthropology, see section IV of the essay "Ecology, Adaptation, and the Ills of Functionalism" in this volume.

are not clear. While it may be possible to do anything with a tangless adz that can be done with a tanged adz, for example, it is less likely that the variety of fish that can be taken on two-piece hooks corresponds exactly to that which can be taken on one-piece hooks. In eastern Polynesia both one- and two-piece hooks are found, whereas in western Polynesia only two-piece hooks are known. Archaeology has yet to decide for us whether these differences are differences in the hook inventories of the immigrant groups, or whether they are a result of subsequent differentiation from initially similar bases, a less likely possibility. If the latter is the case, we may have an example of technological "adaptive differentiation." If the former, we have an initial difference which may have made for slightly different impacts on more or less similar marine ecosystems.

It is extremely unlikely that the biological variation among different founding populations can ever be fully known; but studies of differences among contemporary populations may help to illuminate the possible importance of biological variation in the ability of particular populations to participate in particular ecosystems. Maude (1963) tells us "... while I could scarcely drink the well water in many Gilbertese villages, particularly in times of drought, the people of Bangai on Tabiteuea, situated on a remote sandy islet, have apparently become accustomed to drinking water so brackish that even the Gilbertese, when visiting them, are reported to bring their own bottled supplies." It cannot be asserted, of course, that the ability to use resources which others cannot use indicates genetic difference. It is probable that the people of Bangai had, through lifelong use, simply become conditioned to water which others were unable, or preferred not, to tolerate. However, the possible biological basis of this ability, genetic or not, does merit investigation. Answers to this and similar questions, particularly those concerning the dietary requirements of various populations, may demonstrate that interpopulation biological differences may be significant variables in the interaction of men and ecosystems.

We should also consider differences between founding populations in those portions of their cultures which comprised the means for ordering elements in the ecosystems into meaningful categories. To be noted here are such questions as: what was immediately recognized as food and what was not; what restrictions, if any, were placed upon the exploitation of various portions of the biota, or on specific practices of exploitation; how close a correspondence there was between what were *seen* to be the critical relationships pertaining among biotic elements and the operational relationships which did, *in fact,* pertain among the same elements.

To deal with these questions, it may be useful to make a distinction between the "operational environment" of a population and what could be termed its "cognized environment." The term "operational environment" was originally proposed by Marston Bates (1960: 554), who quotes a definition of environment constructed earlier by Mason and Langenheim:

The environment of any organism is the class composed of the sum of those phenomena that enter a reaction system of the organism or otherwise directly impinge upon it to affect its mode of life at any time throughout its life cycle as ordered by the demands of the ontogeny of the organism or as ordered by any other condition of the organism that alters its environmental demands.

The cognized environment may be seen as the class composed of the sum of the phenomena ordered into meaningful categories by a population. The operational and cognized environments will include many of the same elements, but they may differ extensively in the structuring of relationships between elements.

It is probable that in the case of human populations in small Pacific islands no operational nor cognized environment is, or ever was, coterminous with a particular ecosystem. Both the cognized and operational environments of such populations included elements best seen as components of several distinct ecosystems; that of the dry land, and those of the sea. On the other hand, it is clear that no cognized environment will ever include all of the elements in any ecosystem, and it is possible that some elements in an ecosystem will be so remote, functionally, from a population in the same ecosystem that these elements may be considered to be outside that population's operational environment.

As in the case of their biological components, it will never be possible to reconstruct the cognitive systems of founding populations in the Pacific, much less map their cognized environments. However, the analysis of contemporary folk taxonomies in such areas a ethnobotany and ethnozoology, a study already pioneered by Conklin and others, should yield important insights into the roles played by distinctive cognitive capacities and limitations in structuring the interaction of particular populations with particular ecosystems.

III

Among the numerous and varied elements of the established island ecosystems and the elements introduced into them an almost infinite number of specific interactions is conceivable. The data are deficient on the interactions that actually took place, but it is evident that not all exotic forms could find a place in the islands to which they were conveyed. Among the forms that might be rejected were human beings themselves. There are islands in the Pacific which were reached by people in pre-European times but seem never to have supported permanent human populations. In some, such as Phoenix Island, it was probably the terrestrial, rather than the reef-lagoon system which was inhospitable to man. We have no evidence to indicate that the reef-lagoon system of Phoenix Island differed markedly from those of nearby inhabited atolls, but we do know that Phoenix was considerably smaller than its inhabited neighbors; too small, according to Maude, to provide a home for a sufficient number of humans to form a viable community. Further, and associated with its small size and local atmospheric conditions, there was quite possibly a deficiency of fresh water on Phoenix. Rainfall was slight and irregular, and when, in 1937, Maude dug six wells to a depth of twelve feet, he was unable to find a fresh water lens (Maude 1952: 77).

While it is probable that in most uninhabited low islands deficiencies in terrestrial rather than in reef-lagoon systems were crucial, it is clear that not all reef-lagoon systems are equally utilizable by humans. It seems, in fact, that factors in some reef-lagoon systems have severely hindered, or even prevented, human colonization. The recent history of the Gilbertese colony on Sydney Island in the Phoenix group is an example. While the size of the island was sufficient for a viable colony, and while coconut cultivation was possible, Maude (1963) writes that "the configuration of the shore-line afforded no adequate lee for the deep sea fisherman, and with many of the reef fish toxic . . . and no fish in the lagoon . . . the colony had to be abandoned after twenty years." The sea channel into the lagoon, according to Maude, had dried up, resulting in a level of salinity in the lagoon too high to maintain marine biota.

Maude also suggests that some islands were differentially hospitable to different immigrant populations:

> . . . there existed many environments so uncongenial to some immigrants that sooner or later they preferred to risk all the perils of the deep rather than remain; whereas on these same islands others more accustomed to making the best use of strictly limited ecosystems were later able to establish comfortable and permanent homes. . . . The more limited the environmental potentialities, the fewer and more specialized the human populations willing to add themselves to the establishment.

The importance of possible interpopulation cognitive and perhaps biological variation is suggested here.

On other islands, conditions permitted the establishment of humans, but excluded certain of the species associated with them. Thus, certain plants such as sweet potatoes and kava, widely cultivated in Polynesia, could not be grown on many atolls. Certain commensals and parasites conveyed inadvertently by man may likewise have failed to become established. This may have been especially true of weeds associated with food crops that came to be cultivated in new ways and under new conditions.

Of the exotic forms *not* rejected, some were established less easily and less extensively than others. On coral atolls, for instance, the establishment of introduced root crops, most commonly taro-like plants, generally required painstaking modification of the cultivation sites. Also, certain arboreal forms were not readily established in coral atolls. Whereas the cultivation of breadfruit was possible there, it was limited by calcareous soils (Catala 1957: 11) and by the sensitivity of the trees to salt water in the form of spray or occasional inundation (Fosberg 1953: 5, 8). That there could be difficulty in establishing and maintaining even that important and widely distributed food plant, the coconut, is suggested by its reported near-absence from a number of atolls prior to the advent of the copra trade (Danielsson 1955: 64–65). The limiting factor probably was drought.

On the other hand, some animals, after being brought by man to certain islands, apparently became established readily and were by no means confined to areas modified by human activities. Most notable of such animals were rats. Cook (1784: 217) found rats on uninhabited Palmerston in 1777. An abundance of the animals was noted by Mayor in 1920 on Rose Atoll, which has never been inhabited (Sachet 1954: 20), and Sharp (1956: 136) states that at least five Polynesian islands had rats but no people at the time of European discovery. Certain insects probably were transported by people. On uninhabited Alone islet in Ant Atoll, Marshall (1957: 5) found swarms of cockroaches. The ability of some animals to establish themselves without much help from man is indicated also by the fact that on some islands, especially the larger ones, domesticated animals have escaped and have maintained themselves in the "wild." In Moorea in the Society Islands, "wild" pigs and chickens have become established in the mountainous and more or less inaccessible interior, and have recently been joined by "wild" goats and cattle as well. There are interesting examples from lower and smaller islands too. Maude (1952: 76–77) found rabbits on uninhabited Phoenix in 1937, and Green (1961) has seen goats on Kamaka, an uninhabited island in the Mangarevan Islands.

Man himself as an exotic biotic element in island ecosystems must not be forgotten. Like many other immigrant species populations, humans found ecological vacuums in the ecosystems they entered. Population growth must frequently have been explosive. A model proposed by Birdsell (1957) suggests that populations in "open" environments are likely to double, at least initially, in each generation. Densities exceeding 1,000 per square mile were eventually reached on some islands.

It seems probable that, generally, the flora transported inadvertently and introduced by pre-European human populations did not become dominant. Merrill (1954: 212) believes that in 1769, when Banks and Solander made their collections in Tahiti, there were relatively few introduced weeds and that the flora had not been greatly altered as to constituent species. It may be that, in general, the establishment of most introduced floral elements was restricted in pre-European times to sites modified by human activities. This seems so for the important food plants, all of which except pandanus were introduced by man. The same kind of restriction for weeds is suggested by Merrill's interpretation, but the data are deficient.

While it is possible, as Maude suggests, that many islands were congenial to some human immigrants and not to others, immigrant populations were rarely confronted with kinds of ecosystems about which they knew nothing. For example, since most high islands have fringing reefs, often with coral islets on them, atolls would not have been entirely strange even to many immigrant high islanders (Goodenough 1957: 151–152). Nevertheless, no two Pacific islands have ever been alike in all important respects; elements apparently similar in two islands might turn out to differ significantly. Thus, some fish, especially red snappers, groupers, jacks and barracuda, are toxic within rather narrow geographical limits, harmless in nearby areas (Banner 1959: 31). This means that the occurrence of toxicity or nontoxicity, even among recognized fish, could not be taken for granted by immigrant groups.

The classifications and reclassifications that humans made of both flora and fauna had a bearing upon the interaction between themselves and island ecosystems. Edible plants and such fauna as sharks and sea-slugs might be utilized, depending upon whether they had been classified as edible or otherwise in the islands from which the people came. There might have been some reclassifications. An emergency food, for example, might have been reclassified as a staple. This was true of *Portulaca oleracea* (purslane) among Gilbertese settlers of the Phoenix Islands (Turbott 1959; 1954). On occasion, people were confronted by plants that they did not know at all. Cumberland tells us that the principal staple vegetable food of the Maoris was the starchy root of the *Pteridium esculentum,* a fern that must have been unknown to the first settlers of New Zealand.

Occasionally, man's introductions resulted in the complete elimination and replacement of certain pre-existing forms, or, more frequently, the range and numbers of those forms were reduced. Such reductions were not always directly due to man. In Hawaii the rat played an important part in bringing some plants and certain ground-nesting birds to the brink of extinction (Zimmerman 1963). But human activities in many cases did have a direct influence. Certain plants and animals were eliminated or substantially reduced, not because they were pests, nor because, being useful, they were overexploited, but simply because they were in the way. This must have been true in localities where sedentary horticulture was instituted. In most areas of tropical Polynesia and Micronesia where swidden agriculture was being practiced, secondary forest usually replaced virgin forest. On Moala Island in Fiji, however, where the lands around long-established villages were deforested as a result of swiddening, replacement was by a thick cover of reed (Sahlins 1957: 458:459). Some plant and animal populations were undoubtedly eliminated or reduced through direct overexploitation. This may have been the reason for moa extinction in New Zealand, although, as Sharp (1956: 136) suggests in a speculative reconstruction, rats and dogs may also have been responsible for the extinction of these birds. Certain shellfish, particularly the more accessible or more visible ones on reefs or close to shorelines, may have been brought to near extinction through overexploitation. Pertinent information on this should become available with the publication of the midden analyses of recent archaeological excavations in Mangareva and in the Society and Hawaiian Islands.

Some plants or animals were the victims of human activities directed against other plants or animals. The use of fire in connection with the hunting of wild fauna could destroy much natural vegetation, and Cumberland indicates that many acres of forests in New Zealand may have been eliminated in this manner in Moa-hunter times. A more recent example is available from tropical Polynesia. Some years ago, when Tahitians began to use fire for hunting pigs in the highlands, large portions of Tahitian uplands were burned. These areas are now covered by weeds largely of American origin, rather than by indigenous arboreal vegetation.

Man's activities sometimes provided new opportunities for certain indigenous species. Coconut groves planted by man were, for instance, an attractive habitat for a number of indigenous plants. Certain of these, such as morinda and pandanus, may so flourish under coconut trees as to threaten to choke out the plantations (Fosberg 1953: 11).

Nonliving components of the ecosystems were also significantly affected by man. When sea-birds were frightened away by human settlements on coral atolls, the soils could no longer be replenished with the phosphate and nitrate contents of guano (Fosberg 1953: 3; Hatheway 1953: 61). In modern times, additional phosphate has been lost from island ecosystems through the export of large quantities of phosphorus-rich copra (Fosberg 1953: 11). In the Tahitian uplands, where human activities have recently effected a replacement of arboreal flora, the water-retaining capacity of the soil has been seriously impaired; streams that previously flowed all the time are now dry for part of the year.

IV

Man's introductions affected levels of productivity and the organization of biotic communities differently in each of the three kinds of Pacific island ecosystems.

The terrestrial systems of high islands were probably the most vulnerable to processes resulting in changed productivity and changed community organization. In general, these systems were extremely hospitable to most new organisms; and there was, no doubt, substantial change in the organization of some biotic communities simply concomitant to the introduction of new species. These introductions increased organic diversity, on the genus level at least, but it is improbable that in themselves they had an important effect upon the general productivity of the ecosystems. Much more important changes, particularly involving processes lowering productivity, could have resulted directly from human activities. Evidence of such processes in pre-European Polynesia and Micronesia are generally lacking, but in Melanesia such degradation is clear. In the latter area, indeed, Barrau (1958: 19) usually credits the formation of grassland, scrub, savannah, and savannah woodland, at the expense of forest, to human activity: "In most areas, man is responsible for spreading these herbaceous formations, which have developed as a result of damage caused to the original vegetation by shifting agriculture or by burning for hunting purposes. Burning was also used in some places to facilitate foraging. . . ."

First, the replacement of forest by grassy cover affected the water supply. Barrau suggests (1958: 25) that the development of a definite dry season in large areas of Melanesia was a result of the replacement of arboreal by herbaceous formations. Such replacement of forest over hilly areas too limited in size to affect the rainfall regime might still reduce the effective water supply over larger regions. A recent case observed in Tahiti has been mentioned above, and Gourou (1963) notes a similar case in nineteenth-century Mauritius. Second, the replacement of forest by other vegetation on slopes may have brought about soil erosion.

It is possible that the replacement of arboreal by herbaceous climaxes was not unknown in pre-European tropical Polynesian and Micronesian high islands. The lack of evidence, however, suggests that in those areas in which primary forests were removed, they were usually replaced by secondary forest rather than by nonarboreal covers. The productivity rates of these fast growing secondary forest formations were probably not at great variance with those prevailing in the primary forests and, further, the long-range tendency toward re-establishment of the original climax was not destroyed. It would seem that on the high islands of Micronesia and Melanesia serious degradation of the terrestrial ecosystems was not frequently or widely induced by human populations, despite their size and density, occupancy of one to three millennia, and removal of primary forest cover from large areas. This is in marked contrast to some larger and less densely populated regions in Melanesia.

The terrestrial systems of atolls were less vulnerable to change induced by pre-European man. While there was possibility of drastic reduction of productivity rates on high islands through the replacement of climax forest by scrub, weed, or grass, the agricultural possibilities presented by atolls precluded such extensive degradation. The cultivation of root crops on atolls was not only restricted to areas under which the water table was relatively low in salinity, but restricted to sites which had been painstakingly modified by excavating and composting. The areas thus transformed were generally small, relative to total island size. Furthermore, it is probable that primary productivity in taro pits was higher than in any unmodified portion of the ecosystem. Great emphasis on tree cultivation is largely recent; a response to the European demand for copra. Nevertheless, it can be assumed that on many atolls cultivated trees, particularly coconut and to a lesser extent breadfruit, were significant in pre-European ecosystems. Tree cultivation necessitated at least partial replacement of indigenous arborescent forms, but trees were replaced by trees. Changes in community structures were, therefore, less profound than in those high islands on which trees were replaced by very different vegetations. Furthermore, since coconut groves sometimes sheltered a lower story of indigenous species such as pandanus and morinda, it is doubtful whether pre-European tree cultivation in itself served to lower levels of primary productivity. It must be noted, however, that cultivated trees were more vulnerable to drought than the indigenous varieties, and that during periods of water shortage primary productivity must have decreased more markedly in cultivated groves than in areas of indigenous vegetation. Furthermore, the cultivation and consumption of coconut has induced depletion of phosphorus in atoll soils, contributing to long-run lowering of productivity. This has become serious on some atolls in recent times, but to what extent it was a problem in pre-European times is uncertain.

Atoll water supplies, while more precarious than those of high islands, were less vulnerable to damage by man. Derived mainly from a hydrostatic lens under a relatively flat surface, they were generally unaffected by human activity.

Reef-lagoon ecosystems were least affected by human participation. Community structure and productivity rates probably always remained, as they still do, quite constant. There is no clear-cut evidence of either the introduction of new organisms into pristine reef-lagoon systems by man or of the complete elimination of any of the constituent species populations by man, although both may have occurred.* Quite possible the numbers of certain species dropped drastically from time to time,

---

*An exception to this may be pointed out in the Palmyra Island lagoon, where the ecological conditions and the biota were completely modified when free circulation of ocean water was cut off (see E. Y. Dawson, *Pacific Naturalist* 1(2): 1–51, 1959).

and it is even possible that occasionally the total biomass of the faunal components of some communities was reduced significantly because of human activities. Such events, however, must have been of short duration, for the primary producers of the reef-lagoon community, in contrast to those of terrestrial systems, could hardly be affected by man. Essentially calcareous algae and zooxanthellae, these primary producers could not be utilized directly as food by man, nor could the space they occupied be turned by man to other uses. Therefore species or whole faunas which had been temporarily reduced could always find the nutriment with which to regenerate their numbers.

V

The kinds of communities emerging from interactions between pristine ecosystems and introduced elements, including man, may be broadly categorized according to man's place in them. On the reef, in the lagoon, and in the sea there continued to be relatively unmodified communities, composed of generally the same elements in generally the same relationships as those that obtained prior to man's arrival. The ecological niche or niches exploited by human populations belonging to such communities depended mainly upon the biotic elements present before the advent of man; the presence, location, and quantity of these elements were subject to little or no control by human beings.

Within Pacific island terrestrial ecosystems, there emerged rather different kinds of biotic communities, which may be designated as "anthropocentric." In such communities, both the presence of the main biotic elements, particularly the primary producers, and the decisive relationships among them depended upon the ecological niches that human beings had arranged for themselves according to their criteria of self-interest. The nature and composition of the communities were the result of attempts by human populations to construct and dominate simplified ecosystems consisting of short food chains.

These anthropocentric communities were delicate. Because they usually did not extend over all of a locality in which similar climatic and edaphic conditions prevailed, the territory of anthropocentric communities might be subject to reconquest by the unmodified biota at community borders. Within the anthropocentric communities were weeds and animal pests that threatened either to subvert the entire communities or, at least, to divert substantial organic matter from food chains leading to man. Moreover, the perpetuation of the anthropocentric communities depended upon the continuing presence of a large class of things not within the "cognized" environment of the human population: nitrogen-fixing bacteria and trace elements, for example. The functional

requisites of even known elements were not necessarily clearly understood and might at times fail to be provided by appropriate human action.
Thus the disruption of anthropocentric communities might come about
through too great a difference between the structures of the cognized
and the operational environments.

Human intraspecies competition placed anthropocentric communities
in jeopardy. During warfare the human population might be unable to
burn the bush or to plant cultigens at the proper times, and enemy plantations might be deliberately destroyed. This is said to have been true of
the native wars of such Polynesian high islands as Tahiti, Hawaii, Samoa,
and Mangaia (Vayda 1956: 240; Williamson 1939: 36–38). Regarding
Tuamotuan coral atolls, Lucett (1851: 260) wrote in the middle of the
nineteenth century that warriors from the island of Anaa "some years
ago . . . overran nearly every island in the group . . . rooting up and destroying every cocoa-nut tree standing, which accounts for their scarcity
at the other islands."

VI

Factors noted in earlier sections may help to account for the remarkable
differences in social stratification prevailing in Polynesian societies when
they were first observed by European voyagers. Consideration of the
relationship of these factors to aspects of Polynesian social orders is,
moreover, pertinent to the continuing discussion within anthropology of
the place of ecosystemic processes and ecological principles and methods
in accounting for cultural differences, and of the utility and propriety in
anthropological formulations of a special cultural ecology on the one
hand and of a general biological ecology on the other.

As Sahlins noted in his bold pioneering study of adaptive radiation,
Social Stratification in Polynesia (1958), differences in prerogatives, rights
and honor were more highly developed on volcanic high islands than on
coral atolls. Not only did structurally complex ranking distinguish three
strata of persons in the most highly stratified archipelagos—Hawaii,
Tonga,* Samoa, and the Society Islands—but the rights vested in each of
these ranks were distinct from those of the others. The highest rank
usually claimed title to land and lagoons, controlled communal production, had call upon the harvests reaped and the fish landed, managed
redistributions, possessed confiscatory prerogatives, could mete out pun-
ishments as severe as banishment or death, and were highly sanctified.

---

*Tongan society, very highly stratified by all accounts, seems anomalous. The dominant
island, Tongatabu, is neither a high island nor an atoll but a raised coral island. In area,
however—about 100 square miles—and in the presence of volcanic soil, it resembles
high islands more than atolls.

Other high island societies—Mangareva, Mangaia, Easter, the Marquesas, Tikopia—seem to have been less stratified than those of Hawaii, Tonga, Samoa, and Tahiti; but the least stratified of all Polynesian societies occupied coral atolls. There were only two status levels in Puka Puka, Ontong Java, and Tokelau (Sahlins 1958: 12, ch. 5) and virtually all other atoll societies, and the prerogatives of the upper or chiefly strata were limited. On only a few atolls were any members of the upper stratum freed from physical labor; chiefs were not usually important in distribution and they did not play much of a part in the management of communal lands. They were not highly sanctified and their ability to punish was slight.

Sahlins attempted to account for differences in the degree of social stratification of Polynesian societies by differences in their productivity. In my view differences in productivity, if they existed at all, had no significance in this respect, but other ecosystemic differences discussed earlier in this essay were, in fact, salient. Sahlins's argument is an important one, however, and it deserves recapitulation. It is founded upon the assumption that greater productivity produced larger surpluses, a portion of which could be used to free chiefs and, in some instances, their retainers as well as "bureaucrats" and craft specialists, from laboring in food production. Freed from horticulture and fishing, the chief could devote himself to the administration of the distribution of that portion of the surplus not required to support him and his establishment. The chief's duties or functions in the domain of distribution would have served, Sahlins argued, as a ground for the extension of his prerogatives into other aspects of social life.

If there is a separation on the basis of status between producers and regulators of general distribution, certain consequences would follow regarding the separation of statuses in many other operations. First there would be a tendency for the regulation of distribution to exert some authority over production.... A degree of control of production implies a degree of control over the utilization of resources, or, in other words... property rights. In turn, regulation of these economic processes necessitates the exercise of authority in interpersonal affairs.... Finally, all these differentials would be validated in ideology and ceremony. Sacredness and ritual superiority become attributes of high rank [1958: 4].

Atoll societies were least stratified because least productive in Sahlins's view. Although it is not altogether clear, he may have considered their relatively low productivity to have been a function of their relatively heavy reliance, compared to societies inhabiting high islands, upon the bounties of the reef, the lagoon, and the open sea. He observes that "in most environments horticultural activities are usually more productive than collecting activities since the reproduction of the energy source is directly controlled" (p. 10). This general rule served Sahlins, at any rate, as a subsidiary ground for assessing productivities, the comparison of which formed the demonstration of his thesis.

Sahlins defined productivity in two rather different ways. First, "the ability to derive need-serving goods from the external world may be called the productivity of the culture" (p. 107); second, productivity is "considered to mean the ability of the wielders of the technology to produce strategic goods beyond their consumption needs" (p. 149). The second of the two seems to identify productivity with surplus and, in the absence of quantitative data on agricultural yields, fish landings, and consumption, Sahlins approached the problem of assessing differential productivity through an attempt to assess and order the surpluses generated in the various societies he considered. He took "the greatest number of people encompassed in a single redistributive network" to be "a fairly accurate indication of the ability to produce S_i, or immediate surplus" (p. 109), which he defined as "the ability of food producers to acquire, in a single exploitative activity, an amount of food beyond their immediate consumption needs, or an amount greater than would be needed before production is resumed again" (pp. 108–109). "Cyclical surplus," that which was produced during a complete production cycle in excess of the needs of those engaged in subsistence production, was also taken into consideration. "Other things being constant, the greater the [cyclical surplus] the greater the proportion of people in the society divorced from food production, that is, the greater the proportion of specialists" (p. 109).

The inferential chain forged by Sahlins to estimate comparative productivity and to associate it with comparative degrees of social stratification was a long one, and some of its links were weak. The identification of surplus with productivity is questionable, for one thing. For another, a procedure that takes the size of the distributive network to be a criterion of productivity *ipso facto* prejudices the results in favor of the larger societies, even when the frequencies of the distributions are taken into account. Indeed, Sahlins's summary table of comparative productivity (p. 132) reveals what may be a perfect correlation between estimated population size and productivity. This would seem to reduce his general formulation to the correlation of social stratification with population size. Such a correlation may, indeed, have prevailed. Most anthropologists would be hesitant, however, to assign an important causal or enabling role in the development of stratification to population size *per se,* although it may be that some atoll populations were simply too small to maintain stratified relations among their members.

Another objection to Sahlins's procedure for estimating immediate surplus was pointed out by Goodenough (1959). If the scope of the distributive prerogative vested in chiefs is to be considered an aspect of stratification and if stratification is to be accounted for by productivity, to read productivity from the size of distributive networks is to come perilously close to circularity.

It may also be suggested that Sahlins's attempt to estimate cyclical surplus from reports of the presence of craft specialists is also dubious. For one thing, the relationship of such specialists to subsistence activities is not entirely clear. Moreover, other criteria for estimating cyclical surplus would have yielded different results. For instance, the stone ceremonial structures found throughout Polynesia represent investments of labor which must have been supported from surpluses, either "immediate" or "cyclical." The largest stone structures in Polynesia are dance platforms in the Marquesas, an archipelago in which stratification was much less strongly developed than elsewhere, and Emory (1947: 42) found that at least thirteen maraes existed on Nupaka, an atoll in the Tuamotus with a land area of not much more than a square mile.

The criteria employed by Sahlins to infer surpluses were, then, questionable and, moreover, the relationship of surplus to productivity is ambiguous. If the confiscatory prerogatives of a chief are supported by severe physical sanctions, that which he takes into his hands, whether he consumes it or redistributes it, may not be surplus, if by "surplus" is meant the quantity of goods exceeding the consumption needs of those who produced them. If, on the other hand, chiefly redistributions served to provide a population with a portion of its *requirements,* as they may sometimes have in Hawaii (see Sahlins, 1958, especially pp. 17–18), it would be difficult to argue that what is redistributed represents *surplus.* Hawaii notwithstanding, however, the part played by large-scale chiefly redistributions in the actual provisioning of the populations of high islands is unclear but is, nevertheless, suspect. For one thing they did not occur very often. For another, in all but a few of the very largest islands the full range of plants and animals contributing significantly to subsistence flourished in locations convenient to all residences. These considerations combine to suggest that the importance of large-scale chiefly *redistributions* in the routine *distribution* of foodstuffs was slight (although they may have had a more important role during emergencies). If the role of the chiefs in distribution was not, in fact, important in provisioning, it could hardly have served as the ground from which their authority could be extended into the realm of production and property rights on the one hand and into interpersonal affairs on the other.

To say, however, that the economic and nutritional importance of chiefly redistributions was probably not great on most high islands is not to derogate their significance, which seems to have been largely "symbolic." To respond to the chief's call for provisions, most of which would be quickly redistributed to those who had donated them, was not merely to recognize his primary rights in the land, the lagoon, the sea, and the fruits thereof, but to give substance to that recognition. Chiefly collections and redistributions were material representations—that is to say, substantiations—of social relations.

It may be noted in passing that to characterize redistribution as *symbolizing* social relations is inadequate. In Charles Peirce's (1960: 143ff.) sense they *demonstrated, displayed,* or *indicated* the character and state of those relations. There were, possibly, two classes of information transmitted in those demonstrations. First, as we have already noted, the message of subordination to the chief was intrinsic to making contributions to redistributions. The term "message" may not be sufficiently strong. Subordination was *realized* in the contribution, which is to say that contributing may not only have been performative in J. L. Austin's (1962) sense (see "On Cognized Models" and "The Obvious Aspects of Ritual" in this volume), but meta-performative, not only establishing the subordination of the particular participants themselves, but ever re-establishing the conventions of subordination. Second, it may be that fluctuations from one distribution to another in the volume of goods flowing to the chief and back from him indicated to both the chief and others fluctuations in productive success. Such information would, however, have probably been freely available. If, however, chiefs could infer from their redistributive operations whether or not there had been changes in the number of their supporters or in the configuration of the groups over which they presided, then their ceremonial redistributions were providing them with important information that they otherwise might not have come by. The size of such networks could not, however, have told them, or us, much if anything about either surplus or per capita productivity.

In sum, Sahlins's criteria for assessing productivity were questionable, resting heavily upon what was probably a misinterpretation of redistribution, and his conception of productivity was itself rather vague. It is important to note that, aside from his remark that horticulture is generally more productive than collecting, his criteria for assessing productivity were social. This led him into tautology. If it is to be demonstrated that aspects of the social order are contingent upon productivity, it is inadmissible to read productivity from the same or closely related aspects of the social order.

It may be suggested that the logical and methodological difficulties that Sahlins encountered derived from the metaphysics of the approach to environmental relations called "cultural ecology" (Steward 1955: 30ff.). This approach, which took its goal to be a "determination of how culture is affected by its adaptation to the environment" (ibid.: 31), assumed that biological and cultural ecology each require their own distinctive concepts and methods, and therefore distinguished itself from biological ecology. The methodological implication of the divorcement of cultural from biological (or general) ecology and, by implication if not entailment, the conceptual divorcement of cultural from biological processes, may have been that organic criteria became inadmissible in assessing processes such as those associated with productivity, which were, perhaps, regarded as cultural. Be this as it may, if it is to be demonstrated that aspects of the social order are contingent upon productivity, it seems best to avoid social indicators of productivity altogether. That which is produced, whether or not its production is socially guided and whether or not it is put to social ends, it not itself social. Being produced are quantities of material, in the Polynesian case foodstuffs. As Sahlins puts it, "productivity is best understood, if cross-cultural comparisons are to be made, in terms of the ability to produce food" (1958: 107). The term "ability" is troublesome in this as in other of Sahlins's statements concerning productivity. At best the term is superfluous, at worst it transforms the straightforwardly and simply material into the vague and ambiguously cultural, social, or psychological. (What is the nature of ability?) It therefore seems advisable to drop ability from consideration and simply to compare the food production of the societies under consideration. In the absence of direct harvesting and landing information a certain organic aspect of Polynesian populations may provide an appropriate and non-tautological criterion for the assessment of production. I refer to their density.

The equation of comparative population density with comparative productivity may require some discussion, noting at the outset that it is in accord with the concept of productivity developed in general ecology, which Eugene Odum (1959: 58) has expressed as follows:

Basic or primary productivity of an ecological community, or any part thereof, is defined as the rate at which energy is stored by photosynthetic and chemosynthetic organisms (chiefly green plants...) in the form of organic substances which can be used as food materials... the rates of energy at consumer and decomposer trophic levels are referred to as secondary productivities.

Productivity in this sense may be expressed as biomass or energy generated in an area of specified size during a specified length of time, for instance, grams or calories per square meter per day or kilograms or tons per square kilometer per year. The notion of rate is as intrinsic to the concept of productivity as is quantity of biomass or energy, but in instances in which the productivities of closely related populations of the same species operating in different ecosystems are to be compared it may be acceptable to assume that rates (of growth, aging, and metabolism) are similar, and therefore to ignore them. The comparison is then made between "standing crops," that is, the biomass of populations per unit of area. When dealing with populations as closely related as those of Polynesia, it is reasonable, when approximations are sufficient and data are lacking, to assume that the organisms composing the populations compared are of roughly similar size, and thus to take population densities to indicate standing crops. Population density, this is to say, indicates productivity in the ecological sense.

It may be argued that ecological productivity differs from productivity in the economic sense implicit in the identification of productivity with surplus or in the extractive sense implicit in its definition as the "ability to derive need-serving goods from the external world." However, for purposes of comparing societies possessing similar material cultures from which power machinery is absent and in which production (in the extractive sense) is for use rather than for profit, it is reasonable to consider ecological productivity, indicated by population density, and economic productivity to be one and the same. Population density, this is to say, indicates the amount of "need-serving goods [extracted] from the external world" in such societies.

It is fortunate that gross and approximate results are sufficient for our purposes because estimates of Polynesian populations at the time of contact are unreliable, good estimates of the proportions of land cultivable on various islands are unavailable, and the proportions of lagoon, sea, and land in the total area exploited vary between societies. It is, nevertheless, of considerable interest that some of the highest densities in the Pacific were reached on coral atolls. This is probably related to the community productivities of coral reefs, which are among the highest of the world's ecosystems (Odum 1959: 357). At any rate, the population of Puka Puka, for example, with only two square miles of land, not all of which could be cultivated, varied between 435 and 632 persons during the period 1906 to 1925, according to the Beagleholes (1938: 21), but it may have stood between 1,000 and 2,000 persons before being devastated by a tsunami around A.D. 1600. Densities reckoned against total land area varied, this is to say, between 217 and, possibly, 1,000 persons per square mile. Economic density, that is, density reckoned against arable area, would, of course, have been much higher. In contrast, Western Samoa, with a total area of 1117 square miles and 505 square miles of arable area (Stace, 1956), had a population estimated at 50,000 at the time of contact (Burrows's figure, accepted by Sahlins, 1958: 133), yielding a gross density of 45 persons per square mile and an economic density of 99 per square mile. Even doubling or tripling these figures, perhaps to be justified because Samoa may have supported a larger population than Burrows estimated, does little more than bring Samoa into the lower portion of the Puka Puka range. Taking marine environments into consideration would only reinforce the comparison, for Puka Puka encompasses a lagoon of only five square miles. Most Samoans had considerably more than five square miles of lagoon available to them and, of course, much larger areas of open sea stood in the lee of Samoa than of Puka Puka.

Other cases may be cited. Ontong Java, with not much more than two square miles of land, may have supported as many as 5,500 people in 1907 (Naval Intelligence 1944: 603, 668). In 1935 the population of Kapingamarangi, with less than one-half square mile of dry land, stood at 399 (Naval Intelligence 1945: 410ff.). Tikopia, a high island with a land area of three square miles and no lagoon, had a population of approximately 1250 persons at the time of Firth's visit in 1929. If 50 percent of the land was arable, a generous estimate, the economic population density stood at 833 persons per square mile. Tikopia was much less stratified than Hawaii, Tonga, Tahiti, or Samoa, in all of which densities were considerably lower. Four of Mangareva's eleven square miles of dry land may have been arable (my estimate from maps). The population at contact probably stood at around 2,500 (Roger Green, personal communication, estimated from church records), yielding an economic density of 625 per square mile, also higher than densities on the most stratified islands. The accuracy of these estimates are, of course, dubious. They are, nevertheless, sufficient to discredit the contention that social stratification in Polynesia was even correlated with, let alone was caused, enabled, or encouraged by, high productivity, and inversely correlated with, or discouraged or precluded by, low productivity.

It may be, however, that the contrasts between the ecological community types discussed in section V were significant in this regard. Of particular importance were differences in the extent to which productive and extractive processes in unmodified systems on the one hand and anthropocentric systems on the other could be controlled. The presence, location, quantity, and periodicity of the species constituting the unmodified systems of the reef, lagoon, and sea were largely beyond the control of humans altogether, and fishing and reef-combing are not well-suited to management by anyone other than the immediate participants. It is seldom even realistic for anyone else to set quotas for fishermen to fulfill. The management of fishing, therefore, generally must be left in the hands of the individuals or small groups directly engaged.

Although they do not have an important part to play in the productive processes of unmodified marine systems, or in extracting resources from them, more inclusive units may be important in the distribution of marine products once they are landed. Such distribution does not, however, require management by powerful central authorities, at least among populations as small as those inhabiting atolls, or, for that matter, the size of the redistributive networks on many of the high islands. On coral atolls generally all persons enjoyed full access to a full range of the products they required by vitrue of membership in a range of groups, each based upon kinship co-residence, joint rights in resources, or joint participation in subsistence activities (Sahlins 1938, ch. 11). Distribution could be effected quickly and efficiently through the networks intrinsic to the membership of all individuals in such pluralities of groups. Central management, particularly by administrators who, being divorced from direct participation in extractive activities, had to be supported in manners befitting their stations, offered few benefits with respect to the exploitation of unmodified marine ecosystems in Polynesia. If advantages of centralized management by superordinate authorities form one of the grounds of social stratification, social stratification was not likely to emerge out of the exploitation of the reef, the lagoon, and the sea by atoll populations. If, on the other hand, control of resources or extractive activities is also prerequisite to the development of social stratification, it is unlikely to develop on coral atolls because marine species are subject to no more than the most limited control, and the same may be said for the activity of fishing. The exploitation of marine resources in the Pacific neither establishes a need for social stratification, nor does it provide opportunity for its development.

We cannot, however, account for differences in stratification between the high islands and the atolls by taking high islanders to be horticulturists and atoll inhabitants marine hunters and gatherers. Cultivated plants were as crucial to the survival of atoll populations as they were to those occupying high islands. General differences among the anthropocentric communities of high islands on the one hand and atolls on the other must now be considered.

I noted in an earlier section that few plant species could establish themselves in the saline and calcareous soils of coral atolls. Horticulture on such islands was possible only in occasional swamps like that on Puka Puka, or in small, laboriously prepared areas, such as taro pits. Horticulture in such an environment does little or no damage to the ecosystem. Primary productivity is probably increased in the areas cultivated and, as experience on Canton Island demonstrates, exotic species flourishing in the cultivated areas usually cannot establish themselves outside of them. Coral atolls are harsh and forbidding environments in which to attempt horticulture but, as we noted in section IV, they are relatively invulnerable to degradation by subsistence cultivation. Atoll crops are, however, especially vulnerable to catastrophic reduction by natural disasters such as typhoons, tsunamis, droughts, and even prolonged periods of hot clear weather following heavy rain. At such times the water in the taro pits could be heated to temperatures lethal to the growing plants (Beaglehole 1938: 20). Atoll populations themselves were also, of course, in much greater jeopardy from catastrophe than were high islanders.

Horticulture was much easier in the volcanic soils of the high islands than on coral atolls but, as we have noted, the terrestrial ecosystems of high islands are delicate compared to those of coral atolls. Horticulture undertaken on high islands could easily cause erosion, soil depletion, general floral change including deforestation, and changes in water regime. Whereas atoll populations could do little to damage their ecosystems, but were vulnerable to catastrophe, the converse was the case on high islands. High islands were hardly subject to drought, typhoons struck them only infrequently and were not as devastating as they were on coral atolls, and much of the land on high islands lies at altitudes above the reach of tsunamis. High island populations were relatively invulnerable to catastrophe, then, but their own activities could seriously damage the terrestrial ecosystems from which they derived the major portion of their sustenance. Such degradation is not widely evidenced in pre-European tropical Polynesia, however, and it may be suggested that the large, stratified, and, in some degree, centralized organizations found on the high islands served to protect inherently unstable ecosystems from the kind of degradation observed in Melanesia, where no such large-scale organizations developed. To be more specific I suggest that the development of large, stratified social units on Polynesian high islands was a managerial response to the need of large and perhaps expanding populations to derive stable or increasing food supplies from the anthropocentric communities of spatially limited ecosystems in which man's activities could easily induce degradation. In contrast, no amount of management could prevent the catastrophically induced fluctuations, not only of harvests but of human populations themselves, that unpredictably afflicted coral atolls. The uncontrollable and unpredictable nature of the factors directly threatening human populations as well as their resource bases on coral atolls, along with the generally greater reliance of atoll peoples upon foodstuffs taken from unmodified and generally uncontrollable marine ecosystems, may well account for the weak development of social stratification on the low islands. Quite simply, stratification offered few, if any, adaptive advantages in the atoll environment, but it did on high islands.

REFERENCES CITED

Austin, J. L.
    1962   *How to do things with words.* Oxford University Press.
Banner, A. H.
    1959   Fish poisoning reports wanted for University of Hawaii study. *South Pacific Commn. Quart. Bull.* 9(3):31.

Barrau, Jacques
　　1958　*Subsistence agriculture in Melanesia.* B. P. Bishop Mus. Bull. 219.
　　　　　Honolulu.
Bates, Marston
　　1960　Ecology and evolution. In *Evolution after Darwin,* vol. 1, ed. Sol Tax,
　　　　　pp. 547–568. Chicago: University of Chicago Press.
Beaglehole, Ernest and Pearl
　　1938　*Ethnology of Puka Puka.* B. P. Bishop Mus. Bull. 150. Honolulu.
Birdsell, Joseph
　　1957　Some population problems involving Pleistocene man. *Cold Spring
　　　　　Harbor Symp. Quant. Biol.* 22:47–68.
Catala, René L. H.
　　1957　*Report on the Gilbert Islands: some aspects of human ecology.* Atoll Rsch.
　　　　　Bull. 59. Washington, D.C.: National Research Council.
Cook, James
　　1784　*A voyage to the Pacific Ocean . . . performed . . . in the years* 1776 . . . 1780,
　　　　　vol. 1. London: Nicoll and Cadell.
Danielsson, Bengt
　　1955　*Work and life on Raroia.* Stockholm: Saxon and Lindstroms.
Degener, O., and E. Gillaspy
　　1955　*Canton Island, South Pacific.* Atoll Rsch. Bull. 41. Washington, D.C.:
　　　　　National Research Council.
Emory, Kenneth P.
　　1947　*Tuamotuan religious structures.* B. P. Bishop Mus. Bull. 191. Honolulu.
　　1961　Personal communication.
Fosberg, F. R.
　　1953　*Vegetation of Central Pacific atolls: a brief summary.* Atoll Rsch. Bull.
　　　　　23. Washington, D.C.: National Research Council.
Goodenough, Ward
　　1957　Oceania and the problem of controls in the study of cultural and
　　　　　human evolution. *J. Polynesian Soc.* 66:146–155.
　　1959　Review of *Social stratification in Polynesia.* In *J. Polynesian Soc.* 68(3).
Gourou, Pierre
　　1963　Pressure on island environment. In *Man's place in the island ecosystem,*
　　　　　ed. F. D. Fosberg, pp. 207–225. Honolulu: Bishop Museum Press.
Grace, George W.
　　1961　Austronesian linguistics and culture history. *American Anthropologist*
　　　　　63:359–368.
Green, Roger C.
　　1961　Personal communication.
Hatheway, William
　　1953　*The land vegetation of Arno Atoll, Marshall Islands.* Atoll Rsch. Bull.
　　　　　16. Washington, D.C.: National Research Council.
　　1955　*The natural vegetation of Canton Island, an equatorial Pacific atoll.* Atoll
　　　　　Rsch. Bull. 43. Washington, D.C.: National Research Council.
Hiatt, R. W., and D. W. Strasburg
　　1960　Ecological relationships of the fish fauna on coral reefs of the Mar-
　　　　　shall Islands. *Ecol. Monogr.* 30:65–127.
Lucett, Edward
　　1851　*Rovings in the Pacific, from* 1837 *to* 1849, vol. 1. London: Longman,
　　　　　Brown, Green, and Longmans.

Marshall, J. T., Jr.
  1957   *Atolls visited during the first year of the Pacific Islands Rat Ecology Project.* Atoll Rsch. Bull. 56. Washington, D.C.: National Research Council.
Maude, H. E.
  1952   The colonization of the Phoenix Islands. *J. Polynesian Soc.* 61:62–89.
  1963   Discussion in *Man's place in the island ecosystem,* ed. F. R. Fosberg, pp. 171–174. Honolulu: Bishop Museum Press.
Merrill, Elmer Drew
  1954   The botany of Cook's voyages and its unexpected significance in relation to anthropology, biogeography and history. *Chronica Botanica* 14(5/6):161–384.
Naval Intelligence Division [British]
  1944   *The Pacific islands.* Vol. 3, *The western Pacific: Tonga to the Solomon Islands.* Geographical Handbook Series.
  1945   *The Pacific islands.* Vol. 4, *The western Pacific: New Guinea and islands northward.* Geographical Handbook Series.
Niering, William A.
  1956   *Bioecology of Kapingamarangi Atoll, Caroline Islands. Terrestrial aspects.* Atoll Rsch. bull. 49. Washington, D.C.: National Research Council.
Odum, Eugene P.
  1959   *Fundamentals of ecology.* 2nd ed. Philadelphia: Saunders.
Odum, Howard T., and Eugene P. Odum
  1955   Trophic structure and productivity of a windward coral reef community on Eniwetok Atoll. *Ecol. Monogr.* 25:291–320.
Pierce, Charles
  1960   *Collected papers of Charles Sanders Pierce.* Vol. 4, *Elements of logic,* ed. Charles Hartshorne and Paul Weiss. Cambridge, Mass.: Harvard University Press.
Sachet, Marie-Hélène
  1954   *A summary of information on Rose Atoll.* Atoll Rsch. Bull. 29. Washington, D.C.: National Research Council.
Sahlins, Marshall
  1955   Esoteric efflorescence on Easter Island. *American Anthropologist* 57: 1045–1052.
  1957   Land use and the extended family in Moala, Fiji. *American Anthropologist* 59:449–463.
  1958   *Social stratification in Polynesia.* American Ethnological Society Monograph. Seattle: University of Washington Press.
Sharp, Andrew
  1956   *Ancient voyagers in the Pacific.* Polynesian Society, Mem. 32. Wallington, N.Z.
Stace, V. D.
  1956   *Western Samoa—an economic survey.* South Pacific Technical Paper 91. Noumea.
Steward, Julian
  1955   *Theory of culture change.* Urbana: University of Illinois Press.
Turbott, I. G.
  1949   Diets, Gilbert and Ellice Islands colony. *J. Polynesian Soc.* 58:36–46.
  1954   Portulaca: a specialty in the diet of the Gilbertese in the Phoenix Islands, Central Pacific. *J. Polynesian Soc.* 63:77–85.

Van Zwaluwenburg, R. H.
   1955   *The insects and certain arthropods of Canton Island.* Atoll Rsch. Bull. 42. Washington, D.C.: National Research Council.
Vayda, A. P.
   1956   Maori warfare. Unpublished Ph.D. dissertation, Columbia University, New York.
   1959   Polynesian cultural distributions in new perspective. *American Anthropologist* 61:817–828.
Williamson, Robert W.
   1939   *Essays in Polynesian ethnology,* ed. Ralph Piddington. Cambridge: Cambridge University Press.
Zimmerman, Elwood C.
   1963   Nature of the land biota. In *Man's place in the island ecosystem,* ed. F. R. Fosberg, pp. 57–64. Honolulu: Bishop Museum Press.

Ritual Regulation

of Environmental Relations

among a New Guinea People

Most functional studies of religious behavior in anthropology have as an analytic goal the elucidation of events, processes, or relationships occurring within a social unit of some sort. The social unit is not always well defined, but in some cases it appears to be a church, that is, a group of people who entertain similar beliefs about the universe, or a congregation, a group of people who participate together in the performance of religious rituals. There have been exceptions. Thus Vayda, Leeds, and Smith (1961) and O. K. Moore (1957) have clearly perceived that the functions of religious ritual are not necessarily confined within the boundaries of a congregation or even a church. By and large, however, I believe that the following statement by Homans (1941: 172) represents fairly the dominant line of anthropological thought concerning the functions of religious ritual:

Ritual actions do not produce a practical result on the external world—that is one of the reasons why we call them ritual. But to make this statement is not to say that ritual has no function. Its function is not related to the world external

This essay was originally published in *Ethnology* 6: 17–30, 1967. The field work upon which it is based was supported by a grant from the National Science Foundation, under which Professor A. P. Vayda was principal investigator. Personal support was received by the author from the National Institutes of Health. Earlier versions of this paper were presented at the 1964 annual meeting of the American Anthropological Association in Detroit, and before a Columbia University seminar on Ecological Systems and Cultural Evolution. I have received valuable suggestions from Alexander Alland, Jacques Barrau, William Clarke, Paul Collins, C. Glen King, Marvin Harris, Margaret Mead, M. J. Meggitt, Ann Rappaport, John Street, Marjorie Whiting, Cherry Vayda, A. P. Vayda and many others, but I take full responsibility for the analysis presented herewith.

to the society but to the internal constitution of the society. It gives the members of the society confidence, it dispels their anxieties, it disciplines their social organization.

No argument will be raised here against the sociological and psychological functions imputed by Homans, and many others before him, to ritual. They seem to me to be plausible. Nevertheless, in some cases at least, ritual does produce, in Homans' terms, "a practical result on the world" external not only to the social unit composed of those who participate together in ritual performances but also to the larger unit composed of those who entertain similar beliefs concerning the universe. The material presented here will show that the ritual cycles of the Tsembaga, and of other local territorial groups of Maring speakers living in the New Guinea interior, play an important part in regulating the relationships of these groups with both the nonhuman components of their immediate environments and the human components of their less immediate environments, that is, with other similar territorial groups. To be more specific, this regulation helps to maintain the biotic communities existing within their territories, redistributes land among people and people over land, and limits the frequency of fighting. In the absence of authoritative political statuses or offices, the ritual cycle likewise provides a means for mobilizing allies when warfare may be undertaken. It also provides a mechanism for redistributing local pig surpluses in the form of pork throughout a large regional population while helping to assure the local population of a supply of pork when its members are most in need of high quality protein.

Religious ritual may be defined, for the purposes of this paper, as the prescribed performance of conventionalized acts manifestly directed toward the involvement of nonempirical or supernatural agencies in the affairs of the actors. While this definition relies upon the formal characteristics of the performances and upon the motives for undertaking them, attention will be focused upon the empirical effects of ritual performances and sequences of ritual performances. The religious rituals to be discussed are regarded as neither more nor less than part of the behavioral repertoire employed by an aggregate of organisms in adjusting to its environment.

The data upon which this paper is based were collected during fourteen months of field work among the Tsembaga, one of about twenty local groups of Maring speakers living in the Simbai and Jimi Valleys of the Bismarck Range in the Territory of New Guinea. The size of Maring local groups varies from a little over 100 to 900. The Tsembaga, who in 1963 numbered 204 persons, are located on the south wall of the Simbai Valley. The country in which they live differs from the true highlands in being lower, generally more rugged, and more heavily forested. Tsembaga territory rises, within a total surface area of 3.2 square miles, from an elevation of 2,200 feet at the Simbai river to 7,200 feet at the ridge crest. Gardens are cut in the secondary forests up to between 5,000 and 5,400 feet, above which the area remains in primary forest. Rainfall reaches 150 inches per year.

The Tsembaga have come into contact with the outside world only recently; the first government patrol to penetrate their territory arrived in 1954. They were considered uncontrolled by the Australian government until 1962, and they remain unmissionized to this day.

The 204 Tsembaga are distributed among five putatively patrilineal clans, which are, in turn, organized into more inclusive groupings on two hierarchical levels below that of the total local group. Internal political structure is highly egalitarian. There are no hereditary or elected chiefs, nor are there even "big men" who can regularly coerce or command the support of their clansmen or co-residents in economic or forceful enterprises.

It is convenient to regard the Tsembaga as a population in the ecological sense, that is, as one of the components of a system of trophic exchanges taking place within a bounded area. Tsembaga territory and the biotic community existing upon it may be conveniently viewed as an ecosystem. While it would be permissible arbitrarily to designate the Tsembaga as a population and their territory with its biota as an ecosystem, there are also nonarbitrary reasons for doing so. An ecosystem is a system of material exchanges, and the Tsembaga maintain against other human groups exclusive access to the resources within their territorial borders. Conversely, it is from this territory alone that the Tsembaga ordinarily derive all of their foodstuffs and most of the other materials they require for survival. Less anthropocentrically, it may be justified to regard Tsembaga territory with its biota as an ecosystem in view of the rather localized nature of cyclical material exchanges in tropical rainforests.

As they are involved with the nonhuman biotic community within their territory in a set of trophic exchanges, so do they participate in other material relationships with other human groups external to their territory. Genetic materials are exchanged with other groups, and certain crucial items, such as stone axes, were in the past obtained from the outside. Furthermore, in the area occupied by the Maring speakers, more than one local group is usually involved in any process, either peaceful or warlike, through which people are redistributed over land and land redistributed among people.

The concept of the ecosystem, though it provides a convenient frame for the analysis of interspecific trophic exchanges taking place within limited geographical areas, does not comfortably accommodate intraspecific exchanges taking place over wider geographic areas. Some sort of geographic population model would be more useful for the analysis of the relationship of the local ecological population to the larger regional population of which it is a part, but we lack even a set of appropriate terms for such a model. Suffice it here to note that the relations of the Tsembaga to the total of other local human populations in their vicinity are similar to the relations of local aggregates of other animals to the totality of their species occupying broader and more or less continuous regions. This larger, more inclusive aggregate may resemble what geneticists mean by the term population, that is, an aggregate of interbreeding organisms persisting through an indefinite number of generations and either living or capable of living in isolation from similar aggregates of the same species. This is the unit which survives through long periods of time while its local ecological (*sensu stricto*) subunits, the units more or less independently involved in interspecific trophic exchanges such as the Tsembaga, are ephemeral.

Since it has been asserted that the ritual cycles of the Tsembaga regulate relationships within what may be regarded as a complex system, it is necessary, before proceeding to the ritual cycle itself, to describe briefly, and where possible in quantitative terms, some aspects of the place of the Tsembaga in this system.

The Tsembaga are bush-following horticulturalists. Staples include a range of root crops, taro (*Colocasia*) and sweet potatoes being most important, yams and manioc less so. In addition, a great variety of greens are raised, some of which are rich in protein. Sugar cane and some tree crops, particularly *Pandanus conoideus,* are also important.

All gardens are mixed, many of them containing all of the major root crops and many greens. Two named garden types are, however, distinguished by the crops which predominate in them. "Taro-yam gardens" were found to produce, on the basis of daily harvest records kept on entire gardens for close to one year, about 5,300,000 calories* per acre during their harvesting lives of 18 to 24 months; 85 percent of their yield is harvested between 24 and 76 weeks after planting. "Sugar–sweet potato gardens" produce about 4,600,000 calories per acre during their harvesting lives, 91 percent being taken between 24 and 76 weeks after planting. I estimated that approximately 310,000 calories per acre is expended on cutting, fencing, planting, maintaining, harvesting, and walking to and from taro-yam gardens. Sugar–sweet potato gardens required

---

*Because the length of time in the field precluded the possibility of maintaining harvest records on single gardens from planting through abandonment, figures were based, in the case of both "taro-yam" and "sugar–sweet potato" gardens, on three separate gardens planted in successive years. Conversions from the gross weight to the caloric value of the yield were made by reference to the literature. The sources used are listed in Rappaport (1966: Appendix VIII).

an expenditure of approximately 290,000 calories per acre.* These energy ratios, approximately 17:1 on taro-yam gardens and 16:1 on sugar–sweet potato gardens, compare favorably with figures reported for swidden cultivation in other regions.†

Intake is high in comparison with the reported dietaries of other New Guinea populations. On the basis of daily consumption records kept for ten months on four households numbering in total sixteen persons, I estimated the average daily intake of adult males to be approximately 2,600 calories, and that of adult females to be around 2,200 calories. It may be mentioned here that the Tsembaga are small and short-statured. Adult males average 101 pounds in weight and approximately 58.5 inches in height; the corresponding averages for adult females are 85 pounds and 54.5 inches.‡

Although 99 percent by weight of the food consumed is vegetable, the protein intake is high by New Guinea standards. The daily protein consumption of adult males from vegetable sources was estimated to be between 43 and 55 grams, of adult females 36 to 48 grams. Even with an adjustment for vegetable sources, these values are slightly in excess of the recently published WHO/FAO daily requirements (Food and Agriculture Organization of the United Nations 1964). The same is true of the younger age categories, although soft and discolored hair, a symptom of protein deficiency, was noted in a few children. The WHO/FAO protein requirements do not include a large "margin for safety" or allowance for stress; and, although no clinical assessments were undertaken, it may be suggested that the Tsembaga achieve nitrogen balance at a low level. In other words, their protein intake is probably marginal.

Measurements of all gardens made during 1962 and of some gardens made during 1963 indicate that, to support the human population, between .15 and .19 acres are put into cultivation per capita per year. Fallows range from 8 to 45 years. The area in secondary forest comprises approximately 1,000 acres, only 30 to 50 of which are in cultivation at any time. Assuming calories to be the limiting factor, and assuming an unchanging population structure, the territory could support—with no

---

*Rough time and motion studies of each of the tasks involved in making, maintaining, harvesting, and walking to and from gardens were undertaken. Conversion to energy expenditure values was accomplished by reference to energy expenditure tables prepared by Hipsley and Kirk (1965: 43) on the basis of gas exchange measurements made during the performance of garden tasks by the Chimbu people of the New Guinea highlands.

†Marvin Harris, in an unpublished paper, estimates the ratio of energy return to energy input on Dyak (Borneo) rice swiddens at 10:1. His estimates of energy ratios on Tepotzlan (Meso-America) swiddens range from 13:1 on poor land to 29:1 on the best land.

‡Heights may be inaccurate. Many men wear their hair in large coiffures hardened with pandanus grease, and it was necessary in some instances to estimate the location of the top of the skull.

reduction in lengths of fallow and without cutting into the virgin forest from which the Tsembaga extract many important items—between 290 and 397 people if the pig population remained minimal. The size of the pig herd, however, fluctuates widely. Taking Maring pig husbandry procedures into consideration, I have estimated the human carrying capacity of the Tsembaga territory at between 270 and 320 people.

Because the timing of the ritual cycle is bound up with the demography of the pig herd, the place of the pig in Tsembaga adaptation must be examined.

First, being omnivorous, pigs keep residential areas free of garbage and human feces. Second, limited numbers of pigs rooting in secondary growth may help to hasten the development of that growth. The Tsembaga usually permit pigs to enter their gardens one and a half to two years after planting, by which time second-growth trees are well established there. The Tsembaga practice selective weeding; from the time the garden is planted, herbaceous species are removed, but tree species are allowed to remain. By the time cropping is discontinued and the pigs are let in, some of the trees in the garden are already ten to fifteen feet tall. These well-established trees are relatively impervious to damage by the pigs, which, in rooting for seeds and remaining tubers, eliminate many seeds and seedlings that, if allowed to develop, would provide some competition for the established trees. Moreover, in some Maring-speaking areas swiddens are planted twice, although this is not the case with the Tsembaga. After the first crop is almost exhausted, pigs are penned in the garden, where their rooting eliminates weeds and softens the ground, making the task of planting for a second time easier. The pigs, in other words, are used as cultivating machines.

Small numbers of pigs are easy to keep. They run free during the day and return home at night to receive their ration of garbage and substandard tubers, particularly sweet potatoes. Supplying the latter requires little extra work, for the substandard tubers are taken from the ground in the course of harvesting the daily ration for humans. Daily consumption records kept over a period of some months show that the ration of tubers received by the pigs approximates in weight that consumed by adult humans, i.e., a little less than three pounds per day per pig.

If the pig herd grows large, however, the substandard tubers incidentally obtained in the course of harvesting for human needs become insufficient, and it becomes necessary to harvest especially for the pigs. In other words, people must work for the pigs and perhaps even supply them with food fit for human consumption. Thus, as Vayda, Leeds, and Smith (1961: 71) have pointed out, there can be too many pigs for a given community.

This also holds true of the sanitary and cultivating services rendered by pigs. A small number of pigs is sufficient to keep residential areas clean, to suppress superfluous seedlings in abandoned gardens, and to soften the soil in gardens scheduled for second plantings. A larger herd, on the other hand, may be troublesome; the larger the number of pigs, the greater the possibility of their invasion of producing gardens, with concomitant damage not only to crops and young secondary growth but also to the relations between the pig owners and garden owners.

All male pigs are castrated at approximately three months of age, for boars, people say, are dangerous and do not grow as large as barrows. Pregnancies, therefore, are always the result of unions of domestic sows with feral males. Fecundity is thus only a fraction of its potential. During one twelve-month period only fourteen litters resulted out of a potential 99 or more pregnancies. Farrowing generally takes place in the forest, and mortality of the young is high. Only 32 of the offspring of the above-mentioned fourteen pregnancies were alive six months after birth. This number is barely sufficient to replace the number of adult animals which would have died or been killed during most years without pig festivals.

The Tsembaga almost never kill domestic pigs outside of ritual contexts. In ordinary times, when there is no pig festival in progress, these rituals are almost always associated with misfortunes or emergencies, notably warfare, illness, injury, or death. Rules state not only the contexts in which pigs are to be ritually slaughtered, but also who may partake of the flesh of the sacrificial animals. During warfare it is only the men participating in the fighting who eat the pork. In cases of illness or injury, it is only the victim and certain near relatives, particularly his co-resident agnates and spouses, who do so.

It is reasonable to assume that misfortune and emergency are likely to induce in the organisms experiencing them a complex of physiological changes known collectively as "stress." Physiological stress reactions occur not only in organisms which are infected with disease or traumatized, but also in those experiencing rage or fear (Houssay et al. 1955: 1096), or even prolonged anxiety (National Research Council 1963: 53). One important aspect of stress is the increased catabolization of protein (Houssay et al. 1955: 451; National Research Council 1963: 49), with a net loss of nitrogen from the tissues (Houssay et al. 1955: 450). This is a serious matter for organisms with a marginal protein intake. Antibody production is low (Berg 1948: 311), healing is slow (Large and Johnston 1948: 352), and a variety of symptoms of a serious nature are likely to develop (Lund and Levenson 1948: 349; Zintel 1964: 1043). The status of a protein-depleted animal, however, may be significantly improved in a relatively short period of time by the intake of high quality protein, and high protein diets are therefore routinely prescribed for surgical patients and those suffering from infectious diseases (Burton 1959: 231; Lund and Levenson 1948: 350; Elman 1951: 85ff.; Zintel 1964: 1043ff.).

It is precisely when they are undergoing physiological stress that the Tsembaga kill and consume their pigs, and it should be noted that they limit the consumption to those likely to be experiencing stress most profoundly. The Tsembaga, of course, know nothing of physiological stress. Native theories of the etiology and treatment of disease and injury implicate various categories of spirits to whom sacrifices must be made. Nevertheless, the behavior which is appropriate in terms of native understandings is also appropriate to the actual situation confronting the actors.

We may now outline in the barest of terms the Tsembaga ritual cycle. Space does not permit a description of its ideological correlates. It must suffice to note that the Tsembaga do not necessarily perceive all of the empirical effects which the anthropologist sees to flow from their ritual behavior. Such empirical consequences as they may perceive, moreover, are not central to their rationalizations of the performances. The Tsembaga say that they perform the rituals in order to rearrange their relationships with the supernatural world. We may only reiterate here that behavior undertaken in reference to their "cognized environment"—an environment which includes as very important elements the spirits of ancestors—seems appropriate in their "operational environment," the material environment specified by the anthropologist through operations of observation, including measurement.

Since the rituals are arranged in a cycle, description may commence at any point. The operation of the cycle becomes clearest if we begin with the rituals performed during warfare. Opponents in all cases occupy adjacent territories, in almost all cases on the same valley wall. After hostilities have broken out, each side performs certain rituals which place the opposing side in the formal category of "enemy." A number of taboos prevail while hostilities continue. These include prohibitions on sexual intercourse and on the ingestion of certain things—food prepared by women, food grown on the lower portion of the territory, marsupials, eels, and while actually on the fighting ground, any liquid whatsoever.

One ritual practice associated with fighting which may have some physiological consequences deserves mention. Immediately before proceeding to the fighting ground, the warriors eat heavily salted pig fat. The ingestion of salt, coupled with the taboo on drinking, has the effect of shortening the fighting day, particularly since the Maring prefer to fight only on bright sunny days. When everyone gets unbearably thirsty, according to informants, fighting is broken off.

There may formerly have been other effects if the native salt contained sodium (the production of salt was discontinued some years previous to the field work, and no samples were obtained). The Maring diet seems to be deficient in sodium. The ingestion of large amounts of sodium just prior to fighting would have permitted the warriors to sweat normally without a lowering of blood volume and consequent weakness during the course of the fighting. The pork belly ingested with the salt would have provided them with a new burst of energy two hours or so after the commencement of the engagement. After fighting was finished for the day, lean pork was consumed, offsetting, at least to some extent, the nitrogen loss associated with the stressful fighting (personal communications from F. Dunn, W. McFarlane, and J. Sabine, 1965).

Fighting could continue sporadically for weeks. Occasionally it terminated in the rout of one of the antagonistic groups, whose survivors would take refuge with kinsmen elsewhere. In such instances, the victors would lay waste their opponents' groves and gardens, slaughter their pigs, and burn their houses. They would not, however, immediately annex the territory of the vanquished. The Maring say that they never take over the territory of an enemy for, even if it has been abandoned, the spirits of their ancestors remain to guard it against interlopers. Most fights, however, terminated in truces between the antagonists.

With the termination of hostilities a group which has not been driven off its territory performs a ritual called "planting the *rumbim.*" Every man puts his hand on the ritual plant, *rumbim* (*Cordyline fruticosa* (L.), A. Chev; *C. terminalis,* Kunth), as it is planted in the ground. The ancestors are addressed, in effect, as follows:

We thank you for helping us in the fight and permitting us to remain on our territory. We place our souls in this *rumbim* as we plant it on our ground. We ask you to care for this *rumbim*. We will kill pigs for you now, but they are few. In the future, when we have many pigs, we shall again give you pork and uproot the *rumbim* and stage a *kaiko* (pig festival). But until there are sufficient pigs to repay you the *rumbim* will remain in the ground.

This ritual is accompanied by the wholesale slaughter of pigs. Only juveniles remain alive. All adult and adolescent animals are killed, cooked, and dedicated to the ancestors. Some are consumed by the local group, but most are distributed to allies who assisted in the fight.

Some of the taboos which the group suffered during the time of fighting are abrogated by this ritual. Sexual intercourse is now permitted, liquids may be taken at any time, and food from any part of the territory may be eaten. But the group is still in debt to its allies and ancestors. People say it is still the time of the *bamp ku,* or "fighting stones," which are actual objects used in the rituals associated with warfare. Although the fighting ceases when *rumbim* is planted, the concomitant obligations, debts to allies and ancestors, remain outstanding; and the fighting stones may not be put away until these obligations are fulfilled. The time of the fighting stones is a time of debt and danger which lasts until the *rumbim* is uprooted and a pig festival (*kaiko*) is staged.

Certain taboos persist during the time of the fighting stones. Marsupials, regarded as the pigs of the ancestors of the high ground, may not be trapped until the debt to their masters has been repaid. Eels, the "pigs of the ancestors of the low ground," may neither be caught nor consumed. Prohibitions on all intercourse with the enemy come into force. One may not touch, talk to, or even look at a member of the enemy group, nor set foot on enemy ground. Even more important, a group may not attack another group while its ritual plant remains in the ground, for it has not yet fully rewarded its ancestors and allies for their assistance in the last fight. Until the debts to them have been paid, further assistance from them will not be forthcoming. A kind of "truce of god" thus prevails until the *rumbim* is uprooted and a *kaiko* completed.

To uproot the *rumbim* requires sufficient pigs. How many pigs are sufficient, and how long does it take to acquire them? The Tsembaga say that, if a place is "good," this can take as little as five years; but if a place is "bad," it may require ten years or longer. A bad place is one in which misfortunes are frequent and where, therefore, ritual demands for the killing of pigs arise frequently. A good place is one where such demands are infrequent. In a good place, the increase of the pig herd exceeds the ongoing ritual demands, and the herd grows rapidly. Sooner or later the substandard tubers incidentally obtained while harvesting become insufficient to feed the herd, and additional acreage must be put into production specifically for the pigs.

The work involved in caring for a large pig herd can be extremely burdensome. The Tsembaga herd just prior to the pig festival of 1962–63, when it numbered 169 animals, was receiving 54 percent of all the sweet potatoes and 82 percent of all the manioc harvested. These comprised 35.9 percent by weight of all root crops harvested. This figure is consistent with the difference between the amount of land under cultivation just previous to the pig festival, when the herd was at maximum size, and that immediately afterwards, when the pig herd was at minimum size. The former was 36.1 percent in excess of the latter.

I have estimated, on the basis of acreage yield and energy expenditure figures, that about 45,000 calories per year are expended in caring for one pig 120–150 pounds in size. It is upon women that most of the burden of pig keeping falls. If, from a woman's daily intake of about 2,200 calories, 950 calories are allowed for basal metabolism, a woman has only 1,250 calories a day available for all her activities, which include gardening for her family, child care, and cooking, as well as tending pigs. It is clear that no woman can feed many pigs; only a few had as many as four in their care at the commencement of the festival; and it is not surprising that agitation to uproot the *rumbim* and stage the *kaiko* starts with the wives of the owners of large numbers of pigs.

A large herd is not only burdensome as far as energy expenditure is concerned; it becomes increasingly a nuisance as it expands. The more numerous pigs become, the more frequently are gardens invaded by them. Such events result in serious disturbances of local tranquillity. The garden owner often shoots, or attempts to shoot, the offending pig; and the pig owner commonly retorts by shooting, or attempting to shoot, either the garden owner, his wife, or one of his pigs. As more and more such events occur, the settlement, nucleated when the herd was small, disperses as people try to put as much distance as possible between their pigs and other people's gardens and between their gardens and other people's pigs. Occasionally this reaches its logical conclusion, and people begin to leave the territory, taking up residence with kinsmen in other local populations.

The number of pigs sufficient to become intolerable to the Tsembaga was below the capacity of the territory to carry pigs. I have estimated that, if the size and structure of the human population remained constant at the 1962–1963 level, a pig population of 140 to 240 animals averaging 100 to 150 pounds in size could be maintained perpetually by the Tsembaga without necessarily inducing environmental degradation. Since the size of the herd fluctuates, even higher cyclical maxima could be achieved. The level of toleration, however, is likely always to be below the carrying capacity, since the destructive capacity of the pigs is dependent upon the population density of both people and pigs, rather than upon population size. The denser the human population, the fewer pigs will be required to disrupt social life. If the carrying capacity is exceeded, it is likely to be exceeded by people and not by pigs.

The *kaiko* or pig festival, which commences with the planting of stakes at the boundary and the uprooting of the *rumbim,* is thus triggered by either the additional work attendant upon feeding pigs or the destructive capacity of the pigs themselves. It may be said, then, that there are sufficient pigs to stage the *kaiko* when the relationship of pigs to people changes from one of mutualism to one of parasitism or competition.

A short time prior to the uprooting of the *rumbim,* stakes are planted at the boundary. If the enemy has continued to occupy its territory, the stakes are planted at the boundary which existed before the fight. If, on the other hand, the enemy has abandoned its territory, the victors may plant their stakes at a new boundary which encompasses areas previously occupied by the enemy. The Maring say, to be sure, that they never take land belonging to an enemy, but this land is regarded as vacant, since no *rumbim* was planted on it after the last fight. We may state here a rule of land redistribution in terms of the ritual cycle: *If one of a pair of antago-*

nistic groups is able to uproot its rumbim before its opponents can plant their rumbim, it may occupy the latter's territory.

Not only have the vanquished abandoned their territory; it is assumed that it has also been abandoned by their ancestors as well. The surviving members of the erstwhile enemy group have by this time resided with other groups for a number of years, and most if not all of them have already had occasion to sacrific pigs to their ancestors at their new residences. In so doing they have invited these spirits to settle at the new locations of the living, where they will in the future receive sacrifices. Ancestors of vanquished groups thus relinquish their guardianship over the territory, making it available to victorious groups. Meanwhile, the *de facto* membership of the living in the groups with which they have taken refuge is converted eventually into *de jure* membership. Sooner or later the groups with which they have taken up residence will have occasion to plant *rumbim,* and the refugees, as co-residents, will participate, thus ritually validating their connection to the new territory and the new group. A rule of population redistribution may thus be stated in terms of ritual cycles: *A man becomes a member of a territorial group by participating with it in the planting of rumbim.*

The uprooting of the *rumbim* follows shortly after the planting of stakes at the boundary. On this particular occasion the Tsembaga killed 32 pigs out of their herd of 169. Much of the pork was distributed to allies and affines outside of the local group.

The taboo on trapping marsupials was also terminated at this time. Information is lacking concerning the population dynamics of the local marsupials, but it may well be that the taboo which had prevailed since the last fight—that against taking them in traps—had conserved a fauna which might otherwise have become extinct.

The *kaiko* continues for about a year, during which period friendly groups are entertained from time to time. The guests receive presents of vegetable foods, and the hosts and male guests dance together throughout the night.

These events may be regarded as analogous to aspects of the social behavior of many nonhuman animals. First of all, they include massed epigamic, or courtship, displays (Wynne-Edwards 1962: 17). Young women are presented with samples of the eligible males of local groups with which they may not otherwise have had the opportunity to become familiar. The context, moreover, permits the young women to discriminate amongst this sample in terms of both endurance (signaled by how vigorously and how long a man dances) and wealth (signaled by the richness of a man's shell and feather finery).

More importantly, the massed dancing at these events may be regarded as epideictic display, communicating to the participants information concerning the size or density of the group (Wynne-Edwards 1962: 16). In many species such displays take place as a prelude to actions which adjust group size or density, and such is the case among the Maring. The massed dancing of the visitors at a *kaiko* entertainment communicates to the hosts, while the *rumbim* truce is still in force, information concerning the amount of support they may expect from the visitors in the bellicose enterprises that they are likely to embark upon soon after the termination of the pig festival.

Among the Maring there are no chiefs or other political authorities capable of commanding the support of a body of followers, and the decision to assist another group in warfare rests with each individual male. Allies are not recruited by appealing for help to other local groups as such. Rather, each member of the groups primarily involved in the hostilities appeals to his cognatic and affinal kinsmen in other local groups. These men, in turn, urge other of their co-residents and kinsmen to "help them fight." The channels through which invitations to dance are extended are precisely those through which appeals for military support are issued. The invitations go not from group to group, but from kinsman to kinsman, the recipients of invitations urging their co-residents to "help them dance."

Invitations to dance do more than exercise the channels through which allies are recruited; they provide a means for judging their effectiveness. Dancing and fighting are regarded as in some sense equivalent. This equivalence is expressed in the similarity of some pre-fight and pre-dance rituals, and the Maring say that those who come to dance come to fight. The size of a visiting dancing contingent is consequently taken as a measure of the size of the contingent of warriors whose assistance may be expected in the next round of warfare.

In the morning the dancing ground turns into a trading ground. The items most frequently exchanged include axes, bird plumes, shell ornaments, an occasional baby pig, and, in former times, native salt. The *kaiko* thus facilitates trade by providing a market-like setting in which large numbers of traders can assemble. It likewise facilitates the movement of two critical items, salt and axes, by creating a demand for the bird plumes which may be exchanged for them.

The *kaiko* concludes with major pig sacrifices. On this particular occasion the Tsembaga butchered 105 adult and adolescent pigs, leaving only 60 juveniles and neonates alive. The survival of an additional fifteen adolescents and adults was only temporary, for they were scheduled as imminent victims. The pork yielded by the Tsembaga slaughter was estimated to weigh between 7,000 and 8,500 pounds, of which between 4,500 and 6,000 pounds were distributed to members of other local groups in 163 separate presentations. An estimated 2,000 to 3,000 people in seventeen local groups were the beneficiaries of the redistribution. The presentations, it should be mentioned, were not confined to pork. Sixteen Tsembaga men presented bridewealth or child-wealth, consisting largely of axes and shells, to their affines at this time.

The *kaiko* terminates on the day of the pig slaughter with the public presentation of salted pig belly to allies of the last fight. Presentations are made through the window in a high ceremonial fence built specially for the occasion at one end of the dance ground. The name of each honored man is announced to the assembled multitude as he charges to the window to receive his hero's portion. The fence is then ritually torn down, and the fighting stones are put away. The pig festival and the ritual cycle have been completed, demonstrating, it may be suggested, the ecological and economic competence of the local population. The local population would now be free, if it were not for the presence of the government, to attack its enemy again, secure in the knowledge that the assistance of allies and ancestors would be forthcoming because they have received pork and the obligations to them have been fulfilled.

Usually fighting did break out again very soon after the completion of the ritual cycle. If peace still prevailed when the ceremonial fence had rotted completely—a process said to take about three years, a little longer than the length of time required to raise a pig to maximum size—*rumbim* was planted as if there had been a fight, and all adult and adolescent pigs were killed. When the pig herd was large enough so that the *rumbim* could be uprooted, peace could be made with former enemies if they were also able to dig out their *rumbim.* To put this in formal terms: *If a pair of antagonistic groups proceeds through two ritual cycles without resumption of hostilities their enmity may be terminated.*

The relations of the Tsembaga with their environment have been analyzed as a complex system composed of two subsystems. What may be called the "local subsystem" has been derived from the relations of the Tsembaga with the nonhuman components of their immediate or territorial environment. It corresponds to the ecosystem in which the Tsembaga participate. A second subsystem, one which corresponds to the larger regional population of which the Tsembaga are one of the constituent units and which may be designated as the "regional subsystem," has been derived from the relations of the Tsembaga with neighboring local populations similar to themselves.

It has been argued that rituals, arranged in repetitive sequences, regulate relations both within each of the subsystems and within the larger complex system as a whole. The timing of the ritual cycle is largely dependent upon changes in the states of the components of the local subsystem. But the *kaiko,* which is the culmination of the ritual cycle, does more than reverse changes which have taken place within the local subsystem. Its occurrence also affects relations among the components of the regional subsystem. During its performance, obligations to other local populations are fulfilled, support for future military enterprises is rallied, and land from which enemies have earlier been driven is occupied. Its completion, furthermore, permits the local population to initiate warfare again. Conversely, warfare is terminated by rituals which preclude the reinitiation of warfare until the state of the local subsystem is again such that a *kaiko* may be staged and completed. Ritual among the Tsembaga and other Maring, in short, operates as both transducer, "translating" changes in the state of one subsystem into information which can effect changes in a second subsystem, and homeostat, maintaining a number of variables which in sum comprise the total system within ranges of viability. To repeat an earlier assertion, the operation of ritual among the Tsembaga and other Maring helps to maintain an undegraded environment, limits fighting to frequencies which do not endanger the existence of the regional population, adjusts man-land ratios, facilitates trade, distributes local surpluses of pig throughout the regional population in the form of pork, and assures people of high quality protein when they are most in need of it.

Religious rituals and the supernatural orders toward which they are directed cannot be assumed *a priori* to be mere epiphenomena. Ritual may, and doubtless frequently does, do nothing more than validate and intensify the relationships which integrate the social unit, or symbolize the relationships which bind the social unit to its environment. But the interpretation of such presumably *sapiens*-specific phenomena as religious ritual within a framework which will also accommodate the behavior of other species shows, I think, that religious ritual may do much more than symbolize, validate, and intensify relationships. Indeed, it would not be improper to refer to the Tsembaga and the other entities with which they share their territory as a "ritually regulated ecosystem," and to the Tsembaga and their human neighbors as a "ritually regulated population."

REFERENCES CITED

Berg, C.
    1948   Protein deficiency and its relation to nutritional anemia, hypoproteinemia, nutritional edema, and resistance to infection. In *Protein and amino acids in nutrition,* ed. M. Sahyun, pp. 290–317. New York: Reinhold.
Burton, B. T., ed.
    1959   *The Heinz handbook of nutrition.* New York: McGraw-Hill.
Elman, R.
    1951   *Surgical care.* New York: Appleton-Century-Crofts.

Food and Agriculture Organization of the United Nations
   1964   Protein: at the heart of the world food problem. *World Food Problems*
          5. Rome: FAO.
Hipsley, E., and N. Kirk
   1965   Studies of the dietary intake and energy expenditure of New Guine-
          ans. South Pacific Commission, Technical Paper 147. Noumea: South
          Pacific Commission.
Homans, G. C.
   1941   Anxiety and ritual: the theories of Malinowski and Radcliffe-Brown.
          American Anthropologist 43:164-172.
Houssay, B. A., et al.
   1955   *Human physiology.* 2nd edit. New York: McGraw-Hill.
Large, A., and C. G. Johnston
   1948   Proteins as related to burns. In *Proteins and amino acids in nutrition,*
          ed. M. Sahyun, pp. 386-396. New York: Reinhold.
Lund, C. G., and S. M. Levenson
   1948   Protein nutrition in surgical patients. In *Proteins and amino acids in
          nutrition,* ed. M. Sahyun, pp. 349-363. New York: Reinhold.
Moore, O. K.
   1957   Divination—a new perspective. *American Anthropologist* 59:69-74.
National Research Council
   1963   Evaluation of protein quality. National Academy of Sciences-
          National Research Council Publication 1100. Washington: NAS/NRC.
Rappaport, R. A.
   1966   Ritual in the ecology of a New Guinea people. Unpublished doctoral
          dissertation. Columbia University.
Vayda, A. P., A. Leeds, and D. B. Smith
   1961   The place of pigs in Melanesian subsistence. In *Proceedings of the 1961
          Annual Spring Meeting of the American Ethnological Society,* ed. V. E.
          Garfield, pp. 69-77. Seattle: University of Washington Press.
Wayne-Edwards, V. C.
   1962   *Animal dispersion in relation to social behaviour.* Edinburgh and Lon-
          don: Oliver & Boyd.
Zintel, Harold A.
   1964   Nutrition in the care of the surgical patient. In *Modern nutrition in
          health and disease,* ed. M. G. Wohl and R. S. Goodhart, pp. 1043-
          1064. 3rd edit. Philadelphia: Lee & Febiger.

Ecology, Adaptation,

and the Ills of Functionalism

Several years ago in an essay in *Man* (1974: 444–469) Jonathan Fried-man characterized as species of vulgar materialism "the ecological anthropology of Vayda, Rappaport and others, and, in a more obvious way, the cultural materialism most recently espoused by Marvin Harris" (p. 444). He further associates this ecological anthropology with "the new functionalism" which, he says, "is fundamentally the same as the old functionalism except that the field of application has changed, the interest now being to show the rationality of institutions with respect to their environmeits rather than to other elements in the society" (p. 457). He does, however, seem to modify the harshness of this assessment in some degree: "The new functional ecology, through its *a priori* assumptions, is ... entrenched in the ideological matrix of vulgar materialism even though its ultimate source and possible salvation is the far more productive framework of systems theory" (p. 445). In the course of his argument he also criticizes my analysis and interpretation of the ritual cycle of the Tsembaga Maring of New Guinea for the improper use of a basic systemic concept, namely negative feedback.

I am grateful to Friedman for the opportunity he has provided to clarify some matters relating to ecological concepts, functional formulations, and the relationship between them. I must note at the outset, however, that the highly general nature of Friedman's critique presents

---

Sections IV and X of this article have been added, for this publication, to the first half of an essay entitled "Ecology, Adaptation, and the Ills of Functionalism (Being, among Other Things, a Response to Jonathan Friedman)," originally published in *Michigan Discussions in Anthropology* 2: 138–190, 1977.

certain problems for response. He paints in such broad strokes ("the new functionalism is fundamentally the same as the old") that it becomes necessary to refine or elaborate his arguments before responding to them, a tedious exercise sometimes requiring the recitation of fundamentals. Moreover, he attempts to paint over a very broad canvas ("the ecological anthropology of Vayda, Rappaport and others"). Friedman's critique thus advertises itself as highly inclusive in its applicability, and presumably in its basis. In fact, he attends to only one work of mine (1968) and to a précis of that work published subsequently as an introduction to an argument concerning the relationship of sanctity to certain characteristics of language (1971a). One old work of Vayda's is cited very briefly in a context conflating it with the work of Suttles (1960) and Piddocke (1965). Harris's interpretation of the place of sacred cows in Indian economic and environmental relations is the only other work clearly associated by Friedman with "the new functional ecology" with which he deals at all. Other works appearing among his references are mentioned only in footnotes (particularly footnote 16: "See references for works by Vayda, Collins [1965], Rappaport, etc."). The basis of Friedman's critique of "the new functional ecology," is, thus, much narrower than the scope he claims for it ("the ecological anthropology of Vayda, Rappaport and others," to say nothing of the cultural materialism of Harris). Indeed, it is narrower than would reasonably warrant making it stand for "my" ecological anthropology much less that of Vayda and others.

The context of my discussion will have to be, in some degree, *Pigs for the Ancestors* because it is the battleground that Friedman has chosen. My aim, however, is not so much to defend a work published a decade ago as it is to consider problems of a more general nature, and to correct what I take to be some common misunderstandings.

I

I shall deal first with the matter of vulgar materialism, which Friedman defines as follows:

Vulgar materialism, mechanical materialism, and economism are terms which refer to a simplistic kind of materialism, rejected by Marx, which envisages social forms as mere epiphenomena of technologies and environments, either by direct causation or by some economic rationality which makes institutions the product of social optimisation. This approach has made its appearance in the form of what Sahlins has called the "new materialism" (1969: 30); neofunctional ecology and cultural materialism, both of which are embedded in the functionalist-empiricist ideology which has characterised most of American social science. [1974: 456–457]

I am not sure that this is an adequate characterization of "vulgar materialism" but, after all, vulgar materialism is a vague and pejorative notion rather than a precise theoretical concept. What does seem to be implied by "epiphenomena" (an inaccurate term because, in denoting the secondary and the derivative, it may connote insignificance, mere effect which in itself effects nothing, and no one, so far as I know, has argued this of "social forms") is that social forms are caused by, or emerge out of (perhaps as some sort of by-product), the interactions of environments and technologies. If this is a criterion of vulgar materialism then *Pigs for the Ancestors* is not vulgarly materialistic because it does not attempt to account in any way whatsoever for the emergence of the social forms with which it is concerned, except, perhaps, in a few sentences (1968: 231) which note that there are strong similarities among the ritual practices of different Highlands peoples, and that the variations among them may be the result of "differences in the ecological circumstances of various populations." This brief suggestion followed an earlier article by Vayda and me (1967) in which we (also briefly) suggested that cultures generate (in accordance with their own constraints) ranges of forms from among which environments select in a manner that may be generally similar to the ways in which natural selection operates upon populations of organisms. I grant that this formulation was vague, that it was hardly original and that it does not constitute an adequate account of the relationship of culture to environment, particularly of the mutually causal and constraining processes that characterize the evolution or "emergence" of human social forms, anthropocentric ecosystems and even humanity itself. I simply assert here that it is an account that does not take social forms to be mere epiphenomena of technologies and environments. Friedman would have to agree that such a formulation is not vulgarly materialistic because he himself proposes something very similar (1974: 451) as if it were an insight vouchsafed to us for the first time by the conjunction of structuralism and Marxism. I would respectfully suggest that inasmuch as he claimed that his charge of vulgar materialism is applicable to the new ecology generally, it was Friedman's responsibility to take this published proposition into account, and then to remark on the ways it differs from or resembles his proposal that environments, as it were, select from among the range of possible transformations of structures those that do, in fact, occur.

I am led here to a second point in Friedman's characterization of vulgar materialism. If I understand him correctly he also considers to be vulgarly materialist a view which would take as causal an economic rationality, which makes institutions the products of social optimization. The charge is difficult to deal with because of the vagueness of the terms, a vagueness that may mask fallacy and certainly encourages confusion.

What, for istance, is meant by "rationality" not only in Friedman's characterization of vulgar materialism but elsewhere in his article? (See his discussion of the "deadly weakness of functionalism" [1974: 459], which I, in turn, will discuss below.) He seems to be referring to some general property of social systems as wholes. Such a usage seems to me to be improper. It is either a translation of terms like "function" or "adaptiveness" into a different jargon or a vague and facile metaphor confusing two levels of analysis and abstraction (the individual and his decisions on the one hand, society and its structure on the other).* Nothing seems to be gained and considerable clarity is lost by using the term "rational" in such a way, and I would urge that it be reserved to refer to processes inhering in individuals or discrete decision-making agencies.

As far as economic rationality is concerned, then, I understand it to be a process located in the thought of individuals and, derivatively or metaphorically, in certain of the activities of corporations acting more or less as individuals. The term "rationality" implies, if it does not entail, consciousness, purpose, and deliberateness. The term "economic" when combined with it implies that consciousness and deliberateness are put to the task of weighing alternatives with respect to differences in the advantages they may be expected to confer upon those who have the opportunity to select among them. The goals of economic rationality, it is generally assumed, are highly specified and it is generally further assumed that the aim of economic rationality is to maximize these specifics, whatever they may be.

Pigs for the Ancestors did, of course, consider behavior that may aptly be described as economic. Individual choices are made with respect to the disposal of pigs; women, I suppose, assess the degrees to which their backs ache against their goals of their husbands; people must be concerned with trade-offs between the work of pig raising and the trouble following garden invasions on the one hand, and the satisfaction of their allies with the pork they are given on the other, and so on. Whether all of these and other considerations are weighed rationally is not a matter which need concern us. One of the main points of the analysis, however, was that Maring ritual regulation is surely not to be understood as an outcome of the economistic behavior of individuals but as providing an order such that (1) the fulfillment of the goals of individuals is given culturally defined and sanctified meaning, and (2) *in the particular case at hand* made consonant with the perpetuation of groups as biological and social entities and with the perpetuation of the Maring as a whole. Maring ritual regulation *stands against* or constrains the economic (and political) goals of individuals and even of corporate groups. In some

---

*Robert Hefner, personal communication.

instances it induces them to behave in ways which do the opposite of maximizing their positions vis-à-vis others. This argument seems to me to be implicit throughout *Pigs for the Ancestors,* but was made explicit in at least one passage (1968: 239), and has been argued at length elsewhere (Kelly and Rappaport 1975).

I have argued that ritual regulation among the Maring is consonant with ecosystemic imperatives and, were it not for the fallacy inherent in attributing rationality to societies, a charge of *ecological* rationality might have been more apposite. Ecological rationality, which may be observed in some individuals, is not simply an extension of economizing rationality into the environmental domain. It is a "rationality" which, concerned with the persistence of systems in which the actor participates and upon which his continued existence is contingent, is *contradicted* by a rationality which is concerned with the maximization of the immediate interests of the actor vis-à-vis that system. It was made clear very early in the book, however, that the conscious purposes of the Maring were not ecological, that is, the ecosystemic regulatory functions of the ritual cycle were mystified by its sacred aspects, although some Maring were surely aware of them.

That the consonance of the religious logic of the ritual cycle with ecosystemic imperatives was not accounted for adequately is a shortcoming of the book, but it seems hardly surprising that social and ecological regulation in an unstratified and undifferentiated society in which production is domestic and in which only a simple technology is available is preservative of the ecosystem. I did not assert that social and cultural forms and the relations among them always and everywhere somehow absorb ecosystematic imperatives and institute ecologically sound practice. Such is not the case among all tribal peoples, and strip-mining, clear-cutting, offshore oil-drilling and continued use of fluorocarbons, among other things, would make nonsense of such an assertion were it to be extended into the "developed" world. I have, in fact, argued in a number of publications (especially 1971b, 1971c, 1976, 1977) that sociocultural forms and ecosystemic considerations often are, are likely to be, indeed may inevitably come to be, at odds. If cultural forms can be contradictory to ecosystemic processes it is hard to see how they can be mere epiphenomena of technologies interacting with environments.

In sum, I think the charge, as made by Friedman, that *Pigs for the Ancestors* is an instance of a vulgar materialism inherent in ecological formulations generally, fails. Later we shall touch upon a related charge, raised by Marshall Sahlins, that of "ecology fetishism."

II

We may now turn to more substantial matters. Friedman identifies the "new ecology" with the "new functionalism" and the "new functionalism" with the old. There are difficulties in dealing with this rather complex matter. For one thing, I do not wish to defend the ill-defined corpus of doctrines designated by the term "functionalism" from criticisms with which I have agreed in print (1968, 1971c; see also Vayda 1968; and Vayda and Rappaport 1967). Indeed, the fieldwork reported in *Pigs for the Ancestors,* and the analysis attempted in that book were guided by *criticisms* of functionalism, and not functional doctrine *per se.*

Moreover, although Friedman identified "ecological anthropology" and "neo-functionalism" with the "old functionalism," he does not specify very clearly the ways in which he takes them to be similar, and he certainly does not deal adequately with the contentions of Vayda, me (references cited) and others (Collins 1965) that they are different in important respects. By ignoring our statements concerning these differences he merely asserts an identity between us and that which we ourselves have criticized. Such a tactic sets discussion back rather than advancing it. If he wished to make the case that the new ecology is fundamentally the same as the old functionalism it was his responsibility to take into consideration both our aims and our practice, and to show that either or both are not essentially different from those of the old functionalism. His discussion is deficient in this regard. His case also required a more comprehensive critique of functionalism than it has in fact provided. In taking up the problems of functionalism we may, however, begin with points that Friedman has raised.

Following Murphy (1970), Friedman notes two related difficulties associated with the concept of function, and he asserts that they continue to plague the "new ecology."

> *a.* In its more modest form, it dissolves into pure description. The function of the stomach is to digest food; the function of ritual pig slaughter is to regulate pig populations—i.e. the function of x is to do what it does. The word here is totally superfluous and adds no information unless we assume some metaphysical notion of purpose implied in the following.
> *b.* By extension to the teleological meaning, "function" becomes "adaptive function." Here we are still dealing with our first definition, "the function of x is to do what it does," but now the "what it does" is not an observed datum, and we are left with what is basically a description of imaginary relations, where the "function" is assumed rather than demonstrated. [1974: 457]

I would, of course, agree that the term "function" adds little or nothing to statements that simply describe the output, immediate result, or product of the operation of some system, structure, or process. In the analysis of any particular case the term "function" should be reserved for the designation of contributions made by components of defined systems to the unitary character or maintenance of those systems. It was so used in *Pigs for the Ancestors,* both explicitly and implicitly.

Before discussing function *per se,* it seems to me that some things need to be said about description *per se.* Although I agree that functional assertions and simple descriptions should not be confused, I do take description to be in itself worthwhile. The first duty of an ethnographer is to report as thoroughly and accurately as he can. If he cannot "explain" everything that he reports, it is no serious matter. Someone else someday may be able to do so, perhaps long after our currently fashionable modes of explanation have become quaint.

There is more to be said in favor of description, however, than that it reports that which may eventually be explained. First, "what is being done" by an organ or an institution is not always as patent as Friedman's parodied examples might suggest. To follow him in his organic allusion, while men have always had a kind of commonsense awareness of what the stomach, heart, and eyes "do," they have not always had such an awareness of either the outputs of, say, the pancreas, the thyroid, and the vermiform appendix, or of the place of these outputs in the maintenance of the organisms of which they are indubitably parts. Discourse concerning these matters, whether or not it is in some narrow sense explanatory (Hempel [1968] and Nagel [1961] agree that it may be), is not superfluous, and discoveries concerning them are, of course, highly informative. We should beware of confusing explanation with informativeness or understanding (see Bergmann 1975).

It is not the case, however, that analyses generally designated "functional" or "systemic" are always actually concerned with "what *x* does." They may be at least as concerned with how systems work as with what they do, and may even take the latter for granted. Men "knew" that the stomach digested food long before they knew how, but elucidation of the ways in which various organic structures and substances join together in the complex processes of anabolism and catabolism is, obviously, enormously informative, and important as well. Similarly, to leave Friedman's organic example for a cultural one, we might say, for example, that anthropology has known since Durkheim's time that rituals establish or enhance solidarity among those joining in their performance. Indeed, an awareness of this has no doubt been part of general common sense since time immemorial. Yet we have much to learn about just *how* ritual creates this solidarity.

In sum, whether or not they are "explanatory" (and if properly formulated and appropriately applied I take them to be), statements of "what it does" and "how it does it" may well be among the most informative, important, and interesting that may be made concerning an organ, an institution, or a convention. To put this a little differently, among the most informative things that can be said about structures or systems, be they organic, social, cultural, or ecological, are statements concerning how they maintain, order, reproduce, and transform themselves. To make such statements concerning structures or systems requires, of course, some elucidation of the parts played by their elements. In the work that Friedman seems to have been attempting to parody in his reference to the ritual regulation of pig populations, I was concerned not merely to note the direct outcome of pig sacrifices, but with the operation of a protracted ritual cycle of which pig sacrifices are a part, and the place of that cycle in a complex system that included ecosystemic, economic, and political relations.

Friedman seems contemptuous of pure description, but does not indicate what he means by the term. For instance, a statement to the effect that ritual pig slaughters *regulate* pig populations could not be counted as "pure description," if we mean to denote by the phrase "pure description" accounts of events. A sentence stating, simply, that a ritual sacrifice has reduced the number of living pigs would be closer. The term "regulate," however, which predicates the sentence that Friedman offers, also and inescapably refers to phenomena external to the event being described and, because regulation is not a directly observable datum, it also implies or even entails some sort of analytic operation. A similar observation can be made with respect to the term "digest" in Friedman's stomach sentence. When their predicates are spelled out these sentences denote relationships between their subjects and larger structures or systems. Moreover, the relationships denoted by the terms "regulate" and "digest" are supportive, and properly designated "functional" in the narrowest sense of the term. Digestion is, after all, necessary to the maintenance of life in organisms, regulation to the persistence of dynamic systems of all classes. Thus, even those sentences that Friedman adduces, in virtual parody, as instances of pure description are probably not what he means by pure description, but are better taken as examples of the second class of functional sentences he identifies, a class he summarily dismisses as descriptive of merely "imaginary relations," in which an adaptive function is assumed rather than demonstrated. Friedman provides us with no definition of "adaptation" or "adaptive function," and the imaginary nature of the relations under consideration is asserted as a derogation rather than demonstrated or even discussed (1974: 457).

The question of "imaginary" versus "real" relations is, of course, sticky. I would only note that all analytic constructs are, in a sense, "imaginary." To disregard this is to fall into the error of misplaced concreteness. Analytic models should make "facts" intelligible, but such models are not themselves "the facts" nor, for that matter, facts at all except as artifacts of metaphysics and epistemology. (N.B.: I speak here of elements of *analytic* models, not components of actors' models.)

If analytic models are imaginary, then the relationships among their components cannot be other than imaginary. This is not, however, to claim that no "real" relations exist in the world. The more or less unified entities with which anthropologists, ecologists, and, for that matter, all scientists are concerned are made up of parts. Relations among these parts and the units of which they are parts, be they conceived as processes or as things, are not imaginary. Whether or not an analyst gets these relations straight—that is, whether or not these relations are accounted for by his imaginary model—is another matter. Friedman's assertions concerning the imaginary nature of "adaptive functions" do not lead me to abandon my belief that analytic terms like "adaptation" and "adaptive function" correspond to processes occurring in the real world. It still seems to me too that the systemic and ecological model applied in *Pigs for the Ancestors* so far as it went (and it should not be forgotten in this regard that it subsumed a structural account of the oppositions of Maring religious logic and their mediation, in accordance with which regulatory activities were performed), provided a reasonable account of the Maring materials. Others may disagree and are free to offer alternative accounts. If I were doing the analysis now rather than a decade ago, I probably would give more attention to the place of individual strategies in the allocation of pork concomitant to the major sacrifices at the end of the *kaiko,* if only to avoid fruitless argument. The data did not suggest to me when the analysis was undertaken, however, nor do they now, that these considerations accounted for the *size* of the pig herd deemed sufficient to perform the *kaiko.*

III

Assertions that the concept of function "in its more modest form dissolves into pure description," and "by extension to the teleological meaning" becomes "what is basically a description of imaginary relations" (1974: 457), together with attempts to illustrate these assertions, hardly constitute an adequate account of the ills of the "old functionalism," let alone grounds for asserting that the "new ecology" is heir to them. It is with some reluctance that I reopen this old can of worms, but in order to respond usefully to the general charge that "ecological anthropology" is "fundamentally the same as the old functionalism except that the field of application has changed . . . to show the rationality of institutions with respect to their environments" (1974: 457), I am afraid that it is necessary to cite more comprehensive critiques of functionalism than Friedman provides. Doing so will allow me to make some of my own views concerning functionalism's limitations explicit, and to indicate some important differences between the "old functionalism" and the ecological perspective of at least some present-day workers.

We may turn here to the critiques of Brown (1963), Hempel (1968), and Nagel (1961), critiques with which, as I indicated in *Pigs for the Ancestors* (especially chapter 6), I am in general agreement. Although its concerns were primarily substantive, *Pigs for the Ancestors* was written with these criticisms in mind and it may be regarded as a more or less explicit, although not altogether successful, attempt to take them into account.

I should remind readers at the outset that the objections the philosophers I have named, and others as well, have addressed to functionalist thought and practice were parts of attempts to specify the proper limits of functional statements and to purge functional analyses of the faults that may, and often do, vitiate them. They were not attempts to do away with the notion of function, which they took to have a valid place in the social sciences, a position with which Friedman surely must agree inasmuch as he proposes, incorrectly I think,* that the elements that make up the hierarchical structures which he calls social formations are simply functional distinctions (1974: 445).

Hempel (1958) argues that functional formulations in the social sciences often fail for several reasons (which can only be outlined in their general form here). First, they are often untestable because their key terms lack empirical import. The entities to which functional assertions refer are frequently not specified with sufficient precision (to which may be added Brown's [1963] objection that these entities are not always

---

*The social formation in Friedman's scheme is a hierarchy, bifurcated in the first descending level into "infrastructure" and "superstructure." Superstructure subsumes two elements or subsystems, one labeled "juridico-political," the other "ideological." Infrastructure is bifurcated into "relations of production" and "forces of production," the latter again bifurcated into "means of production" and "organization of production." While a term like "juridico-political" may designate in a vague sort of way activities of a certain sort, it is descriptive rather than functional. The term "ideological" denotes phenomena of a certain ontological nature. It does not, in itself, propose the contribution that ideology makes to systems in general (meta-function) or to any particular system (function). Terms like "infrastructure" and "superstructure" are of an entirely different order. They are analytic rather than descriptive (ontological) or functional terms. The same may be said for "relations of production" and, possibly, the other terms as well. The "model" seems to be composed of a hodgepodge of terms of different order. Moreover, as it is represented diagrammatically its structure shows no clear relation of command—or dialectic—between the elements of superstructure and infrastructure. It is quite possible that I misunderstand this model, but it seems to me that it betrays a lack of awareness of the distinction between an analytic model which attempts to relate categories with respect to inclusiveness and a systemic model which attempts to represent operating relationships among parts. The latter sort must be system-specific if they are to be useful. The former may be of use for gathering data and organizing them categorically.

*Sahlins (1969) has used this point as a mild criterion of ecological formulations, but it seems to me misplaced as such. The point is well-understood by ecological anthropologists and, moreover, it is implicit in the use of goal ranges in designated variables to specify acceptable or adaptive states.

proper objects of functional assertions), and there is often a failure to provide empirical criteria for such terms as "adequate functioning." Second, there is a failure to make explicit the hypotheses of self-regulation that are implicit in functional formulations and to identify the mechanisms of self-regulation precisely. He also notes certain difficulties in functional logic, and, I might add, there are further confusions with respect to the relationship between universal and system-specific functional formulations. I shall take up these problems later.

These criticisms were, of course, justified, and I attempted to meet them in *Pigs for the Ancestors*. Thus, the units to which the book's functional—I would now prefer to use the term adaptive—assertions in the main referred were specific and concrete: organisms, self-defined groups of organisms, such as local populations; and ecosystems. Procedures for identifying these units were made explicit when necessary, and the choice of these rather than other units was argued on the grounds that they are commensurable with ecological (and adaptive) theory. Whether or not they are proper objects of functional statements is a separate issue (although their appearance in ecological theory, which is systemic in its general outlines, would lead us to believe, *prima facie,* that they are).

Brown (1963: 110) has asserted that functional statements hold only in systems of a certain type, namely those that are "self-persisting." Within them, Brown states, functional statements are, in fact, causal. He is in agreement in this regard with Nagel (1961), who states that functional statements are appropriate in connection with systems incorporating "self-persisting mechanisms." Brown notes that a system can be taken to be self-persisting if it includes self-regulatory devices or mechanisms.

There is clearly no argument between Friedman and me concerning the propriety of including within the class of "self-persisting," "self-maintaining," or "self-regulating" systems both organisms and organized social groups, a class of which local populations are members. It may be asked, however, whether ecosystems are to be included among such systems. Friedman thinks not:

An eco-system is not organized as such. It is the result of the mutual and usually partial adaptation of populations each of which has laws of functioning that are internally determined. [1974: 466]

Vayda and McKay (1975: 229ff.) seem to come close to agreement with Friedman. Citing Colinvaux's (1973: 549) remark, ". . . nowhere can we find discrete ecosystems, let alone ecosystems with the self-organizing properties implied by the concept of the climax . . ." they assert that "the ecosystem is an analytic, not a biological, entity." They continue by proposing that "interactions observed in complex ecosystems need not be regarded as expressing self-organizing properties of the systems themselves; instead they can be understood as the consequences of the various and variable adaptive strategies of individual organisms living together in restricted spaces." (While Friedman favors the "social formation" as an analytic unit, Vayda and McKay assign a priority to the individual organism because natural selection operates on individuals.)

I regard all of this to be rather muddled. The distinction that Vayda and McKay make between the analytic and biological seems to me to be a mistaken one. It is surely the case that there are few, if any, ecosystems less inclusive than the solar system that are hermetically sealed to flows of matter, energy, and information across their borders. Their boundaries must, therefore, be specified analytically, as must those of social formations or, for that matter, social units of any sort. The question of the criteria used to discriminate ecosystems from the continuity of natural phenomena is, of course, strategic. In *Pigs for the Ancestors* the criterion for establishing the boundaries of local ecosystems in what was a continuous biotic association, it is important to note, was human territoriality. The Maring are horticulturalists and, as such, ecological dominants. They set the conditions encouraging or discouraging the presence of other species, and they attempt to construct anthropocentric ecosystems within areas in which the engagement of humans in interspecies exchanges is conventionally regulated. Maring local groups are regulating the ecosystems within which they participate or, to put it in the converse, the domain of the regulatory operations of a local group *defines* an ecosystem. Because a Maring local group is a component of the ecosystem which it regulates (and upon the persistence of which its own persistence is contingent) the ecosystem is by definition self-regulating.

It might be argued that self-regulatory properties are peculiar to anthropocentric ecosystems. I think this is not the case. Self-regulating mechanisms, I believe, inhere in ecosystems *qua* ecosystems *as well as* in their constituent populations. That there are self-regulating mechanisms at one level of organization does not mean that there are none at others. Every population in every ecosystem must have "internally determined laws of functioning" of its own, but this does not mean that there are no self-regulating mechanisms emerging out of relations between and among populations—as in the case of the mutual regulation of predator and prey populations. Ecosystemic self-regulation may be a product of dynamic interaction among a number of species none of whom exercises central control or is even dominant in a less active way. Such diffuse regulation is not unfamiliar to us; it animates, at least conceptually, the "perfect market" of economic mythology.

Ecosystems do seem to be self-regulated, then, and they show other indications of being "organized as such." For one thing they possess well-known structural characteristics. Regardless of what their constituent species may be, ecological systems are roughly cyclical with respect to material flow and pyramidal with respect to the productivity and energy flux of constituent populations, and with respect to population regulation as well. They also seem to possess "self-organizing" properties. They not only transform themselves in response to changes in external conditions, sometimes by replacing all of their constituent species populations with populations of other species, but also through the mutual adaptation of their constituent species to each other. (I am not sure what Friedman means when he asserts that these adaptations are only "partial." Biological adaptation cannot create *ex nihilo*. It can do no more than transform what is present. As such, I suppose it can never be more than partial in some sense. Nevertheless, some astounding relationships [e.g., termites and *Myxotricha paradoxa*] have evolved, relationships of such intricacy and intimacy that the term "co-evolution" should be used to refer to the mutual causal processes through which they have emerged.)

Although ecosystems may include species that have come together accidentally and which are, at the outset, only crudely articulated, the constitutions of such systems are likely to become increasingly elaborate and coercive through time. Many ecologists have believed, and continue to believe, that ecosystemic successions, unless they are arrested or deflected, exhibit certain holistic tendencies and that these tendencies are similar in systems very different in species composition (see Odum 1969; Margalef 1968). Under more or less stable conditions, it is proposed, the number of species of which ecosystems are composed increases, perhaps to some maximum; the species present become increasingly specialized and an increasing proportion of them is composed of large, longer-lived, slower-breeding organisms. Systems as wholes require less and less energy flux per unit of standing biomass to sustain themselves, but productivity per unit of area increases. Material and energy pathways proliferate, as do regulatory mechanisms. Systemic redundancy thus offsets the loss of systemic stability that might otherwise be a concomitant of the increasing specialization of the species present. Colinvaux (1973, chs. 6 and 40 especially) has recently argued that successional properties have been oversimplified and their commonalities exaggerated, but even he does not dismiss them. The adjudication of this argument must be left to biological ecologists. Whatever the outcome of their debate may be, however, there are sufficient grounds for taking ecosystems to be organized as such, to be members of the class of self-persistent systems, and as such they qualify as proper objects of functional formulations. Whether they are appropriate units of such formulations in particular cases is, of course, another matter.

A statement of Robert Murphy's could possibly be taken to be an argument against using the ecosystem as an object of functional statements even though the organized status of such systems is granted:

> Higher order phenomena arrange lower order phenomena to their purposes, though they may not change their properties. Correspondingly, human social systems reach out and embrace ecosystems rather than the reverse proposition, and culture reorders nature and makes appendages of the parts of it that are relevant to the human situation. [1970: 169]

The only qualification that I would voice with respect to this statement is that it may not apply to hunting and gathering populations. With food production—or at least with plant cultivation—men become ecological dominants, the populations setting the conditions encouraging or discouraging the presence of populations of other species. The burden of regulating anthropocentric ecosystems rests, of course, upon the men dominating them. To say that men put nature to their own purposes (i.e., regulate ecosystems in accordance with what they take to be their own self-interest) is true to the point of truism, but this is hardly the end of the matter. We want to know how this is done; what the purposes and understandings of the actors may be; to what degree these purposes are themselves constituted, coerced, or constrained by environmental characteristics; the degree to which they conform to, or are even explicitly concerned with or informed by, an awareness of the requirements of ecosystemic perpetuation; and, of course, whether actions guided by such purposes are ecologically destructive. My study of the Tsembaga suggested to me that there was such conformity in this case, and I have argued elsewhere (1971c) that this may not be unusual in small highly self-sufficient preindustrial social groups all of whose full members are actively engaged in gardening.

To insist upon the self-regulating, self-organizing characteristics of ecosystems is not to claim that only ecosystems are organized as such and that functional statements properly apply only to them. Well-defined social units and individual organisms are also constituted systems with "laws of functioning that are internally determined." To note that ecosystems are constituted is not to deny to the organisms and populations of organisms (including human groups) participating in them their relative autonomy. Conversely, to recognize the relative autonomy of a social unit is not to deny the organization of the ecosystem of which it is a part, any more than to recognize the relative autonomy of individuals is to deny the organization of the social units of which individuals are always members. To deny the organization of more inclusive systems to protect conceptually the autonomy of the systems they include is not to argue for the relative autonomy of the latter. It is tantamount to arguing for the absolute autonomy of systems at one or another level of inclusiveness (laissez-faire capitalists would, for instance, take the autonomous systems to be, properly, individuals or corporations) operating in larger fields which are not systematic or the systemic qualities of which are purely derivative. The complexity of the world does not warrant such a view even for analytic or heuristic purposes. We must recognize that more inclusive entities are indeed organized systems, made up of components that are themselves relatively autonomous. Ecosystems, for instance, include populations which are, in turn, composed of individuals. While it may be that generally similar principles organize systems at various levels of inclusiveness, as systems theory proposes, we must also recognize that there are important differences in their more specific "laws of functioning."

A difference to which little attention has been given, and which is perhaps closely related to relative autonomy, is that of the differential degrees of coherence that systems of different classes both require and can tolerate. By "relative coherence" I refer to the degree to which changes in one component of a system effect changes in other components of the system. A fully coherent system is one in which any change in any component results in an immediate and proportional change in all other components. As no living system could be totally incoherent, neither could any living system be fully coherent, for disruptions anywhere would immediately spread everywhere. Perhaps because their functining depends upon fine, quick, and continual coordination of their parts, organisms are, and must be, more coherent than social systems. Conversely, the degree of coherence continually required by organisms would probably be intolerable for social systems (which may attain levels of coherence comparable to that of organisms only in extraordinary circumstances for relatively brief periods). Ecosystems are probably less coherent than social systems, at least human social systems (perhaps because orderly relations within them depend more on increasing redundancy of food and energy chains than upon coordination). Their low degree of coherence may well be in large part responsible for our frequent failure to recognize their systemic characteristics.

It is, of course, obvious that the maintenance of systems and the purposes of their relatively autonomous components do not always coincide. Men can surely do violence to the structure and function of the ecosystems that they come to dominate, just as certain subsystems of societies, such as industries, can do violence to the social entities that they come to dominate. Although such violation is not unexampled among tribal peoples, its likelihood is increased and its effects extended and intensified by increased differentiation of society, alienating or at least separating the economic rationalities of individuals from direct ecological imperatives by production for gain rather than use and by industrialization.

The imperatives of individual existence often bring men into conflict with the social systems of which they are members; the cultural imperatives of social systems may lead to actions at variance with ecological principles. Contradiction between constituted systems on various levels of inclusiveness—between men and societies, between societies and ecosystems—are inevitable. Sahlins (1969) and Friedman err, I think, in taking ecological or adaptive formulations to be "innocent of a concern for contradiction." Elsewhere (1969a, 1974, 1976, 1977, and see "Adaptive Structure and Its Disorders" in this volume) I have discussed maladaptation in structural terms, proposing that it is to be understood as, or as resulting from, interlevel contradiction. Indeed, it seems to me that it is Friedman's argument, and not adaptive and ecological formulations, that is analytically innocent of a concern for interlevel contradiction. In insisting, as I think he should, upon the relative autonomy of certain social entities, he mistakenly, in my view, denies reality or organization to the systems that include the systems he favors. But if reality or organization is denied to ecological systems how is it possible to discover contradictions between them and the social entities participating in them? By asserting the autonomy of his chosen systems and by banishing to virtual irrelevance others Friedman may not only miss much of explanatory importance but also much of what is problematic or even poignant or tragic in the human condition. The impoverishment of the perspective is increased if relevance is also denied to the relative autonomy of the individuals composing the social entities with which he is concerned. It should not be forgotten that one of the perennial concerns of human thought about the human condition is with the problems congregating in the relationship between individuals and the societies of which they are members, problems which are conceptually summarized in such phrases as "the problem of freedom"—or of happiness, duty, honor, authenticity, ambition, responsibility, obligation, or ethics.

IV

More needs to be said about populations as referent units in ecological formulations before we proceed to further problems of functional formulations. The use of populations as environed units distinguishes most clearly what others have called the "new ecology" from the "cultural ecology" of Steward (1955) and others (e.g., Sahlins, 1958), in which cultures are taken to be the environed units. Friedman has raised no explicit objections to the use of populations (although his own choice would seem to be the "social formation"), but others have. Marshall

Sahlins has argued that in the "translation" of a "social order" into a "population of organisms ... everything that is distinctively cultural about the object has been allowed to escape" (1976a: 298). Because the propriety of an analytic choice of almost two decades ago remains a matter of discussion and, I believe, a matter of misunderstanding, it may be well, even at this late date, to clarify it and some of the considerations that led to it.

First, difficulties are entailed by the uses of cultures or their parts (e.g., Steward's "culture core") as environed units in ecological analyses, and when cultures are combined with an ecosystemic concept of the environment these difficulties are increased. An awkward analogy is implicit in the simple formulation of cultures in ecosystems, but before making it explicit I would suggest that such a choice is the result of a rather subtle methodological or even logical confusion, a confusion between an explicandum on the one hand and, on the other, the primary units of analysis, the major components of analytic or descriptive models, the elements seen to stand in relation to each other.

This confusion is easy to fall into, and it is understandable that anthropologists interested in the formative effects of environments on cultures would take cultures, or parts of cultures, to be their primary units of analysis. The conception of culture as an order of phenomena distinct from the psychological, biological, and inorganic has been one of anthropology's important contributions to Western thought. Inasmuch as cultural phenomena may be distinguished from other phenomena and inasmuch as culture, however it is understood, is what most cultural anthropologsts wish to elucidate, cultures or their constituents have seemed obvious choices for referent units in ecological as well as other anthropological formulations. Indeed, it may be that such a choice seems almost inevitable when it is remembered that culture is conceived by many anthropologists to be not only ontologically distinct from biological, psychological, and inorganic phenomena, but processually independent of them as well. Culture, it is said, obeys laws of its own, laws distinct from those governing organic and inorganic processes.

At the same time that cultural ecology took cultures, distinct from the organisms bearing them, to be interacting with environments, it borrowed the concept of ecosystem from general ecology. In the formulation resulting, cultures simply interact with ecosystems. But cultures and ecosystems are not directly commensurable and cannot simply be squeezed together in such fashion. An ecosystem is a system of matter and energy transactions among populations of organisms of various kinds, and between each of them and all of them on the one hand, and non-living substances, things, and processes on the other. Culture is the category of phenomena distinguished from others by its contingency upon symbols. A culture consists of the cultural phenomena distinguishing a particular group or category of people from others. The incommensurability of ecosystems and cultures becomes clear when the analogy implicit in the notion of cultures (independent of, or at least conceptually separated from, culture-bearing organisms) interacting with other components of ecological systems is made explicit.

CULTURE : ECOSYSTEM :: ANIMAL POPULATION : ECOSYSTEM

It is ironic to note that the choice of cultures as primary units of analysis in "cultural ecological" formulations aimed to protect the uniqueness of culture against the dissolving power of ecological principles, but it has the opposite effect, for the processual equivalence of cultures and animal populations is logically entailed by it. This not only implies that they have similar requirements that must be fulfilled in similar ways and are similarly limited by environmental constraints, but also that cultures, far from obeying laws of their own, are directly subject to the same laws as those governing animal populations. No cultural ecologist has ever taken such a position, of course, and, I am sure, none ever intended to do so. It is nevertheless intrinsic to the eclectic conjunction of incommensurable and incongruent terms that characterizes the cultural ecological conception. Eclectic formulations bring together the disparate terms they subsume only by violating some or all of them. In the case at hand the violence is wreaked upon the notion of culture, for it, or some of its aspects, such as the social order, may be conflated with biological phenomena. This problem is illustrated by difficulties experienced by Marshall Sahlins in *Social Stratification in Polynesia.* It was his thesis in that work that certain differences in the social orders of Polynesian societies, in particular differences in social stratification, were to be accounted for by differences in productivity. The term "productivity" must refer in societies such as those of Polynesia to the yields of horticulture and fishing. In the absence of direct production data he attempted to estimate the comparative productivity of the societies in question by comparing the size of the largest networks through which garden, grove, and fishing yields were distributed in each society, making the assumption that the larger the network and the more frequently it operated, the greater the surplus and therefore the higher the production. The relationship between surplus and productivity is problematic, however, and there is no reason to believe, *prima facie,* that a society of a certain size organized into a single distributive network produces more per capita than a smaller society, or more than one of the same size organized into a number of smaller networks. Moreover, if the scope of the distributive prerogatives vested in chiefs is an aspect of stratification, and if stratification is to be accounted for by productivity, to read productivity from the size of redistributive networks brings the argument perilously close to circularity.

The dubiety of a long inferential chain and the dangers of circularity are avoidable, however. Productivity in an ecological sense is understood as the amount of biomass or energy produced per unit of area per unit of time. The horticultural productivity of societies can thus be compared in such terms as tons per acre per year. In the absence of harvest and landing data indices may or must be used, but the size of redistributive networks is not an appropriate one. In relatively undifferentiated non-industrial societies like those of Polynesia, however, in which production is for use rather than for gain, and in which populations are closely related genetically, it is reasonable to infer comparative productivity, or production, from a comparison of the densities of the populations supported by that production. Such a comparison indicates that there was probably no correlation between social stratification and productivity in aboriginal Polynesia, but the point I wish to make here is that I believe Sahlins's difficulties have followed from a failure to distinguish an aspect of social orders—the size of redistributive networks—from a biological characteristic of populations, namely their densities.

Synthetic formulations in contrast to those which are merely eclectic subsume the subject matter of what had previously been separate realms of discourse under terms of sufficient generality to accommodate both without distortion. They do not ignore or deny distinctions but employ terms of sufficiently high logical type to encompass distinct phenomena as separate subclasses. The first step in moving toward any synthesis is to find terms expressing commonalities. In the case of the place of humans in ecosystemic processes, instead of attending only to that which distinguishes the human species from other species, synthesis begins with what is common to them and then proceeds to whatever may distinguish them. We thus begin with the simple observation that the human species is, after all, a species among species and that, as such, humanity's relations with its physical and biotic environments are, like those of other animals, continuous, indissoluble, and necessary. It follows that it is not only possible but proper to take populations of the human species to be an environed unit in ecological formulations.

An ecological population is an aggregate of organisms sharing distinctive means for maintaining a common set of material relations with the other components of the ecosystem in which they together participate. An ecosystem, as we have already noted, is the total of ecological populations and nonliving substances bound together in material exchanges in a demarcated portion of the biosphere. The terms "ecosystem" and "human population," taken in the ecological sense (and not, for instance, in the sense of a simple census count in a polity of some

sort) are fully commensurable and congruent. I have discussed procedures for discriminating ecosystems and populations of various sorts
elsewhere (1968, 1969b, 1971c) and need not discuss them further here.

But what of culture? *For purposes of ecological formulations,* cultures or
their constituents may be regarded as *properties* of populations. In this
view, culture is not analogous to animal populations but is, *in part,*
analogous to the distinctive means by which populations or other species
maintain their environmental relations. It is important to emphasize,
however, that to say that a population's means for meeting its needs are
cultural is surely *not* to say that cultures are mere instruments in the
service of organic phenomena. Far from being merely instrumental,
cultures have, as it were, needs and purposes of their own; some are
material and some may be at odds with the organic needs of the populations in which they occur. That the cultural properties of human populations can be inimical to their organic properties is as inherent to this
view of the relationship between cultural and organic phenomena as is
the recognition that aspects of culture are properly regarded as instrumental. Indeed, the contradiction, perhaps inevitable, between the cultural and biological is, in my view, the most important problem of an
ecologically aware anthropology. It is well to make clear, however, that
such an anthropology does not, or should not, attempt to account for all
of culture in ecological terms. It does not constitute a general theory of
culture, although it may be that some anthropologists, including me
(Rappaport 1971c; Vayda and Rappaport 1967), have come close to
trying to make it so from time to time. Be this as it may, no violation of
culture or any of its parts is *entailed* when cultures are taken to be
properties of populations. Indeed, far from the social order being reduced to the status of a population of organisms, as Sahlins charges
(1976: 298), organisms are more clearly distinguished from the cultural
conventions ordering them than they are in the cultural ecology of
Steward or the early Sahlins.

It may be well to make explicit further epistemological and metaphysical implications of the population unit. Although anthropologists
like to think of themselves as especially free of ethnocentrism, they have
traditionally been concerned with those aspects of human existence that
are unique to the species. Anthropology is, in short, anthropocentric
and, of course, it would be surprising if it weren't. But by focusing upon
those aspects of human existence that are unique to humanity we tend to
ignore other aspects of human existence that, although not unique to
human life, are nonetheless parts of it. Such a stance may lead us to
separate ourselves from or even oppose ourselves to the rest of nature in
our daily lives and public affairs, with the unhappy consequences we see

developing in the environment around us. Moreover, in our more formal attempts to understand our relation to the rest of the world we are encouraged to seek special explanations, explanations which, founded upon assumptions of uniqueness, can cover only one, or at best a narrow range, of cases, and we are dissuaded from attempts to understand cultural phenomena in terms of principles that apply to other species as well. Whether such general principles as those concerning adaptation, homeostasis, and cybernetic operation have much to contribute to our understanding of culture or the human condition is touched upon later in this essay. Here it may be suggested that formulations that illuminate similarities rather than emphasize differences should have a place in our epistemologies. It may even be proposed that the exposure of similarities among a class of phenomena, such as organisms, populations, or even living systems, generally precedes adequate understanding of the differences among them. Unless similarities are recognized and understood, the magnitude and significance of differences cannot be comprehended. What to a more general perspective might seem to be variations on a common theme may appear to a narrower perspective to be enormous differences.

It seems to me, finally, that the use of the human population in ecological analyses preserves a view of man as part of nature at the same time that it recognizes the uniqueness conferred upon him by culture. As such it preserves the terms defining the condition of a creature that can live only in terms of meanings, largely culturally constituted, in a world to which law is intrinsic but meaning is not.

V

Let us now return to the ills, real and putative, of functional formulations *per se.* That they often seem to identify what Friedman calls the rationality of elements while ignoring the rationality or irrationality of the system is surely true. Friedman is, however, incorrect in asserting that this is a "deadly weakness of functionalism" if he is proposing (1) that it is intrinsic to the logic of functional (or systemic) analyses, or (2) that it is peculiar to them. He is wrong in a more specific way in regard to formulations that include ecological variables. As far as the general charge is concerned, Vayda has observed that "a concern with how extant systems operate by no means commits the analyst to the proposition that no other systems could operate better" (1968: x), and Harris (1966) has also been explicit about this. Friedman is, of course, free to demonstrate that the practice of these writers contradicts their explicit statements, but he did not attempt to do so.

It should be kept in mind that adaptation is not a maximizing, or even an immediately optimizing process. Adaptations need not be the best possible solutions to problems, but only "good enough." (In fact, "good enough" is, in the long run, often better than "best" because maximization, or even optimization, of immediate material returns is likely to require specializations which reduce long-term flexibility [see Bateson 1963; Slobodkin and Rapoport 1974; see also "Adaptive Structure and Its Disorders"].)

The weakness of which Friedman speaks is not peculiar to functionalism *per se*. It is, rather, intrinsic to the doctrine of cultural relativism with which functional formulations have often been associated. Obviously required to obviate the problem are supra-cultural criteria in accordance with which both the operations of particular systems and the effects of their operations may be assessed. Ecological theory and general systems theory (the latter being concerned, among other things, with the *structure* of self-regulating and self-organizing processes) provide such criteria. What Friedman might mean by "the rationality" of systems, and at least what I mean by the adaptiveness of systems as well as of elements, may be assessed with respect to (1) their ecosystemic consequences and (2) the extent to which their structures are self-regulating and self-organizing.

Although ecological theory and the theory of adaptive structure do provide criteria in terms of which the operation of systems may be assessed, I do not claim that they alone provide such criteria. Half a century ago, for instance, Sapir suggested that cultures may be judged "genuine" or "spurious" in terms of their internal consistency and the opportunities they provide to individuals for personal realization (1924). The application of one such set of criteria does not preclude the simultaneous application of others, and I raise no objection in principle to the application of standards, such as those that Sapir suggested, to sociocultural systems generally. If they are derived from an explicit theory and if some sort of objective import can be given to their key terms, they are strengthened by claims to empirical testability; but even if their terms cannot be given hard objective meaning they may have a subjective or intuitive validity not to be discounted, even though great caution is required when subjectivity and intuition are at play.

A variety of supra-cultural criteria might be put to the task of assessing sociocultural systems. It may be suggested, however, that ecological (and I may add, biological) and adaptive criteria are indispensable. I do not wish to press this point, but the following arguments may be adduced in its support. First, and least important, ecological criteria, and biological criteria in general, enjoy a high degree of objectivity. Ecological criteria are material, often amenable to quantification, and viable limits for ecological and biological variables can sometimes be established. Adaptive criteria are structural and quasi-logical. (This point is elaborated in the essay "Adaptive Structure and Its Disorders.") Systems which are characterized by, or defined by, adaptive processes, a class that includes all living systems (organisms, populations, and ecosystems), seem to be, and probably must be, organized both hierarchically and cybernetically. While much work remains to be done on the conceptualization of the adaptive processes, it does already seem possible to specify some of the structural features requisite to systems if orderly adaptive processes are to continue within them (Bateson 1963; Pattee 1973; Piaget 1971; Simon 1969; Slobodkin and Rapoport 1974). If these structural features can be identified, then violations of them can be recognized and taken to be maladaptive.

Second, and more obvious, relating as they do to matters of survival, ecological, biological, and adaptive criteria are, in a crucial sense, fundamental.

Third, and most problematic, ecological, biological, and adaptive theories, including as they do in their formulations such units as organisms and associations of organisms, are not only commensurable with theories pertaining to all of life, but may also provide a framework within which some criteria drawn from other substantive theories could be organized and related to each other in orderly fashion. Even psychological and humanistic criteria might be accommodated. For instance, adaptive structures are in their nature self-regulated. Adequate regulation requires, among other things, that the regulation contain informational variety equivalent to the variety manifested in the phenomena to be regulated. Because humans play regulatory roles in sociocultural and ecological systems this argues against their narrow specialization, a matter that troubled Sapir long ago. Let me reiterate, however, that I do not claim for ecological, biological, and adaptive criteria that they have exclusive rights with respect to the assessment of social systems or that they can order or dominate all other criteria. They surely cannot subsume all of the humanistic concerns that properly reside in humans and that should not be discounted because they are intangible.

To summarize, the procedure adopted in *Pigs for the Ancestors* met a general criticism of functional analyses, namely that the units to which functional statements refer are usually not adequately specified. Ecosystems, being themselves self-regulating and self-organizing, qualify as objects of functional statements, but they are not the only units that do. So do social groups and individual organisms, and *Pigs for the Ancestors* gave them an attention equal to that which it gave the ecosystem. The recognition of the ecosystem as one of the significant units, however, makes it possible to discover contradictions between their imperatives and the internally determined imperatives of the units they include. Far from denying the relative autonomy of the latter, that autonomy is regarded as an inevitable source of real world problems. It is possible that *Pigs for the Ancestors* did, in fact, fail to illuminate contradictions between social, ecological, and organic levels of organization. Nevertheless, that a particular case may be free, or relatively free, of interlevel contradiction does not suggest that such harmony is usual. Finally, I reiterate that the inclusion of ecological, biological, and adaptive criteria (the latter not emphasized in *Pigs for the Ancestors*) provides a method for assessing what Friedman calls "the rationality of systems" as well as elements.

Friedman, it may be recalled, has asserted that the "new ecology" is "fundamentally the same as the old functionalism except that the field of application has changed, the interest now being to show the rationality of institutions with respect to environments, rather than to other elements in the society" (1974: 457). The implication of the last portion of my argument is that the inclusion of ecosystems in the analysis is more than a mere extension of functional analysis to a new domain. It is a more fundamental change, for it exposes interlevel contradiction and provides criteria for *systemic* assessment.

V

I turn now to the matter of the failure of functional formulations to provide empirical import for such key terms as "adequate functioning," "survival," "homeostasis," and so on. That this criticism is justified is indubitable, but it is also fair to say that there was a serious attempt to meet it in *Pigs for the Ancestors*. That attempt was only partially successful, but its shortcomings, I think, had the virtue of exposing specific difficulties, only partially of a metrical sort.

The procedure was patent, but I shall reiterate it here. Having defined the units to be considered, an attempt was made to give "homeostasis," or "adequate functioning," empirical import in variable-specific terms. It was conceived, in accordance with the strictures of Hempel (1958) and Nagel (1961), as a set of "goal ranges" (i.e., ranges of viability) on variables which, for reasons *independent* of the mode of operation of the system under consideration, were taken to be crucial to the persistence of that system. Thus, for ecological reasons, "carrying capacity" and nutritional variables were among those selected. An attempt was made to assign values to them on the basis of observation, measurements, and reference to more or less general theories. These attempts at quantification were only partially successful.

While upper limits were assigned to the tolerable size of pig and human populations, lower limits were not. The values assigned to upper limits were themselves suspect. It was not possible, for instance, to ascertain directly just how long fallow periods had been, much less how long they needed to have been. All that could be done—or at least was done—was to adduce evidence indicating that they had been adequate. No value was assigned to the frequency of warfare, much less to viable frequencies of warfare. Since there remained important lacunae in the quantitative data, the study remained an "exploratory sketch," to use Collins's (1965) term.

An important feature of the method, noted in passing in the last paragraph, deserves emphasis. I stipulated that the assignment of limits to goal ranges is to be made by reference to considerations distinct from the values at which the relevant variables (e.g., numbers of pigs) are, in fact, equilibrated. This stipulation is necessary if another common failing of functional formulations, namely that they fall into tautology, is to be avoided. (I came perilously close to this with respect to the length of fallow periods.) If the level at which a variable is in fact equilibrated is taken *ipso facto* to represent an equilibrium or homeostatic value for that variable, there is, *ipso facto,* tautology. However, if homeostasis is defined by reference to independent criteria, tautology is avoided. Reference values (the values with respect to which equilibration or regulation takes place) and goal ranges (the ranges of values defining "homeostasis," adequate functioning, survival, etc.) *must* be established independently. In establishing them independently it is possible to discover instances in which reference values fall outside of goal ranges. Such a condition may define "dysfunction" *under stable conditions.* The possibility that reference values may well violate goal ranges is indicated in the last pages of *Pigs for the Ancestors* in a discussion of cognized and operational models.

There is a yet more fundamental difficulty intrinsic to the procedure I have outlined. In a changing world even goal ranges may change. The introduction of a new crop, for instance, may change carrying capacity. That this difficulty was, in fact, recognized in the book does not dissolve it. The method, as I have outlined it, suffers from the limitations of the static, a point that Friedman did not raise, but that must be made explicit. In another essay in this volume, "Adaptive Structure and Its Disorders," I deal with ways in which change may be dealt with in general systemic terms.

VI

I have been using terms more familiarly associated with systemic than with functional analysis, and Hempel, in his critique of functional analysis, in effect called for the replacement of vague functional formulations by more rigorous systemic constructions. That he made no sharp distinction between the two constituted a tacit recognition on his part that the latter may be regarded as a reform of the former. Be this as it may, *Pigs for the Ancestors* constituted an attempt at systemic analysis, an analysis in which the units are clearly specified, the goal ranges and reference values of key variables are given objective import, and the regulatory mechanisms identified. That it failed to meet the rigorous requirements of systemic analysis in all respects must be freely admitted, and it is thus vulnerable to criticism in its own terms. It is important to point out here, however, lest anyone be bemused by Friedman's suggestion that the "ultimate source and possible salvation" of the "new functional ecology" lies in systems theory (1974: 445), that systems analysis, at least (systems theory is another matter), has problems of its own.

Systemic analysis makes no prescription concerning the variables to be included in the analytic system. Their selection is a product of hypotheses concerning interrelations among the phenomena under investigation. While the rigorous specification of systems ameliorates the vagueness that often vitiates looser functional formulations, it increases the danger that crucial components or aspects of the natural or cultural system being represented will be omitted. Since systemic analyses, like looser functional formulations, are concerned to elucidate the ways in which order is maintained in systems that naturally tend toward disorder or entropy, it may be—although it is not logically entailed that this should be so— that there is a tendency to ignore the disorderly and to include only the orderly, even though the notion of self-regulation, virtually intrinsic to the notion of system, implies response to *perturbation*. Nevertheless, by giving himself the system, so to speak, the maintenance of which he takes it to be his task to elucidate, the analyst may affirm whatever assumptions concerning harmony and orderliness he entertained at the outset without fear of overthrow. The dilemma is, simply, that the abstraction necessary to derive analytically tractable systems from the complexity of nature and culture puts systemic formulations in danger of becoming unreal or unfalsifiable. This, of course, is not very different from the difficulties besetting all of science. The point here is that this difficulty is *exacerbated* by increased rigor; more specifically, by increasingly rigorous canons of specification. The problem is not hopeless, of course. Systemic analyses do not usually take place in contexts devoid of substantive theories. Such theories usually include references to units that can be taken to be the systems forming the object of investigation, and also are likely to include criteria for establishing the goal ranges of the variables which they specify as crucial to systemic persistence. Ecology provides one such body of theory, discriminating discrete units on several levels of inclusiveness, many of which are directly available to observation (e.g., organisms), and some of which correspond to self-defining and self-bounding entities (e.g., Maring local populations). For the analyst to take such units to be those with which his analysis is concerned is to go far toward avoiding the problems implicit in "giving himself the system," but this remains an ever-present danger.

VII

We have continually returned to the matter of regulation, and may now deal with another of the important criticisms of functionalism raised by Hempel, namely that the self-regulatory mechanisms implicit in functional formulations are not made explicit. I claim that *Pigs for the Ancestors* met this criterion adequately. The self-regulatory processes inhering in the ritual cycle of the Tsembaga were described in narrative form in the work itself in sufficient detail to make possible its computer modeling without, on the part of the modeler, requests for additional data from me (Shantzis and Behrens, 1973). In a later work of mine (1971c), the Tsembaga system, including its regulatory mechanisms, was represented diagrammatically (see "On Cognized Models" in this volume).

Friedman, however, takes issue with my analysis of Maring ritual regulation, arguing that I have misused the general concept of negative feedback. His first point is a general one. He defines negative feedback systems as "systems in which certain variables are kept within certain crucial limits by the operation of other variables which are *dependent functions of those limits*" (1974: 459; italics original), and says that he fails "to see that the environment limit is involved at all [in the Tsembaga case], since . . . the [ritual] cycle is triggered way below carrying capacity, and other groups probably come closer to that limit" (1974: 460). Later he elucidates his argument with the following analogy: "If a thermostat is set for 75 degrees, but the furnace which it regulates breaks down at 65 degrees every time, then we cannot speak of negative feedback" (1974: 460).

A misunderstanding of negative feedback is evident here. Negative feedback is simply a process in which deviations from *reference values* initiate operations tending to return the state of the deviating variable to its reference value. The relationship of reference values to *goal ranges* (what Friedman probably means by "limits," i.e., the possible range of viable or homeostatic states) is a separate question, and a very important one, which, as I have already pointed out, was considered *in italics* in the closing pages of the Maring book. In a discussion of the relationship between cognized and operational models I called attention to problems that may develop in cybernetic operation itself. I said the following, italicizing the main point in the original so that its significance would not be missed. (Evidently this strategy was not successful.)

First, what is the relationship between signs and the processes they are taken to indicate? Is it the case, for instance, that such processes as environmental degradation are detected (indicated by signs) early, or only when they are well advanced? Second, to what extent do reference values, which are likely to reflect people's wants rather than their needs, correspond to the actual material requirements of the local population, the ecosystem, or the regional population? In other words, *what is the relationship between the reference value or ranges of values of the cognized model and the goal ranges of the operational model?* [1968: 240–241]

I did not make explicit that the "wants" referred to in this passage are culturally determined, are a product of ideology, ambition, social relations, or social structure. I simply took that for granted and assumed that anyone who read the book would also take it for granted. It may be that I should have discussed more fully the possible sociocultural factors that entered into the reference value for pig herd size, but as I have already mentioned, I argued that although the slain pigs were put to culturally determined ends, the reference value itself is a reflection of a local population's tolerance for the labor requirements of pigs or the disruptive capacity of pigs. The more important point I wish to reiterate here is that the reference values upon which negative feedback operation is equilibrated *may lie outside of independently specified goal ranges.* To paraphrase Friedman's thermostat-furnace analogy, we could set a thermostat at 40° and sit around shivering, or at 110° and collapse from heat prostration. More to the point, our own society offers a large number of instances of economic reference values, which are of course culturally determined, being maintained outside of environmental and physiological goal ranges. I think we can say that this is "dysfunctional" or "maladaptive" even if the economic system is working well for the time being (which, of course, it isn't). This is to say that negative feedback need not be homeostatic.

This leads to an important point raised by Friedman. He notes that "while it is valid to *describe* [italics original] the ritual cycle as operating to keep the pig population below a certain level, it is incorrect to claim that it is a *homeostat* [italics added] when no relation has been shown to exist between the limit and the triggering of the cycle" (1974: 460). This point must be taken seriously, and it does, I think, rightly point to a deficiency in *Pigs for the Ancestors*. I showed no intrinsic relationship between women's labor and carrying capacity, and there may not be any. I did argue, however (1968: 160ff.; see also pp. 116 and 70), that in more densely populated areas the depredations of pigs, rather than their labor requirements, may trigger *kaiko*s. I further argued that the frequency of garden invasions by pigs is density-dependent and as such may be related, in a rough way, to environmental limits. In terms that I was not aware of at the time, what was implied (but in all fairness to Friedman was surely not adequately expressed) was multi-phasic regulation (Vayda 1974), in which at low densities women's labor is operative while at high densities environmental considerations predominate. Friedman relegates his discussion of garden invasions by pigs to a footnote in which he seems to dismiss the possible relationship of density dependence to environmental limits and in which he also is guilty of an ethnographic error. (A more careful reading of the work would have indicated to him that conflicts concerning pigs are not generated in "the nuclear phase of a pulsating settlement pattern," but throughout the dispersal which they in part motivate.) Be this as it may, my argument concerning the density-dependent nature of pig-caused conflict and the relationship of this density-dependence to environmental limits was not supported by sufficient data and, therefore, was no more than hypothetical. Moreover, I did not, in accordance with the strictures of Hempel, specify the range of conditions (e.g., human demographic) under which the regulatory mechanism of the ritual cycle would keep pig herd size within environmental capacity. My case, then, for asserting that the regulatory operation of the ritual cycle is homeostatic, was incomplete. It is worth noting, however, as I did in the book (1968: 163), that the problem under discussion here is not altogether one of analysis, but is a reflection of how natural systems operate. It is certainly the case that maximal pig population size among the Tsembaga was equilibrated well below limits. This is not unusual. As Wynne-Edwards (1962), Birdsell (1958) and others have noted, populations of many species are regulated in the first instance by endogenous mechanisms operating well below carrying capacity, and it is not always clear how such regulatory operations relate to environmental limits. It may be that instances of humans who are not maximizing occasion some surprise, but such surprise is surely engendered by economistic preconceptions. Adaptation is not a maximizing process, and the imperatives of Maring social structure do not encourage maximizing.

Friedman raises one other problem concerning Maring regulation that remains to be discussed.

The principal limit of the system as it is described by Rappaport is the point at which physical strain on women builds up. Since it is they who are burdened with the task of feeding and managing the pigs, they are the first to feel the diminishing returns on increased labor. All the evidence he presents indicates that it is this strain in the system which triggers the cycle. Yet his own "explanation" appears to turn the whole thing upside down since he assumes that it is the ritual cycle which regulates labour and not the converse. [1974: 459–460]

Friedman is certainly correct in his reading of the ethnography when he notes that it is "the strain" of too many pigs that triggers the *kaiko*. I tried very hard to argue that very point, and the attempt to use it in criticism of the analysis suggests to me a misunderstanding of cybernetic operation. The very same point could be made concerning thermostats, which, I am sure, Friedman will admit to the class of cybernetic regulators. It is a rise in room temperature, an outcome of the furnace's operation, that triggers the regulatory reaction of the thermostat, namely to turn off the furnace. Similarly, it is the increase in pig population to intolerable limits, as indicated by complaints concerning labor and conflicts resulting from porcine depredations, that triggers the regulatory reaction of the ritual cycle, namely the *kaiko*, which "turns off" the pigs. If the ritual cycle is not a regulatory mechanism, neither is the thermostat.

We note in these examples that cybernetic or negative feedback regulation takes the form of a closed loop: it has a circular causal structure. A change in the value of a variable itself initiates a process that either limits further change or returns the value to its former level. The basic difficulty in Friedman's argument seems to be that it attempts to impose a notion of linear causality upon a system which is in its nature circular. The linear assumption is implicit in the view that *either* the *kaiko* *or* the labor is causal.

Granting the circular structure of cybernetic systems, it still might be asked why it should be said that the ritual cycle regulates pig demography, warfare frequency, etc., and not that they regulate the ritual cycle. The same question may be asked about the regulatory relationship of the thermostat and the furnace.

The self-regulatory operations of all systems in which they occur are, of course, contingent upon the dynamic interaction of these systems' components, and in some systems discrete regulators are not to be distinguished. Nevertheless, there surely are grounds for taking thermostats and ritual cycles to be regulators. I would note first that the Maring ritual cycle contains, so to speak, a set of standard corrective responses to deviations in the values of variables external to itself; for instance, the labor of which Friedman speaks. One basis for saying that the ritual cycle regulates labor and not vice versa is the fact that "amount of labor" is not a regulatory response, but rather a variable which may deviate from a reference value or goal range (thus requiring regulation). It is important to make clear, however, that the ritual cycle is not simply a set of corrective responses. It itself *constitutes* those responses. It is the locus of the conventions in accordance with which the corrective responses are undertaken and conducted. It embodies a set of instructions for a communal corrective program. Thermostats, analogously, also contain instructions, albeit rather simple ones (e.g., when the temperature of the room reaches the value set on the dial, switch off the furnace; when it drops 3° below that value, switch on the furnace). The regulator is that component of a circular causal system which contains the instructions in accordance with which the system operates. In the sorts of systems exemplified by the Tsembaga and their relations with other species and groups, the regulator is the dominant information processing component in systems of matter and energy transactions. The information processed is culturally encoded, and it goes without saying that, as such, it is not only founded upon cultural perceptions of natural processes (which perceptions may be "objectively" inaccurate), but it is also selected by socially determined motives and goals, and in accordance with the imperatives of social relations and structures. I shall reiterate, however, that in small undifferentiated societies such as that of the Maring, in which all adult members are directly and continuously engaged with the natural environment and in which corrective informational feedback from the environment is direct, observable, and relatively quick, we may expect a close correspondence between culturally specified motives and goals and the requirements of ecosystemic processes.

It may be possible to add another justification to those already offered for taking the ritual cycle to be regulator rather than regulated, although this may be little more than a translation of the preceding argument into other terms. The ritual cycle constitutes, or at least codifies, the relations of production of Maring society. To use Friedman's definition, "relations of production are those *social relations* which dominate (i.e. determine the economic rationality of) the material process of production in given techno-ecological conditions.... More specifically they determine... the use to be made of the environment... the division of productive labour ... the forms of appropriation and distribution" (1974: 446). The ritual cycle is a sacred structure within which productive and reproductive activities (ecological, biological, and social) proceed and in terms of which social, political, and ecological relations are defined and given meaning. It may be suggested that ritually regulated societies comprise a mode of production commensurable with feudalism, capitalism, and oriental despotism. Because the operation of ritually regulated societies does not entail social stratification or even ranking, ritual itself may constitute a very old if not the primordial mode of production.

VIII

There remains the criticism that systemic as well as functional formulations suffer from the fallacy of affirming their consequents. Now it surely is invalid to claim, as some functional analyses seem to do, that an "item" or "trait" is present in a system because the system functions adequately if and only if a certain condition is met, and that the item present meets the condition. To say that a particular item meets the condition is not to say that only that item could meet the condition. It might be met equally well by other items. Only in cases in which the item present and only the item present could meet the condition can a functional statement account for the item's presence in the system, but such functional indispensability is empirically difficult or even logically impossible to demonstrate. This criticism was presaged before the turn of the century by Durkheim (1938: 90).

It is true that in a brief passage in *Pigs for the Ancestors,* to which allusion has already been made, it was indeed suggested that the Maring ritual cycle might be a local variation of a generalized Highland form and that the peculiar characteristics of the local variation might be accounted for by local environmental conditions. This proposal, it may be suggested, is not a simple functional proposal, but an adaptive one, implying, as it does, a model of adaptive radiation. Be this as it may, the aim of the book was not to account for either the presence or the origin of the ritual cycle, and it was not asserted that the regulatory functions ascribed to the cycle could not be fulfilled by other mechanisms. The ritual cycle was taken as a given, and the aim of the book was simply to elucidate its place in the operation of a particular system during a particular period in its history.

The general criticism, that function does not account for presence or origin, is not relevant to *Pigs for the Ancestors,* and Friedman did not raise it explicitly. It is nevertheless worth discussing for two reasons. First, Friedman's charge that the "new ecology" is essentially the same as the old functionalism seems to imply that it embodies all of the vices of the old functionalism. Second, and more important, the critique itself is not without difficulties.

Taking up the simplest of these difficulties first, it is surely true that functional statements alone cannot account for origin or presence, but they may form indispensable components of more elaborate formulations that can. Although "items" other than those present could conceivably fulfill indispensable functions at a particular time and place, given the limited cultural materials (structural, ideological, technical, social, political, or whatever) usually available, only the item or form present, or a limited range of them, could have emerged. It might be supposed, for instance, that a king or a bicameral parliament could have done everything that the Maring ritual cycle was doing, and done it better, but given the cultural materials available, a ritual cycle, and neither kings nor parliaments, did, in fact, emerge.

To use Aristotelian terminology, neither final nor efficient nor material cause is alone sufficient to account for presence or origin, but taken together they may be. Environmental changes or perturbation are of the class of processes that can qualify as efficient causes, inducing a system to respond (change its state or structure) within the constraints of its previously existing constitution (material cause) in such a way as to perpetuate itself (final cause, or what is ordinarily meant by "function"). This is all obvious, but two general comments should be made.

First, we are no longer speaking of simple functional formulations, which are no more than final causal, but of adaptive formulations which also include material causal and, of course, efficient causal considerations as well. I take ecological and systemic formulations to be, at least implicitly, adaptive rather than merely functional, although I have myself to blame for labeling *Pigs for the Ancestors* (in the first sentence of the first chapter) a functional study. I did not fully comprehend what I was, in fact, trying to do. I shall return to adaptive formulations later.

Second, Aristotle proposed a fourth type of cause, namely formal cause. He wasn't very clear about it, but I take it to refer to the entailment of operations of particular sorts by the formal characteristics of structures. We are led here to the second major difficulty with the general critique of functional formulations presently under discussion. It grows out of a confusion resulting from a conflation of formal and final causal accounts under the label "functional." Raymond Kelly and I (1975) have recently attempted to clarify some of the issues: I shall take this opportunity to elaborate our earlier attempt.

In its most common usage the term "function" implies final cause, a functional formulation being one seeking to "explain" or "elucidate" an "item" in a "system" by specifying its "contribution" to the "survival," "persistence," or "adequate functioning" of that system. Although, as I have already noted, they are often improperly constructed, and although their proper limits have often been violated, this concept of function, particularly when expressed in the rigorous terms of an empirically-based systemic analysis and informed by a substantive theory, does have a legitimate place in the social sciences. That it may be impossible to demonstrate the "functional indispensability" of particular items does not vitiate the value of the final causal conception of function. It must be understood, however, that final causal accounts are properly only system-specific. For instance, that a ritual cycle regulates the social, political, and ecological relationships of the Maring people such that the frequency of warfare, the intensity of land use, and the divisive effects of internal quarreling among the members of local groups are all kept within viable limits does not mean that forms or structure that we would recognize as *ritual* perform similar functions anywhere else in the world. The specification of a particular function in a particular system does not entail the specification of the form of the mechanism the output of which is that function. Conversely, the specification of a "category" or "form" or "type" of "item" (e.g., ritual) does not entail the specification of its *particular* contribution to any system in which it appears. This autonomy of form and function with respect to each other is sometimes considered to be lethal to the notion of function as an "explanatory concept." In fact, it simply proposes the limitations of final causal statements.

We may turn now to the other form of argument which is sometimes labeled "functional," but which differs importantly from final causal formulations. In fact, it is formal causal, and as such virtually the inverse of the final causal type. Its aim is not to elucidate the contribution that some "item" or "component" or "form" makes to the system of which it is a part, but to elucidate what is *entailed by, follows from* or is *intrinsic to* a particular *form* or *structure*.

The form of a formal causal account is certainly not limited to, but is nicely illustrated by, cybernetic mechanisms. The term "cybernetic" denotes a *structure* or *form* of a particular sort, that of the closed causal loop. *Intrinsic to,* or *entailed by,* the operation of a *simple* cybernetic structure is "negative feedback," such that deviations of the states of components of the loop from reference values initiate processes tending to return those states to their reference values. (We needn't go into the matter of "positive feedback" or "deviation amplification" here.)

A number of observations are in order. First, because cybernetic structure *entails* regulation, wherever the structure is observed the state of some variable is being equilibrated at or around some reference value. In contrast to simple final causal accounts, which are properly only system-specific, formal causal accounts are universalist.

Second, formal causal accounts are properly applied only to *structures,* that is, to phenomena that may be formally described in terms of enduring *internal* relations. Cybernetic structure is a proper object of such formulations, but the class of such objects is innumerable, certainly including kinship systems, marriage systems, and ritual. Elsewhere, for instance, I have defined ritual as the performance of more or less invariant sequences of formal acts and utterances not encoded by the performers. This definition, specifying as it does not only a number of features but also relations among them, denotes a structure, and I have argued that this structure *entails* social contract, morality, a paradigm of the concept of the sacred and notion of the divine (see "The Obvious Aspects of Ritual").

Third, if particular entailments are intrinsic to a particular structure and only to that structure (e.g., to the cybernetic structure, or to the structure which is ritual) it may be argued that those structures are without equivalents. I have so argued for ritual (ibid.),, and a similar argument could be made for cybernetic structure (see Piaget 1971: 15). If the unique entailments of a particular structure are crucial to the persistence or survival of systems in general then it may be said that that structure is not only without equivalent but indispensable. This may account for the ubiquitous occurrence of such structures as the cybernetic and ritual forms.

Fourth, this argument would seem to contradict the dictum that function cannot account for presence because of the impossibility of demonstrating the indispensability of even those items performing indispensable functions. It seems to propose that there is an aspect or class of phenomena, namely structure or structures, for which claims of functional uniqueness and indispensability can, in fact, be made. The contradiction, however, is more apparent than real because the entailments of structure are not properly regarded as functions in the final causal sense. What is entailed by a structure does not *in itself* constitute a *specific* contribution to the maintenance of any *particular* system in which it appears. To recall an earlier argument, the proposition that a cybernetic mechanism equilibrates the state of a variable around some reference range may sound like a final causal statement. It is not, because it alone does not take account of the relationship of the reference value to the persistence or survival of any particular system. As I observed earlier, we could set our thermostat to maintain temperature at a level that would kill us. Similarly, the proposition that the structure of ritual is such as to invest the contents of ritual with morality does not in itself take into account the relationship of the particular practices or conceptions invested with morality to the "persistence" or "adequate functioning" of the systems of which they are parts. The assertion, then, that ritual makes its contents moral falls short of adequacy as a final causal statement.

Fifth, to recognize that that which is intrinsic to a structure is not *ipso facto* final causal is not to deny its significance. To assert that morality and social contract are intrinsic to the structure of ritual is not vacuous. Statements concerning entailments are not simple functional statements in the final causal sense, but statements of another order. It could be said, I suppose, that formal causal formulations are meta-functional, or perhaps it would be better to say that they are statements concerning meta-functions. They are not properly attempts to stipulate the contribution that a form or structure makes to the persistence of any particular system in which it occurs, but what is intrinsic to that form or structure that makes it suitable to fulfill the range of specific functions its instances do fulfill in the diversity of systems in which they occur.

In summary, I have noted two contrasting types of account, one final-causal and system-specific, the other formal-causal and universalist. The two have not been sufficiently distinguished in anthropological thought (both often being called "functional"), and what Kelly (Kelly and Rappaport 1975) has called "the fallacy of crossed explicanda" has sometimes followed from this confusion. This fallacy, which might be regarded as an error in logical typing (Bateson 1972), occurs when final causal statements are offered in instances in which formal causal statements are apropriate and vice versa. For example, to state that it is *in the nature of ritual* to regulate ecological and political relations in the way that I attempted to demonstrate that it did for the Maring would be to make a final causal assertion where a formal causal statement is appropriate. Such an assertion would tend to trivialize ritual and would also be false on empirical grounds. We can cite innumerable instances in which ritual has nothing whatever to do with political or ecological relations.

Conversely, an attempt to account, let us say, for the division of labor in nineteenth-century France by invoking Durkheim's assertion that organic solidarity is intrinsic to the division of labor, as a final causal statement ("the division of labor in nineteenth-century France enhanced the organic solidarity of French society"), to make, that is, a formal causal assertion where a final causal one might be appropriate, would not be so much wrong as banal, vacuous, and, of course, inadequate (see Bergmann 1975).

IX

Time and transformation remain to be discussed. Although simple functional formulations may be well-suited to the consideration of changes in the states of systems, they are ill-equipped to deal with structural change, and may impose specious assumptions of stasis upon dynamic realities. The temporal limitations of fieldwork may exacerbate this difficulty and ecologically informed research has not been exempt. Indeed, the problem of carrying capacity to which I earlier alluded exemplifies it with especial clarity.

Of course, the problem of static formulation in dynamic context is not exclusive to functional and systemic formulations. Self-consciously structural accounts face problems that are at least similar. Neither systemic nor structural formulations are, however, intrinsically static. Indeed, the theory of evolution by natural selection, a theory concerning structural transformation, is systemic in character.

Both Friedman and I are concerned with problems in the relationship of the temporal to the atemporal, with possibilities for making hypotheses about "social formations" as wholes, and with the general characteristics of order and ordering. Writing of the conjunction of Marxist and structuralist thought, Friedman speaks of "an expanded view of the social field which could render possible hypotheses about social formations as wholes." He continues as follows:

In structuralist terms this would be a framework for handling the as yet unapproachable problem of "l'ordre des ordres" (Lévi-Strauss 1958: 347) or vertical structures which account for societies as entities. Further, it is the only way that one can get at a real theoretical history. For unless we assume that history takes place outside the object of study and according to some meta-social laws of its own, then the problem of diachrony and synchrony must dissolve in the understanding of the dynamic properties of social systems. It is knowledge of the fundamental structural properties of social reproduction which enables us to predict the way society will behave over time. [1974: 445]

I must demur from what I take to be overstatement (e.g., ". . . the *only* way to get at a *real* theoretical history"), and I think that claims of prediction must be set about with elaborate qualification because the specific outcomes of evolutionary processes are, given the unforeseeable nature of the stresses that any living system experiences, low in predictability. In my view, moreover, Friedman's hierarchical schematization of Marx's social formation into, initially, a bifurcation of infrastructures and superstructure, both subsuming other "functional" categories, is, as I indicated earlier (see note, p. 52), incapable of realizing the goals he sets for himself and for anthropology. I am, however, in general sympathy with the aspirations he expresses in this passage, and I would suggest that the concept of adaptation may have much to contribute to the realization of the goals that I share with him.

The term "adaptation" is generally associated—perhaps free-associated—with environment and thus, perhaps, with ecological formulations. It is certainly the case that adaptive processes are manifested or realized only in particular environments, social, cultural, or physical. Nevertheless, a general theory of adaptation is not so much concerned with the particulars of environment as it is with those structural characteristics of systems that make it possible for them to transform themselves in response to environmental fluctuation, change, or opportunity. Adaptive formulations thus have ecological implications, but are not properly subsumed under a category of ecological formulations. It also should be clear that they are neither simple functional formulations because they are concerned with structural change, nor are they simple evolutionary formulations because they are as concerned with the persistence of systems as they are with changes in them. In fact, the distinction between maintenance and change, "diachrony and synchrony," dissolves in the dynamics of adaptive processes. Adaptive formulations, moreover, are formal as well as final causal, emphasizing not only the goals and effects of processes but *processual structure* as well. Indeed, the concept of adaptation is fundamentally structural (in the sense of structure expressed, but hardly originated, by Piaget [1971]) because adaptive operation has certain structural entailments or, to put it differently, orderly adaptive operation is contingent upon the prevalence of certain formal relationships among the components of the systems in which it occurs. This is to say that adaptive systems are characterized by a generally similar architecture, or that adaptive processes are characterized by a generally similar structure. The form of this structure and the consequences of anomalies in it are considered in some detail in the essay "Adaptive Structure and Its Disorders."

X

In light of this essay's movement it may seem unnecessary to take up further problems of functional or ecological formulations. We have, after all, left simple functional and ecological accounts behind as we have approached more complex and synthetic adaptive notions. There remain, however, certain important criticisms that may have more general implications than any of those already discussed, and their discussion, furthermore, will lead us at the end to consider what relationships should prevail among the various modes of explanation and interpretation prevalent in anthropology.

We may turn first to a criticism not only of functional formulations but of social science in general recently published by the philosopher Frithjof Bergmann (1975). He suggests that the often rehearsed objections to functionalism—for instance, that it cannot explain why one rather than some other element fulfills a certain function (1975: 6), or that functional analyses play down the irrational features of cultural institutions in their search for hidden utilities (1975: 3)—really miss the mark. The shortcoming of functional formulations is at once more simple and more profound. The central question is *"how much* of a given phenomenon the postulated function in the end explains" (1975: 3; italics his).

Bergmann's answer is "very little." He notes, as an instance, that attempts to explain language in terms of its functions have encountered a "gross disproportionality," for "the biological and social needs that can postulated as genuine requirements could always be fulfilled by an instrument vastly less complex and powerful than any actual language" (1975: 3). Similarly, the rather simple set of functions postulated for the Maring ritual cycle in *Pigs for the Ancestors* could have been achieved with something much simpler, and therefore only a small portion of the phenomena described in the work are accounted for.

> It is not clear what the prohibition against cooking *marita* and *ma* together, or the belief that this taboo is ended by spitting out a mouthful of pandanus seeds in the nearby forest contribute to the achievement of one or any of these ends. And since this is similarly true of countless other features it may be regarded as the main limitation of the functional approach. [1975: 6]£

Bergmann fits his criticism of functionalism into a larger critique of scientific approaches to the study of social and cultural phenomena generally. Following Monod (1972) he asserts that "the 'principle of objectivity' represents the one indispensable foundation upon which 'science' rests" (1975: 7). This principle prohibits "subjective" principles of explanation to be "exported," that is, applied to natural phenomena. Human activity, however, is precisely the domain of the subjective, and therefore

> in the investigation of cultures or societies, or perhaps of anything distinctive of man (as opposed to inaminate and animate *nature*) the use of "subjective" principles of explanation clearly does not constitute an [improper] "exportation." ... Man has motives and purposes and goals and we have ways of knowing what they are. Therefore we confront a choice: we can ... observe the "principle of objectivity" even in these investigations and in effect model them after other sciences. The price exacted would be much that we genuinely know [which would be excluded because both subjective and only subjectively known].... Alternatively, we can allow "subjective principles" of explanation and ... pay the price of no longer working in real "science." The alternatives are thus between being scientific at the expense of knowledge, and gaining knowledge that will no longer form a science....
> If functionalism is placed against the schema of this choice it appears as an unhappy compromise. It suffers the disadvantages of both alternatives without gaining the full benefits of either. [1975: 8-9]

In Bergmann's view structuralism suffers from kindred deficiencies, and he calls for a deep change in the nature of social studies generally.

> ... at the root lies the erroneous assumption that we need a "science" to know and to understand. What must be disavowed is the epistemology that interpreted the whole of knowledge as analogy to science.
> Once that epistemology has been discarded the investigation of society can be conceptualized in a new way. The main fact is not that the object of this enterprise is too complex or too resistant to the tools of "science." More important is that we have an entirely different epistemic *relationship* to this object: that it in essence is so widely known [from our experience as members

of society] that the highly structured "scientific" forms of knowledge cannot advance us further, but on the contrary become impediments that hold us back. [1975: 21]

Anthropology should, in Bergmann's view, quit whoring after the strange gods of physics and openly declare itself a convert to the humanities.

Raymond Kelly and I, in a response to Bergmann (1975) have agreed that science is one thing and all of knowledge another, and although science may require obedience to a "principle of objectivity" this is not so for all of knowledge. We have also agreed that in the study of anything distinctive of humanity as a cultural species the use of subjective principles is proper. We also indicated that we don't care any more than Bergmann does about whether or not our credentials as scientists are in order. We believe, however, that the choice Bergmann asks of anthropology—to be either one of the sciences or one of the humanities—is unnecessary and mistaken. Anthropology is properly a synthesis of the two. This is not a plea for an easy tolerance of what any and every anthropologist does. What constitutes the proper domains of the subjective on the one hand and the objective on the other is a matter of fundamental importance which remains in some degree ambiguous and even confused. It seems to me certain, however, that clarification will not follow from their radical separation. To choose between subjective and objective principles of elucidation is not only to impoverish our understanding, but also to force us to make the particular set of principles we favor do work for which it is not suited, work properly belonging to the domain of the other. As it is improper to "import" objectivity into the subjective realm, so is it improper to "export" subjectivity into the objective realm. Furthermore, one of the most profound sets of problems with which anthropology should be concerned is that of the relationship of the "subjective domain (that of goals, motives, purposes, feelings, understandings, misunderstandings, hopes, dreads)" to the "objective domain (of rocks, water, trees, animals, metabolism, endocrine secretion, nutrition, growth, decay, entropy)." To choose between objective and subjective principles is to make it impossible from the start to investigate relationships between the domains to which each properly applies, relationships that approximate those between meaning and law, between the performatively constituted and the naturally constituted (see "On Cognized Models"). This relationship is the most distinctive characteristic of the human condition.

It is this relationship with which *Pigs for the Ancestors* was centrally concerned. Through both distinguishing and relating cognized and operational models it attempted to show purposeful men operating in terms of culturally constituted meanings in a purposeless but lawful natural world. Whereas the strategy of distinguishing a subjective cognized model from an objective operational model and then relating them to each other was, I think, proper, I will freely admit that the attempt was flawed. Some of the "objective" data were inadequate and some meanings were missed, misunderstood, or, possibly, infected by what Sahlins (1976a: 298) has called "ecology fetishism," which is associated with a

... materialism [which] allows itself to ignore the distinctive quality of human action as meaningfully organized—that it may proceed to organize meaning as an instrumental mystification of natural reason. Its "empiricism" then consists in the radical practice of the idea that nothing is in fact what it appears, i.e., culturally, but is translated instead into natural coordinates or consequences. The result is a kind of "ecology fetishism" whereby corn, beans and squash become an unbalanced diet ... ritual pig slaughter and distribution to affines a mode of remaining within "the limits of carrying capacity," the social order "a population of organisms.". ...

We are well-warned by Sahlins to guard against simplistic equations of meaning with "instrumental mystifications of natural reason." Some of the interpretations of meanings in *Pigs for the Ancestors*—particularly in matters relating to food consumption—may have been little more than that. I would suggest, however, that Sahlins's discussion, both in the work cited and in *Culture and Practical Reason* (1976b: 87ff.) is not clarifying. To say, for instance, that corn, beans, and squash form an unbalanced diet is, assuming it to be correct, simply to report an "objective fact," i.e., one "belonging to" the objective domain. Such a statement surely does, by itself, "ignore the distinctive quality of human life as meaningfully organized" but it does not provide an instance of "meaning as instrumental mystification of natural reason" simply because it doesn't say anything about meaning at all, nor does it entail or even imply any instructions whatever as to how meaning is to be construed. Because it is devoid of any report, description, or interpretation of the meaning of the corn, beans, and squash trinity for those who live on it, the statement is inadequate as a full ethnographic account. Ethnographies are not, however, composed of single statements, and to say that a statement is by itself inadequate is not to say that it is irrelevant. The relevance to the general ethnographic enterprise of the nutritional qualities of the diets of the peoples with whom anthropologists live and work need not be defended, although I will agree that not all ethnographic fieldwork need attend to such matters.

The account of the Maring ritual cycle's meanings, as provided in *Pigs for the Ancestors,* was largely concerned, first, with the activation, by the events of social life, of certain oppositions between spirits and between qualities; second, with the relationships of categories of persons to those spirits and qualities; and, third, with the mediation and amelioration of those oppositions and the transformation of those relations through the dynamic of the cycle. Nowhere was it argued that any of those elements of meaning emerged out of environmental relations, nor were they transformed into mere "mystifications of natural reason" because the ritual cycle with which they were associated had attributed to it certain regulatory functions—including keeping porcine populations within "the limits of carrying capacity"—by an objective analysis. The meanings remained what those for whom they were meaningful took them to be, regardless of whatever objective regulatory functions may have inhered in the ritual cycle which they invested, and regardless of the fact that, because the Maring acted in ways that those meanings organized, and not in ways dictated by "practical" or "natural" regulatory factors, they *ipso facto* masked, mystified, or made subsidiary those practical or natural factors.

The relationship of meaning to natural processes is hardly a simple one. Meaning is nowhere monolithic. Much of quotidian understanding everywhere is grounded in observations of naturally constituted processes and, through acts of distinction, encoded as "fact" in classifications, either implicit or explicit. Some of these facts are, of course, performatively established, but concordance is generally high between natural processes and what I have elsewhere called "low order meaning," meaning founded upon distinction (see "On Cognized Models"). Higher order meanings, the meanings not of distinctions but of similarities underlying distinctions, the meanings of metaphor, symbol, and value, are not grounded directly in observations of nature and are thus relatively free from constraints to conform to it. They are, this is to say, free to organize action in a variety of ways and thus are free to attempt the subordination of natural processes to whatever ends they define—mollifying ancestors, repaying affines, making profits. I have already suggested that a high concordance between actions organized in terms of higher order meaning and ecosystemic processes in an unstratified and relatively undifferentiated horticultural society such as that of the Maring should not be surprising. Virtually everyone is directly engaged in activities that not only display to them the circularities of those ecosystemic processes but involve them directly in their maintenance. Ancestors and affines are kept happy, but at levels sufficiently modest to avoid ecosystemic degradation.

Such concordance may not pertain in all domains in such societies. For instance, the nutritional soundness of Maring pig husbandry and consumption is probably more dubious than the general ecological soundness of the ritual cycle and probably more dubious than I cautiously suggested in *Pigs for the Ancestors*. Different conventions, which could have included both agistment and regular slaughter at earlier ages with wide distribution of the pork might have enhanced the Maring diet significantly. However, the conventions governing husbandry and slaughter during the period described in the ethnography were crucial to the maintenance and regulation of social and political relations as well as ecosystemic relations and dietary intake. Meaning and the requisites of the social order were thus being served at what might have been significant cost to the health of the organisms whose actions they organized.

To say that meaning is highly valued everywhere borders on the tautologous simply because the concept of value is subsumed by the concept of meaning. Without meaning there is no value. Be this as it may, humans always and everywhere have been willing to labor, to give treasure, to kill, and even to sacrifice their own lives for such meanings as God, Salvation, Fatherland, and Honor. High cost may be prerequisite to deep meaning, and deep meaning may be requisite to the maintenance of social life. It is a vulgar error to consider the costs of meaning—the treasure and labor given to the temple, the bird feathers provided for the chief's cloak, even the lives given for the sake of honor, glory, or salvation—to be exploitative because those who pay them do not necessarily receive material returns. Sometimes, however, too much may be asked of individuals, and sometimes not only individuals but entire social orders may be led into decline by the meanings they entertain. The very survival of populations may be endangered by the requisites of the social orders which are their properties. The concordance existing between higher order meaning and ecosystemic processes among the Maring should not set up a cross-cultural expectation. Contemporary industrial society, for instance, is badly damaging the natural systems upon which it depends in the name of such ideas as progress, free enterprise, "the health of the economy," the communist threat, the abundant life.

Of course some meanings are instruments of the survival of the organisms maintaining them, and of course the actions of the self-same organisms are meaningfully organized in terms of ends that they themselves did not define, that do not emerge naturally out of "natural" or utilitarian considerations, and that may, indeed, be inimical to those who strive toward them. But neither of these two statements by itself constitutes an adequate account of the relationship of the processes of culturally constituted meaning and natural processes, nor, for that matter, do the two together. What they do delineate is a field for investigation, a set of problems corresponding closely to the characteristics of a species that not only must live in terms of meanings but must itself construct those meanings although only loosely constrained by nature from fashioning sefl-destructive follies.

XI

Let us return here to Bergmann's essential point, that the systemic account provided by *Pigs for the Ancestors* (and other such works) finally fails because much that it describes remains unexplained or uninterpreted. The virtues of description for its own sake could once again be raised in defense, of course, but it seemed to Kelly and me that the account of the ritual cycle in that work did not leave readers as completely in the dark about pandanus seeds, marsupial tails, fighting stones, eels, *raua mai,* and other such symbolic phenomena as Bergmann's critique suggested. There was an attempt to indicate, partly through a subsidiary structural analysis made more explicit in later essays (1971c, also "On Cognized Models"), at least some of the ways in which such disparate phenomena as conceptual oppositions between spirits and abstract qualities on the one hand and population trends in pig herds were related to each other through a ritual cycle. We argued, furthermore, that the relations thus elucidated were not among the phenomena already "richly known" through ordinary experience as members of society, either the Maring's experience or our own. Our common sense would not lead us to believe that the sow's ear of ecosystemic regulation would be embroidered by the silken thread of an elaborate succession of rituals, nor would it lead us from the rituals themselves to their regulatory effects. As far as the common sense of the Maring is concerned, it was argued in the conclusion of the work under consideration (and reiterated earlier in this essay), not at all originally, that native understandings must be at some variance from the actual operations of social systems. This is to claim that knowledge not given to us in other ways was gained through the analysis, but it must be agreed that at the end much remained to be accounted for. Surely conceptual approaches other than that which dominated the book could have elucidated aspects of ritual that remained untouched by the analysis.

It may be asked, however, whether the failure of this or any other analysis to account for all the detailed descriptive material with which it is associated should be allowed to disqualify, or even demean, what it did accomplish. To say that an analysis does not illuminate everything does not mean that it illuminates nothing. The most that we can ask of any analysis is that it tell us something that is worth knowing and that we otherwise wouldn't know—in other words, that it add significantly to our understanding. It would be both mistaken and arrogant to claim for the analysis under discussion—or, for that matter, any analysis—that it explained everything "really important" in the phenomena with which it is concerned. Functional or systemic or structural or symbolic or other sorts of analysis impoverish understanding only when their results are taken to be alternative to, rather than enlargements of, knowledge gained through other modes of analysis or through general social experience.

It follows that moving on to other modes of description, analysis, or interpretation, even of the same material, does not constitute a rejection of what has already been done but, simply, a recognition of its limitations. I, for instance, have been led—or pushed—to more recent concerns with the nature of the sacred and the formal characteristics of ritual (see "The Obvious Aspects of Ritual") by the realization that an ecological and systemic analysis of a ritual cycle says nothing about those aspects of rituals that make them rituals, or about the nature and grounds of sanctity. I had, at best, learned something about the functions of ritual and sanctity among the Maring. I had not learned anything at all about ritual or sanctity themselves.

It is the business of philosophers to criticize theories, paradigms, methods, to locate their deficiencies, to discover their limitations, to test their soundness, and anthropologists should listen carefully to what they have to say. We may, however, be too naïvely sensitive to their strictures, and thus too prone to disparage modes of analysis for what they are not, too reluctant to value them for what they are, too quick to dismiss them because they do not account for everything. But there never has been, nor will there ever be, a mode of analysis that will tell us everything worth knowing about anything. To persist in demanding the unattainable is unreasonable, but would be more or less harmless if it merely left us in chronic states of disappointment. It doesn't. It leaves us either with nothing, as we reject everything, or with an undifferentiated everything as we give ourselves too easily to the saving images of the revitalistic movements that, with some regularity, sweep through the discipline promising, if not the keys to the kindgom, the key to the universe— culture and personality in the thirties, the "New Ethnography" and "Cultural Ecology" in the fifties, "Structuralism" and the "New Ecology" in the sixties. Those swept up in such movements are inclined either to impoverish understanding by defining "everything worth knowing" as that which can be known through the doctrines to which they are devoted, or to distort understanding by asking more of their theories, methods, or perspectives than they can deliver. Failures resulting from the exportation of sound but limited modes of explanation into unsuitable domains are likely to be construed not as the abuses of concepts, which they are, but as the bankruptcy of those concepts, which they are not.

To say simply that no mode of explanation illuminates everything and that more comprehensive understanding is grounded in several modes simultaneously applied is to invite a shapeless eclecticism, and as such is not very helpful. A little ecology, let us say, a little Freud, and a few structural embellishments are more likely, when stirred together, to increase confusion than understanding. If a plurality of explanatory principles are to be invoked effectively they must be related to each other in ordered ways. Thus, questions concerning the proper place of ecological principles, of the notion of function, of the concept of system in anthropological understanding dissolve into the larger question of a general ecology of explanation. There is a need, I think, to elucidate the relationship both of modes of explanation and of explanatory principles to each other.

I am not competent to deal with the complex issue of the structure of comprehensive explanation, but I must note that we have been touching on this matter throughout the course of this essay. Earlier in this section, for instance, we considered the relationship of subjective and objective domains. Our discussion in a previous section of the relations pertaining among formal, final, efficient, and material accounts, moreover, suggests one obvious way in which ecological explanations fit into a general ecology of explanation. Environmental perturbations can qualify as efficient causes of events in societies or even of changes in the structures of societies. Systems respond to efficient causes within the constraints of their previously existing orders (i.e., structured contents) which, in this terminology, constitute material cause. To claim that the specific characteristics of environments or perturbations in them cannot account for the specific nature of the responses to them—a common complaint—is, first, simply to say that efficient cause is not material cause (the related complaint that functions do not specify how they are fulfilled in like manner criticizes final cause for not being material cause). Second, and perhaps more important, the claim, if radically construed, is exaggerated to the point of being misleading or even erroneous. With the possible exception of genetic responses, the characteristics of environments and changes in them do more than stimulate adapting systems to random activity. Problems constituted by environments have particular properties that must be accommodated, circumvented, overridden, domesticated, ameliorated, or corrected. Whereas characteristics of the environment or changes in them do not determine the specific nature of responses to them, they may establish the general direction or trajectory of those responses more or less stringently and, of course, it is in terms of them that the appropriateness, adequacy, or success of those responses is minimally assessed. That adaptive formulations can seldom provide "uniquely correct answers," as critics have charged, is, of course, true. Ordered versatility is, after all, the essence of adaptiveness. But to say that the "answers" provided by adaptive formulations are not "uniquely correct" is not to say that they are incorrect or of no account.

A related problem bearing upon comprehensive understanding, touched upon earlier in this essay, is that of contradiction between the requisites, goals, and effects of the operations of included vs. including systems—organisms, populations of various magnitudes, and ecosystems. Considerations of this general problem, which seems to be one of the most crucial of our time, obviously requires consideration not only of the specific "laws of functioning" of systems at various levels, but of relations between levels. It was suggested at the end of our brief discussion of adaptation in an earlier section that if the relationship of included to including systems is to any degree that of part to whole, these hierarchies of interlevel relations may have to possess certain structural characteristics to remain orderly. In the essay "Adaptive Structure and Its Disorders" the possible structural requisites of adaptive organization will be considered in some detail and so will the possible consequences of anomalies in them. Here I will only note, first, that these principles have a logical basis and, second, if the suggestions in that essay are in any way correct they will demonstrate that principles of great generality can increase our understanding of some of the detailed structural characteristics of human social systems.

I will finally note as germane to an ecology of explanation that statements concerning principles of organization generally may be ordered into explanatory hierarchies. Such principles may be associated with classes of organization of greater or lesser generality, for example, Maring society, human society, single species societies, living systems, information processing systems, physical systems, all systems. (Such hierarchies are different from those of included and including systems. Human society, for instance, *subsumes* Maring society as a member, but does not *include* it as a part in the same way that an organism includes a cell.) Certain phenomena are characteristic of each of these "levels" and certain laws, regularities, or orders prevail within each of them. For instance, all physical systems are subject to the thermodynamic laws, and all information processing systems to the logic of analogic or digital coding. All living systems are characterized by adaptiveness, all organisms by metabolism, all animals by sentience, all humanity by cultural processes, all Maring by Maring cultural processes. It seems clear that the laws relating to more inclusive classes limit or bound the subclasses they include. For instance, the operation of metabolism conforms to the thermodynamic laws and may, perhaps, be taken to be special cases of them. It also seems that a relationship of contingency between the processes applying to less and more general classes of systems prevails. Metabolism, for example, is a prerequisite of sentience, or, to put it in the converse, sentience is contingent upon metabolism. The extent to which functional relations correspond to contingency relations is unclear and may have changed in the course of evolution. Whatever sentience is possessed by, let us say, an earthworm, is probably fully in the service of metabolism and reproduction, but such a simple relation between sense and metabolism is not true of humanity nor even, for that matter, of the higher animals. I have, in other terms, repeatedly spoken of this ambiguity as a source of substantive problems.

The hierarchies that we are considering here are hierarchies of specificity and generality. It follows that goals or requisites of more general categories are given specificity in terms of the specific principles of their individual members. It has, however, been suggested that the more general or inclusive the domain of an explanatory principle the less it is able to account for the particulars of any phenomenon. The laws of gravity do not, it is true, tell us much about culture, cultures, or the human condition. We should not, however, permit an oversimplified dictum to constrain us unduly. It does not seem to me that the principles ordering the phenomena characteristic of, or defining, any level should be allowed to monopolize understanding. Various aspects of a particular phenomenon may be illuminated by reference to the principles of various levels and the resulting account is "thicker," richer, and thus more meaningful than an account that is limited to the explanatory principles of a single level. This seems to me to be as true of meaning as it is of adaptation. Consider the meanings inhering in the ritual uprooting of *rumbim* described in the essay "On Cognized Models."

First, there are the meanings encoded in the particular representations appearing in the ritual—*rumbim, amame,* a special form of oven, particular foodstuffs, the acts of removing the charcoal called *ringi* from men's bodies, of sacrificing pigs, of consuming the contents of the oven, of planting the *rumbim* and the *amame* and so on. These multivocalic representations simplify, symbolize, and "iconify" meanings peculiar to Maring culture—certain spirits, qualities, and social conditions, relations among them and relations of the Maring to them. These meanings, being peculiar to Maring culture, are, of course, to be understood in the terms of Maring culture. That these Maring meanings are represented in the contxt of a *ritual,* however, leads us out of the level of the particular culture to meanings of a second and more general sort. I have mentioned in an earlier section that certain meanings—social contract, morality, a paradigm of creation, the concept of the sacred, the notion of the divine—inhere in ritual *per se.* In "The Obvious Aspects of Ritual" I argue that these meanings are entailed by the structure that is definitive of ritual. Ritual, however, is not peculiar to Maring culture. It is a pan-human phenomenon, and it would be a mistake to take its pan-cultural meanings to be specifically Maring meanings. Moreover, the nature of the "meaningfulness" of the specifically Maring meanings is different from the meaningfulness of panhuman ritual. The matter is too intricate to describe in this essay, but is discussed in detail in "The Obvious Aspects of Ritual." Here it must suffice to say that whereas culturally specific representations stand in symbolic and iconic relationships to their culturally specific significations, the meanings peculiar to *ritual* are indexically signaled. Further, the participation (in the ritual) of the sender of ritual messages (who is also their most important receiver) is *ipso facto* participation in the messages themselves. I argue in the essay "On Cognized Models" that the meaningfulness of participation is that of identity, unity, or integration, rather than that of reference, which is the form of meaningfulness characterizing culturally particular meanings by themselves.

There is yet a third level of meaning in ritual: the significance intrinsic to the mere fact of a ritual's performance. I have argued elsewhere (1971d) that the mere occurrence of a non-calendrical ritual may be a signal. Since any ritual included in the repertoire of a people can, at any particular time, be in only one of two possible states—occurring or not occurring—occurrence can transmit a binary signal. Although the occurrence of the ritual transmits a "yes/no" signal, it may have been triggered by the achievement or violation of a particular state or range of states of a continuous, "more-less" variable, or even of a complex state or range of states constellated by relationships among a number of such variables. As such, the occurrence of a ritual may be a simple qualitative representation of complex quantitative information or, to put it differently, the occurrence of a ritual may summarize complex analogic information and translate it into the simplest possible digital signal, one for which there is only one alternative. It is of great importance to note that the simple binary characteristics are not peculiar to Maring rituals. In fact, they are not peculiar to ritual. We are speaking here of a much broader phenomenon, a general characteristic of digital information processing.
binary characteristics are not only peculiar to Maring rituals. In fact, they are not peculiar to ritual. We are speaking here of a much broader phenomenon, a general characteristic of digital information processing.

Our understanding of rituals, then, is increased by appeals to three levels of order. It would have been possible to invoke other levels as well, but our illustrative purposes have not demanded it. The point here is that valuable insights concerning detailed aspects of ritual have been vouchsafed to us by the principles governing three levels of order. Of course the general characteristics of ritual and the panhuman meanings they entail do not account for all of the symbolic and iconic particularities of Maring, Catholic, or any other ritual. Conversely, the particularities of Maring, Catholic, or any other ritual cannot provide an understanding of why they are presented in ritual and not in some other symbolic form. We are led here to a related point. An appeal to more than one level does not simply provide us with several concurrent but more or less autonomous sets of meanings. These sets of meanings are related to each other. For instance, the occurrence of culturally specific representations in ritual contexts sanctifies them and invests them with morality. The performance of a ritual, moreover, entails an acceptance by the performer of an obligation to abide by whatever that ritual encodes. Further implications of the ritual form for what is represented in it are discussed in "The Obvious Aspects of Ritual" and in "Sanctity and Lies in Evolution." Sufficient has been said here to indicate that the ritual form is something like a meta-statement about the culturally specific meanings it encompasses. I say "something like a meta-statement" because rituals possess performative qualities and are not merely statements. I have discussed the meaningfulness of performatives in "On Cognized Models." It is not simply the meaningfulness of description, nor even that of evaluation. It is constitutive. As such it is a meaningfulness very different from that of culturally specific representations by themselves. It is a meaningfulness that is, or comes very close to being, causal.

In sum, our understanding of ritual is not merely enriched by appeals to more than one level of generality. It is, rather, impoverished, incomplete, and inadequate unless we do invoke the meanings of more than one level. The proper citation of the principles of one level does not conflict with the simultaneous citation of those pertaining to other levels. Indeed, to say that the simultaneously invoked principles of the several levels complement each other is inadequate as an expression of the intimacy of their relationship. It would be tempting to say that they complete each other if it were not that our understanding of anything as profound, subtle, various, and ubiquitous as ritual can never be complete, for such things forever demand that new questions be asked of them. It should not be forgotten, furthermore, that the scope of that which anthropology seeks to understand is not well or truly represented by any catalogue of the innumerable cultural categories or phenomena, such as ritual or rituals, with which the distinctions of language can provide us. The task of anthropology is not even to be understood as the elucidation of cultures as systems. As Roger Keesing put it a few years ago, we also

... want to know how human groups organize and sustain their social life; how biology and experience interact... how the nature of that experience shapes personalities; how different—and how similar—are human modes of thought and perception in different times and places; how ways of life change, and what shapes and forms they take in particular settings. [1974: 90]

And, I would add, we want to know how cultures come to be at odds with the creatures who bear them and with the ecological systems in which they are set; in what specific forms such contradictions between "nature" and "culture" manifest themselves and whether the difficulties that follow such disorders can be corrected. We also need to understand better how humans may keep from destroying the systems upon which they depend, and themselves along with them, when the complexity of those systems exceeds any hope of comprehension.

In the face of the world's enormity, demands for "uniquely correct answers," which neither adaptive formulations nor any others can really provide, sound like cries in the dark. Uniquely correct answers may be provided for a relatively small number of precise questions, of course, but there are no uniquely correct questions. Those that may properly be asked are as innumerable as the species and stars of which they are asked and as unbounded as the imaginations of those who would ask them.

REFERENCES CITED

Bateson, Gregory
    1963 The role of somatic change in evolution. *Evolution* 17:529–539.
    1972 The logical categories of learning and communication. In *Steps to an ecology of mind.* New York: Ballantine.
Bergmann, Frithjof
    1975 On the inadequacies of functionalism. *Michigan Discussions in Anthropology* 1(1):2–23.
Birdsell, J.
    1958 On population structure in generalized hunting and collecting populations. *Evolution* 12:189–205.
Brown, Robert
    1958 *Explanation in social science.* Chicago: Aldine.
Colinvaux, P.
    1973 *Introduction to ecology.* New York: John Wiley & Sons.
Collins, Paul
    1965 Functional analyses in the symposium "Man, Culture and Animals." In *Man, culture and animals,* ed. A. Leeds and A. P. Vayda. Washington, D.C.: American Association for the Advancement of Science.
Durkheim, Emile
    1938 *The rules of sociological method,* 8th ed. Edited by George Catlin. Translated by Sarah Soloway and John H. Mueller. New York: Free Press.
Friedman, Jonathan
    1974 Marxism, structuralism, and vulgar materialism. *Man* N.S. 9:444–469.
Harris, Marvin
    1966 The cultural ecology of India's sacred cattle. *Current Anthropology* 7:51–60.
Hempel, Carl
    1958 The logic of functional analysis. In *Symposium on sociological theory,* ed. Llewelyn Gross. Evanston: Row, Peterson.

Keesing, Roger
    1974   Theories of culture. *Annual Review of Anthropology* 3:73-98.
Kelly, Raymond, and R. A. Rappaport
    1975   Function, generality, and explanatory power: a commentary and response to Bergmann's arguments. *Michigan Discussions in Anthropology* 1(1):24-44.
Margalef, Ramon
    1968   *Perspectives in ecological theory.* Chicago: University of Chicago Press.
Monod, Jacques
    1972   *Chance and necessity.* New York: Random House.
Murphy, Robert
    1970   Basin ethnography and ecological theory. In *Languages and cultures of western North America,* ed. Earl Swanson, Jr. Pocatello: Idaho State University Press.
Nagel, Ernest
    1961   *The structure of science.* New York: Harcourt, Brace & World.
Odum, E. P.
    1969   The strategy of ecosystem development. *Science* 164:262-270.
Pattee, H. H., ed.
    1973   *Hierarchy theory.* New York: Braziller, International Library of Systems Theory and Philosophy.
Piaget, Jean
    1971   *Structuralism.* London: Routledge & Kegan Paul.
Piddocke, S.
    1965   The potlatch system of the southern Kwakiutl: a new perspective. *Southwestern Journal of Anthropology* 21:244-264.
Rappaport, Roy A.
    1968   *Pigs for the ancestors.* New Haven: Yale University Press.
    1969a Sanctity and adaptation. *Io* 7 (1970):46-71. (Paper prepared for Wenner-Gren Conference on the Moral and Aesthetic Structure of Human Adaptation, 1969.)
    1969b Some suggestions concerning concept and method in ecological anthropology. In *Ecological essays,* ed. David Damas. National Museum of Canada Bulletin 230.
    1971a Ritual, sanctity, and cybernetics. *American Anthropologist* 73:59-76.
    1971b The flow of energy in an agricultural society. *Scientific American* 225(3):116-132.
    1971c Nature, culture, and ecological anthropology. In *Man, culture and society,* rev. ed., ed. H. Shapiro, pp. 237-268. New York: Oxford University Press.
    1971d The sacred in human evolution. *Annual Review of Ecology and Systematics* 2:23-44.
    1974   Energy and the structure of adaptation. *Coevolution Quarterly,* vol. 1, no. 1.
    1976   Adaptation and maladaptation in social systems. In *The ethical basis of economic freedom,* ed. Ivan Hill, pp. 39-82. Chapel Hill, N.C.: American Viewpoint.
    1977   Maladaptation in social systems. In *Evolution in social systems,* ed. J. Friedman and M. Rowlands. London: Duckworth.

Sahlins, Marshall
  1958 *Social stratification in Polynesia.* American Ethnological Society
       Monograph. Seattle: University of Washington Press.
  1969 Economic anthropology and anthropological economics. *Social Science
       Information* 8:13–33.
  1976a CA comment on "Structural and eclectic revisions of Marxist strategy:
       a cultural materialist critique," by Allen H. Berger. *Current Anthro-
       pology* 17:298–300.
  1976b *Culture and practical reason.* Chicago: University of Chicago Press.
Sapir, Edward
  1924 Culture, genuine and spurious. *American Journal of Sociology* 29:401–
       429.
Shantzis, S. B., and W. W. Behrens
  1973 Population control mechanisms in a primitive society. In *Toward
       global equilibrium,* ed. D. L. Meadows and D. H. Meadows. Cam-
       bridge, Mass.: Wright-Allen Press.
Simon, Herbert
  1969 *The sciences of the artificial.* Cambridge, Mass.: MIT Press.
Slobodkin, L., and A. Rapoport
  1974 An optimal strategy of evolution. *Quarterly Review of Biology* 49:
       181–200.
Steward, Julian
  1955 *Theory of culture change.* Urbana: University of Illinois Press.
Suttles, Wayne
  1960 Affinal ties, subsistence, and prestige among the Coast Salish. *Ameri-
       can Anthropologist* 62:296–305.
Thomas, Lewis
  1974 *The lives of a cell.* New York: Viking Press.
Vayda, A. P.
  1968 Foreword to *Pigs for the ancestors* by R. A. Rappaport, pp. ix–xiii. New
       Haven: Yale University Press.
  1974 Warfare in ecological perspective. *Annual Review of Ecology and Sys-
       tematics* 5:183–194.
Vayda, A. P., and B. McKay
  1975 New directions in ecology and ecological anthropology. *Annual Re-
       view of Anthropology* 4:293–306.
Vayda, A. P., and R. A. Rappaport
  1967 Ecology, cultural and non-cultural. In *Introduction to cultural anthro-
       pology,* ed. J. Clifton, pp. 456–479. Boston: Houghton-Mifflin.
Wynne-Edwards, V. C.
  1962 *Animal dispersion in relation to social behavior.* Edinburgh and London:
       Oliver & Boyd.

On Cognized Models

Nature is seen by humans through a screen of beliefs, knowledge, and purposes, and it is in terms of their images of nature, rather than of the actual structure of nature, that they act. Yet, it is upon nature itself that they do act, and it is nature itself that acts upon them, nurturing or destroying them. Disparities between images of nature and the actual structure of ecosystems are inevitable. Humans are gifted learners and may continually enlarge and correct their knowledge of their environments, but their images of nature are always simpler than nature and in some degree or sense inexact, for ecological systems are complex and subtle beyond full comprehension.

The discrepancy between cultural images of nature and the actual organization of nature is a critical problem for mankind and one of the central problems of any ecologically oriented anthropology. To cope with it I have suggested in earlier essays (1963, 1968, 1971) that the ethnographer must prepare two accounts of his subject matter. One, which I have called the "cognized model," is a description of a people's knowledge of their environment and of their beliefs concerning it. The second, the "operational model," describes the same ecological system (including the people and their activities) in accordance with the assumptions and methods of the objective sciences, in particular the science of ecology. It is, in another jargon, "etic," whereas the cognized model is "emic" (Harris 1976). I have suggested that many components of the physical world are likely to be included in both the cognized and operational models, but their memberships will seldom, if ever, be identical. The operational model includes those substances, organisms, processes, and cultural practices which observations proceeding in accordance with the canons of natural science suggest to the analyst have an effect upon the organisms, populations, and ecosystems under consideration. It may include elements of which the actors are unaware (such as microorganisms and trace elements) but which affect them in important ways. The cognized model, on the other hand, may well include components, such as supernaturals, whose existence cannot be demonstrated by empirical procedures, but whose putative existence moves the actors to behave in the ways that they do.

I have argued that this approach does not imply that cognized models are merely less accurate or more ignorant views of the world than operational models written in accordance with scientific principles, but should, rather, be regarded as parts of populations' distinctive means for maintaining themselves in their environments. The important question concerning cognized models in this view is not the extent to which they are identical with what the analyst takes to be reality but the extent to which they direct behavior in ways that are appropriate to the biological well-being of the actors and of the ecosystems in which they participate. The criterion of adequacy for a cognized model is not its accuracy, but its adaptive effectiveness. Accordingly, the analysis of the ecological ethnographer consists of an integration of the cognized and operational models, an integration that permits him to describe the effects of behavior undertaken with respect to the understanding of the cognized model on both the ecosystem and the population itself as they are represented in the operational model. In this way it becomes possible to assess the adaptiveness not only of overt human behavior, but even of the ideology that informs that behavior.

In this view, the place of cognized models in the material relations of populations is analogous to that of the "memories" of computer controls in cybernetically regulated systems of material exchange and transformations. In such systems reports of current systemic states are continuously or periodically compared to reference values (which may, of course, be continuously adjusted in response to signals from other parts of the system). If discrepancies between states of affairs and the relevant reference values are detected, programs to return the states of affairs to those reference values may be initiated. Such programs are, ideally, discontinued when the discrepancies are eliminated.

In a roughly similar way I have suggested that people compare the states of the systems in which they participate, *as these states are indicated by signs,* with their culturally determined notions of what they think they should be (reference or ideal values). Some important general questions follow. First, what is the relationship between signs and the processes they are understood to indicate? Is it the case that such processes as soil depletion are detected early, or only when they are well advanced? Do those phenomena that are taken to be signs of particular conditions actually indicate what they are understood to indicate? Of even greater importance, to what extent do reference or ideal values, which reflect people's culturally defined understandings and wishes, correspond to their actual material requirements, and to the requirements *and limitations* of the ecosystems in which they participate?

I have put these questions in more formal terms in earlier essays. Operational models, as I proposed to conceive them, may—perhaps even should—include specifications of what are sometimes called in systems jargon "goal ranges" for variables that are, on theoretical or empirical grounds, taken to be crucial to the perpetuation of the systems under consideration. The goal range of such a variable encompasses the range of states that, if maintained, permits the system to continue. Violation of a goal range, conversely, threatens the perpetuation of the system. The population size of local groups in tribal societies may serve as an example. Below a certain size a local group may not be able to defend itself, but if it becomes too large it may degrade its resource base. The goal range lies between the minimum number required for self-defense and the maximum number that can be supported in perpetuity on the land available. Similarly, a goal range for livestock, such as pigs, may lie between the minimum requisite for nutrition and a maximum beyond which environmental destruction would ensue. It is of great importance that the limits of goal ranges be established by procedures independent of those attempting to discover reference values because *reference values, that is, the values around which systems equilibrate themselves, may not correspond to goal ranges, the ranges of states within which systems remain viable.* We return here to the formal expression of the question raised in the last paragraph: *What is the relationship between a reference value, or range of values, which is a component of a cognized model, and the corresponding goal range, a component of an operational model?*

In *Pigs for the Ancestors,* a work dealing with tribal horticulturalists, I argued that among the Maring of New Guinea the upper limit of the reference range for pigs was always likely to remain below the upper limit of the goal range defined as the territory's ability to support pigs (see "Ecology, Adaptation, and the Ills of Functionalism" elsewhere in this volume for a discussion of Jonathan Friedman's criticism of this analysis), but it is important to emphasize that such a nice fit between reference values and goal ranges does not always prevail. I have repeatedly noted that it is entirely possible for reference values to be set *outside* of goal ranges. To say that a system is self-equilibrating or cybernetic is *not* to say that it is, *ipso facto,* adaptive or functional. Systems may be equilibrated at levels that are self-destructive.

I have argued that reference values that violate the goal ranges of biological (including demographic and ecological) variables are, *prima facie,* maladaptive. The concept of adaptation, and the related notion of maladaptation, are considered at length in another essay in this volume ("Adaptive Structure and Its Disorders"), but it is well to note here that maladaptive, dysfunctional, or contradictory equilibration may not be at all uncommon. Although instances can surely be found among the stateless societies traditionally studied by anthropologists, maladaptive equilibration may be encouraged by increases in social scale, complexity, and interdependence. Such enlargements increase the likelihood that local social and ecological systems will be regulated in terms of values external to and distinct from themselves. We come here to a problem more profound than that of simple disparity between reference values and their corresponding goal ranges. The very terms in which reference values are expressed may be alien to and inappropriate for the systems being regulated. Economic terms, for instance, are incommensurable with ecological terms, and the state of the "developed" world strongly suggests that the regulation of ecosystems in accordance with economic reference values is likely to result in environmental destruction, just as the regulation of social relations and health care in economic terms may degrade social relations and obstruct medical treatment.

If the regulation of ecological systems in terms of economics is likely to result in environmental devastation, and is ultimately destructive to the society dependent upon that environment, then it would seem advisable to elevate ecological and other biological principles to positions of ultimacy in cognized models (at the same time demoting economic considerations to the subordinate positions that their short-term, conventional, and contingent nature warrants). I have argued, however, that there may be no simple, direct relationship between the amount of testable empirical knowledge included in a cognized model and the appropriateness of the behavior that it elicits. It is by no means certain that the representations of nature provided us by science are more adaptive than those images of the world, inhabited by spirits whom men respect, that guide the actions of the Maring and other "primitives." To drape nature in supernatural veils may be to provide her with some protection against human folly and extravagance. Indeed, destruction of nature may well be encouraged by a natural view of it. Given the complexity of natural ecosystems it is unlikely that we will ever be able to predict the outcome of all of the actions we undertake in any of them, even if we do understand the principles of ecosystemic operation generally. Because knowledge can never replace respect as a guiding principle in our ecosystemic relations, it is adaptive for cognized models to engender respect for that which is unknown, unpredictable, and uncontrollable, as well as for them to codify empirical knowledge. It may be that the most appropriate cognized models, that is, those from which adaptive behavior follows, are not those that simply represent ecosystemic relations in objectively "correct" material terms, but those that invest them with significance and value beyond themselves.

All cognized models encode values, but all do not value the same things equally, and we may inquire into the adaptiveness of different sets of evaluative understandings. A model dominated by, let us say, the postulates of economic rationality would propose that an ecosystem is composed of elements of three general sorts: those that qualify as "resources," those that are neutrally useless, and those that may be regarded as pests, antagonists, or competitors. In contrast, the Ituri Pygmies take the forest encompassing them to be the body of God. These two views of the world obviously suggest radically different ways of living in it.

*   *   *

The crude first approach to the systemic relationship of cultural understandings to ecological processes just outlined is not devoid of merit but it is surely inadequate, even with respect to its own limited ends. Before discussing its undoubted shortcomings and possible virtues, however, it will be useful to turn, for illustrative purposes, to Maring ethnography. Whereas earlier presentations of this material have emphasized the "objective" terms of the operational model the emphasis here will be upon Maring understandings, in particular those encoded in their ritual cycle. That their ritual cycle embodies Maring conceptions of the divine, cosmological postulates, and the rules guiding social action at the same time that it regulates political and environmental relations proposes that it is of strategic importance in approaching the problems with which this essay is concerned, and we may reasonably expect ritual cycles of at least some other tribal societies to be comparably important.

I shall proceed as follows. After describing the Maring ritual cycle and the understandings that animate it I shall note some of the obvious deficiencies of the earlier formulation of the relationship of the meaningful and material. This will lead to a discussion of the *structure* of cognized models which, I shall propose, are composed of understandings of several orders. I shall suggest that these understandings are organized, or "put in order," along several dimensions. I shall be particularly concerned with the way in which such ordering is accomplished by ritual, and with the adaptive implications of such orders. This discussion will make clear the need for further changes in the formulation of the relationship between the meaningful and material reviewed in the opening pages of this essay.

We shall proceed from the ordering of understanding to a discussion of the order of meaning and meaningfulness. This will lead to consideration of differences in the meaningfulness of cognized models in traditional and modern societies. Differences in the ways in which knowledge is organized in traditional and modern societies will, in turn, lead to consideration of the relationship of knowledge and its distribution to power. In the course of this discussion the predicating force of metaphor and its place in domination and subordination will be examined. This discussion will elucidate the general nature of cognized models, proposing that they are quasi-performative or quasi-illocutionary (Austin 1962), and not simply descriptive. The "naturalization" of the performatively constituted will then be discussed and, finally, the union of the meaningful and material aspects of living processes will be considered.

II

The Tsembaga, who at the time of fieldwork in 1962–1963 numbered 200 people divided among five putatively patrilineal clans, may be considered an ecological population, and their territory, 3.2 square miles of forested land rising from 2700 to 7200 feet on the south wall of the Simbai Valley, an ecosystem. About half of their land is arable, and the Tsembaga, who are slash-and-burn horticulturalists, cut new gardens in the secondary forest up to altitudes of 5400 feet each year. Harvesting continues for a year to two years or more, after which the site must be allowed to lie fallow until the secondary forest developing upon it has reached a certain stage of maturity. This takes from seven to forty years, depending upon the site. Staples are root crops. Taro and sweet potatoes are most important, but yams, manioc, bananas, pandanus, and a great variety of greens are also grown. The Tsembaga also raise pigs which, although domiciled and fed in the women's houses, wander loose during the day and provide themselves with most of their diet. In addition to the rations of tubers given them (an adult pig is given about as much as a man) they consume garbage and human feces as well as what they can root up in abandoned gardens and secondary forest.

Immediately to the east of the Tsembaga, on the same valley wall, lies the territory of the Tuguma, a Maring local group with whom the Tsembaga are friendly. The land immediately to the west is occupied by the Kundagai, against whom the Tsembaga waged war four times in the half-century previous to 1962.

The Tsembaga, like all other Maring, are egalitarian as far as men are concerned. There are no chiefs or other authorities who can command or coerce the obedience of others. But, I have argued, relations between autonomous local populations such as the Tsembaga and the Kundagai, and between such populations and the other species with which they share their territories, are regulated by protracted ritual cycles. Indeed, the operation of these cycles helps to maintain an undegraded biotic and physical environment, distributes local surpluses of pigs throughout a region in the form of pork, and may assure people high quality protein when they are most in need of it. The ritual cycles also limit warfare to frequencies that do not endanger the survival of the regional population but allow occasional redispersion of people over land and land among people, thus, perhaps, tending to correct discrepancies between the population densities of different local groups.*

While observations informed by general ecological and cybernetic principles indicate the regulatory functions of Maring ritual cycles, they are not so understood by the Tsembaga and other Maring. They perform them, they say, to maintain or transmute their relations with spirits.

*   *   *

Two sets of major spirits inhabit the Maring world. One dwells in the upper reaches of clan territories, the other in the lower. The spirits of the high ground include Red Spirits (*Raua Mugi*) and Smoke Woman (*Kun Kaze Ambra*). The Red Spirits are said to dwell in the high altitude forest, and Smoke Woman is thought to reside at the highest point in the group's territory, sometimes flying off to the summit of Mount Oipor, the highest peak in the general area.

Smoke Woman, who was never human, acts as an intermediary between the living and all other categories of spirits. Shamans communicate with her in seances, conducted in darkened men's houses and often lasting all night, by "pulling smoke." They inhale deeply the smoke of strong native cigars and send their *nomane* (a term which in some contexts means thought, refers here to the conscious aspect of the self that survives death) out of their noses to fly to the houses of the Smoke Woman in the high places and to escort her back to the seance. She enters the shaman's head through his nostrils and, speaking through his mouth, informs the living of the wishes of the dead. Shamans commune with the Smoke Woman before all important rituals and upon many other occasions as well.

Although this spirit is female, she has no association with women. Female shamans are virtually nonexistent; the one of whom I know was regarded as preposterous by most men. Smoke Woman has no connection whatsoever with fertility either, and while not antagonistic to women generally, is perhaps antagonistic to the sexuality of living

*See "Ritual Regulation of Environmental Relations among a New Guinea People" earlier in this volume.

women. At any rate, when a man is "struck" by her for the first time, he should abstain from intercourse for a while because, it is said, the Smoke Woman might, out of jealousy, do mischief to any women with whom a novice of hers consorted.

The Red Spirits are spirits of those who have been killed in warfare. Those species included in the category *ma*—mostly high altitude arboreal marsupials—are said to be their pigs, but aside from some concern with the hunting and trapping of these animals, the Red Spirits have no interest in subsistence activities. As they are associated with the upper portion of the territory, so they are associated with the upper part of the body. They may cause illness of the head and chest, and their help is solicited when such afflictions have other causes. Their most important concerns, however, are with the relations of the local group to other local groups, particularly in warfare. Warfare rituals are largely addressed to them, and they enforce the taboos associated with warfare.

Their general qualities are reflected in the terms by which they are addressed in ritual. Often they are called *Norum-Kombri* and *Runge-Yinye. Kombri* are cassowaries, fierce birds living mainly in the high forest. *Norum* are epiphytic orchids with strong stalks growing high on high-altitude trees. *Runge* is the sun, *yinye* is fire. The Red Spirits are said to be *rombanda,* which in other context may mean simply "hot," but in relation to them, as well as in some other contexts, it implies dryness, hardness, strength, and, as seems apparent in some rituals associated with warfare, anger and ferocity as well.

The two classes of spirits that dwell in the lower portions of the territory are sometimes known collectively as *Raua Mai. Mai* in this context seems to mean antecedent in a biological sense: a taro corm from which rhizomes have grown is a *mai;* a woman who has borne children is an *ambra mai;* old men are *yu mai.*

Included among the *Raua Mai* is, first, *Koipa Mangiang,* who, like Smoke Woman, was never human. This spirit is said to be male and to dwell in pools in the streams dissecting the mountainside and, as marsupials are the pigs of the Red Spirits, eels are said to be his pigs.

Living nearby, in the trunks of the largest trees in climax forest remnants, are the *Raua Tukump,* the spirits of those who have died of illness or accident. The term *tukump* refers both to a supernatural corruption that may pollute places and harm people, and to the mold, sometimes said to be faintly luminescent, that develops on rotting objects and substances.

As the Red Spirits are associated with the upper part of the body, so the "Spirits of Rot" are associated with the lower—with the belly, the reproductive organs, and the legs—and they may both afflict those parts and cure afflictions of them. They and *Koipa Mangiang* have minor parts to play in warfare rituals (for instance, when the warriors call the Red Spirits into themselves, they ask the spirits of the low ground to strengthen their legs) but their major concern is, not surprisingly, with fertility generally—with the fruitfulness of women, pigs, and gardens—and rituals concerned with fertility are addressed, in the main, to the spirits of the low ground. *Koipa Mangiang* has authority in these matters, the Spirits of Rot acting as his intermediaries, but his dominion is not limited to fertility. He alone among the major spirits actually kills (although other spirits may request that he do so). *Koipa Mangiang* has, therefore, a fearful as well as a benign aspect.

As the spirits of the high ground are said to be "hot," so those of the low ground are said to be *kinim,* which sometimes means, simply, cold. Here, *kinim* carries an implication of wetness as well: the juice of sugar cane is *kinim.* So is water and all creatures that live in water, and women are said to be so because of their vaginal secretions.

Maring observe that cold and wet conditions induce decay, the dissolution of organic matter and its reabsorption into earth from which it sprang, and decay is seen by them to favor fertility. New life grows from the rot of things once living; that which is living will in its turn dissolve, supporting life yet to come. But whether or not it is beneficial to growth, that which is decaying is, after all, itself dead or dying. Fertility is, thus, closely related to death in Maring cosmology. This closeness is indicated by their union in the figure of *Koipa Mangiang.*

Both hotness and coldness, both strength and fertility are, in the Maring view, qualities necessary to survival—to the successful defense of the land and to its successful cultivation. But the two sets of qualities are inimical to each other. Therefore, some activities must be segregated from others in time and space, and some objects and persons must be insulated from contact with other objects and persons during certain periods or even permanently. Thus, men at war who have taken into themselves the heat of the Red Spirits should avoid contact with women because the coldness and wetness of the women will extinguish their fires and soften their strength. Like many other New Guinea Highlanders, the Maring have well-developed notions, expressed in a welter of taboos, concerning the polluting qualities of women, and too much contact with women at any time is said to be debilitating (see Buchbinder and Rappaport 1976).

In sum, the virtues of the two sets of spirits stand in clear contrast to each other, although we could, perhaps, note within the cosmology, as I have outlined it, some mediation between them. The Spirits of Rot and the Red Spirits were kinsmen in life, and thus, perhaps, stand, in some logical sense, between Smoke Woman and *Koipa Mangiang.* But of greater interest than this logical mediation is the dynamic mediation of

the ritual cycle. It is in terms of this mediation among supernatural entities that the material variables comprising the ecosystem are regulated.

*   *   *

It is convenient to begin a description of the ritual cycle with the
outbreak of warfare. Hostilities erupt when a member of one local group
(such as the Tsembaga) inflicts upon a member of another local group an
injury of sufficient seriousness to demand homicidal revenge. A principle
of balanced reciprocity prevails with respect to homicide including battle
casualties. Injuries requiring vengeance are therefore most often homicides or attempted homicides revenging deaths suffered in previous
rounds of warfare but remaining unavenged. That is, because the spirit of
every person slain demands to be avenged with the life of a member of
the killer's group, more deaths suffered by one side than the other in a
round of warfare serve as grounds for the next round some years later.

We have noted that the Red Spirits are primarily associated with
warfare, and that their characteristics stand in opposition to those of the
spirits of the low ground. Indeed, the virtues of the latter are thought to
be inimical to those of the Red Spirits, and to the assistance that they
might provide during warfare. It is therefore necessary, when warfare is
initiated, to segregate the two sets of spirits and everything associated
with them as much as possible, and to identify the community, especially
the men, more closely with the Red Spirits. This is accomplished in an
elaborate ritual during which certain objects called fighting stones (*bamp
ku*) are hung from the center post of a ritual house. This ritual transforms
the relationship of the antagonists from one of "brotherhood" (*ngui-
ngui:* 'brother-brother') into one of formal and sanctified enmity (*cenang
yu:* 'ax men') if it had not already been so transformed in earlier rounds
of warfare. The territories of enemies may not be entered except to
despoil them, and enemies may not be touched or addressed except in
anger.

In the course of this ritual, in which only men participate, the Red
Spirits are taken by the warriors into their heads, where they are said to
burn like fire. Sexual intercourse is henceforth tabooed, of course,
because contact with the cold, wet, soft women would put out the fires
burning in the hot, hard, dry men's heads, and conversely, women would
be burned by contact with the men. For similar reasons food cooked by
women, moist foods, soft foods, and foods identified with the lower
altitudes become tabooed to the warriors, who also suffer a taboo on
drinking any fluids while actually on the battle ground. The segregation
of that associated with the high from that associated with the low, a
segregation which is at its most extreme when warfare is initiated, is
indicated by these and other taboos. It is perhaps most clearly repre-

sented by the prohibition against consuming marsupials, the pigs of the Red Spirits, together with the fruit of the marita pandanus, which is associated with the Spirits of Rot (parts of whose mortal remains are buried in pandanus groves). Marsupials and pandanus each may be cooked and consumed, but not in mixture or even at the same meal.

Not only are the two sets of supernaturals segregated from each other, but the living are separated from both by heavy obligations. These are owed even to the spirits of the low ground who are asked, when the stones are hung, to strengthen the warriors' legs. Because of these debts a taboo on the trapping of marsupials goes into effect, although they may be eaten if shot. Eels may neither be trapped nor eaten. Men cannot eat them because eels, being cold and wet, would be inimical to their strength. But they cannot be trapped even for consumption by women because they are the pigs of *Koipa Mangiang,* and while a debt to him remains his pigs may not be taken.

Warfare, in sum, tears the universe asunder, for it requires the radical separation of the hot from the cold, the high from the low, the strong from the fertile, male from female. When war is "declared" (by hanging the fighting stones) a great range of taboos prohibiting certain objects, substances, foods, classes of persons, and activities from coming into contact with each other are therefore activated, and heavy debts in favor of the dead are assumed by the living, for the dead must be repaid for their assistance in the fighting.

Fighting could go on for weeks. Oral histories report the occasional rout of one of the parties, and in such cases the victors despoiled the territory of their opponents, then retired to their own ground. Maring say they never seize the land of enemies because, even if they have driven off the living, their ancestral spirits remain to guard it. Usually, however, warfare terminates by agreement between the antagonists that there has been enough fighting and injury and death for the time being.

With the termination of warfare reintegration of the universe commences. Indeed, from the Maring point of view the remainder of the ritual cycle, which began when the fighting stones were hung, is a procedure for mending the world that warfare has broken. Each of the cycle's steps absolves those participating from certain taboos, and thus allows objects, persons, and activities that hostilities have segregated to come together once again. Planting *rumbim* is the first of these rituals. Indeed, the very act of planting *rumbim* by a local group, or, as is usually the case, by its constituent units simultaneously (antagonists plant *rumbim* separately), signifies that it has committed itself to a truce. It is after planting *rumbim* that men and women can once again become intimate, and taboos on certain foodstuffs are also abrogated at this time.

*   *   *

The importance of the *rumbim* planting ritual, which represents or even constitutes the fundamental terms of Maring cosmology and society at the same time that it establishes a sanctified truce, is sufficient to warrant a more or less detailed account. Buchbinder and I have provided such a description elsewhere (1976), but I shall repeat it here.

When it is agreed by the antagonists that warfare is to be discontinued, everyone in the local group—women, children, warriors, and allies— assembles for the events preceding the planting. In preparation, all possible varieties of edible wild animals are taken: marsupials, snakes, lizards, frogs, rats, insects, grubs, birds; and wild greens, chiefly edible ferns, are gathered. These wild foods, along with a little fat from the belly of a female pig, are cooked in a special oven (*pubit*) said to be about three feet square and made of bark. While the food is steaming in the oven, the warriors ritually remove the "hot" charcoal called *ringi* that they had applied to themselves when the fighting stones were hung. When the oven is opened, they, as well as their womenfolk and children, partake of its contents, although mixed throughout it are meats at all other times forbidden to men who have participated in warfare rituals.

What seems to be represented by the oven are both the fruitfulness of nature, and a natural precultural state in which men, like animals, knew no taboos and would eat anything that nature offered them. Perhaps also significant with respect to the lack of distinctions in the state of nature is the very position of the oven—it rests directly upon the ground. In contrast, ovens in which pigs dedicated to the Red Spirits (sometimes called "head pigs") are cooked are raised above the ground, while those in which pigs are offered to the spirits of the low ground ("leg pigs"), as well as those in which non-ritual meals are prepared, are dug into the ground. It may further be suggested for reasons that will become apparent, that the fruitfulness of nature represented in the feast of wild foods and the oven itself are associated with procreation.

The feasting finished, the women are sent away and a young *tondoko,* a red-leafed variety of *rumbim* (*Cordyline fruticosa*), is planted in the middle of the emptied oven. It is called the *yu min rumbim* (*yu*/man, *miñ*/shadow, life stuff). Each man clasps the *rumbim* as it is planted, and some men say that by laying hold of it their *min* flows into the plant where it remains for safekeeping. At any rate, although the *rumbim* may be planted primarily for the well-being of those planting it (women may not even touch it), it is not planted for their benefit only. It is said that after they plant *rumbim,* the children begotten by the participants will quickly become "hard" (*anč*); that is to say they will grow quickly, become strong and remain well.

By joining in the planting of *rumbim,* a man who was previously an outsider is attached to a territory and assimilated to the group occupying that territory. Thus, *rumbim* seems not only to be associated with individual men, and with the quality of hardness or strength, but also with claims to territoriality. Claims to territory reside in corporations of men who are, ideally, agnatically related, but by grasping the *rumbim* an outsider mingles his *miñ* with theirs, taking the first step toward the assimilation of his descendants into the agnatic clan claiming the territory. Although the several patrilineal clans that form a local population coordinate the planting of *rumbim* (in fact, such coordination defines them as a local population), they usually plant it separately, each clan on its own ground. *Rumbim* is, thus, associated with patrilineality as well as with territoriality and with men's well-being and strength. By grasping the *yu min rumbim,* not only does an outsider seemingly mingle his *miñ* with those of the clansmen, thereby taking the first step toward assimilation, but he incidentally resettles his ancestors at his new home, for he accompanies his participation in this ritual with the sacrifice of pigs, and he calls out to his dead to come to the new place to partake of it.

Although it is with their *miñ* that men invest the *rumbim,* it may be that the association of *miñ* with agnatic corporations imbues the commingled *miñ* that infuses the *rumbim* with, if not immortality, a perdurance beyond that of individual lives. By clasping *rumbim,* a man participates in, as it were, a corporate life whose span is greater than his own. Such a view of clan *miñ* is suggested by a standard phrase in the speech of heroes in accounts of how brave men have faced death. "It does not matter if I die. There are more Merkai (or Kamungagai, or Kwibigai, etc.) to hold the land and father the children." The clan is not immortal, but it is subject to extinction rather than death, and thus its mortal span is prolonged beyond that of the individual. In a sense, it evades death, and *rumbim* is associated with this extended life span as well as, or as a function of, its association with both individuals and territorial corporations. The spiritual qualities of *rumbim* are yet more encompassing, however, for it is also associated with the Red Spirits. *Tondoko* has red leaves, and the Red Spirits are addressed when it is planted. They are thanked for their help in warfare, promised offerings of pork in the future, and asked to guard the *rumbim* so that the men will remain well and the children begotten by them healthy. Spirituality, strength, health, agnation, territoriality, continuity, and something like immortality are thus represented in the planting of *rumbim.* (We may be reminded here of the *Mudyi* tree of the Ndembu people of Zambia whose many significations have been masterfully analyzed by Victor Turner [1967a]).

When the men unclasp the *rumbim,* they plant *amame* around the oven. The belly fat of pig cooked with the wild foods has been reserved and is buried among the *amame,* which is called, in fact, the *konč kump amame* (pig belly *amame*). While it is being planted, the spirits of the low ground are entreated to care well for it, that the pigs will be fertile and grow fat, that the gardens flourish, and that the women be healthy and bear children. As the oven rots, the *amame* overruns it. When it has, cuttings are taken from it to plant at the women's houses for the sake of the human and porcine residents.

The sexual symbolism of the *rumbim* and the oven seems obvious, but the planting of *rumbim* in the oven probably does not represent the procreative act in any simple sense. It seems to employ a relationship between objects similar to that of male and female organs in intercourse to represent metaphorically a more abstract union which will be described below. The spatial relationship of these objects does suggest, however, that the oven is in some sense a vaginal representation. This identification receives some support from the oven's bounty: as human children emerge from vaginas, so the fruits of the earth emerge from the oven. Although neither Buchbinder nor I got corroborating exegeses from Maring informants, and would not have expected them, this interpretation does not rest entirely on exogenous theories of symbolism. There is a theme in Maring stories of an apparently pregnant woman from whom bursts forth not a child, but a great flood of wild vegetables and animals. The story of such a miracle reached one of us in the field as the report of a current event in a distant community.

To say that the oven represents a vagina through which the fruits of the earth come forth is to assimilate the earth to other entities possessing vaginas, notably women. The earth and women, this is to say, are members of a class sharing certain qualities or attributes. Both are fruitful, and as we observed earlier, the fruitfulness of both soil and women is related to their "coldness." This coldness, however, is dangerous as well as fertile. In the light of this, it may now be suggested that the spatial relationship of *amame* and *rumbim* to each other produced by their planting and by the subsequent growth of the *amame* over the area occupied by the oven recalls the spatial relationship of these two plants on burial sites. This is to say that as *rumbim* and *amame* are spatially related to the oven, so are they related to graves. It is further to suggest, if the oven is a vaginal representation, that vaginas and graves are conflated. As the earth possesses a vagina in the oven, so women possess, in their vaginas, graves. In the symbolism of ritual, then, we find corroboration of the identification of fertility and death implicit in avoidance behavior and almost explicit in cosmology, and we gain some insight into the nature of men's pollution fears. As that which emerges from the earth is eventually reabsorbed by the earth, so re-entry by men into that from which men emerge, although necessary for procreation and pleasurable as well, is dangerous. As the earth dissolves the creatures sprung from it, so can those sprung from vaginas be dissolved by entry into vaginas. It is of interest that pollution by women is said to cause a severe putrescence, a condition of deterioration resembling that of corpses (a process with which the Maring are familiar because they expose cadavers on raised platforms, where they are attended by widows or close female agnates until reduced to skeletons). In light of this it may be suggested that Maring men's fear of pollution by women's sexuality on the one hand and by the association of women with corpses on the other, are one and the same.

The process of the natural world is the cycle of fertility, growth, and death, and the planting of *rumbim* and *amame* seems to represent an attempt by men to impose their own cultural order upon the bounties and dangers of the nature by which they are both sustained and threatened. If the oven is a representation of a vagina, it may signify not only that the bountifulness of the wild is an aspect of the wild's fecundity, but that fecundity itself is an aspect of the wild. This is to say that the planting of *amame,* itself a cultigen, around the oven which it eventually overruns is an attempt to capture for the cultivated the fecundity of the wild. Since the *amame* is explicitly planted for the benefit of women, domestic pigs, and gardens, to plant it is to lash sociocultural ends onto natural processes, or to assimilate the processes of nature into those of society.

It is of importance to note here that the opposition of wild to cultivated is not foreign to the Maring. The distinction between *t'p wombi* and *t'p demi,* approximating that between things domestic and things wild, is important in Maring thought. It is in accordance with our general discussion, however, that *demi* may carry the meaning of dangerous as well as wild, and that some creatures or entities not in a meaningful sense either cultivated or uncultivated, such as enemies and the ghosts of those who have not been given proper mortuary rites, are said to be *demi.*

Whereas the planting of *amame* may be interpreted as the imposition of cultural purposes upon the fruitful but dangerous and purposeless processes of nature, the planting of *rumbim,* a plant that men clasp and invest but women may not even touch, makes clear that insofar as the cultural order is in the hands of mortals, it is literally in the hands of men. Moreover, since Red Spirits are associated with the *rumbim* as well as with the living men who plant it, since the *amame* is associated with the spirits of the low ground, and since seances with the Smoke Woman always precede the planting of *rumbim,* the cultural order that men dominate is a spiritual order as well.

The planting of *rumbim* in the oven does not represent a procreative act in any simple sense but, rather, the union of nature, associated with death and fertility, with spirituality, associated by the Maring with the cultural order. It is of interest in this respect that the word *nomane,* which means in some contexts thought or "soul," can in other contexts be glossed as custom or culture. This union implies, we may note, an ordering of living and nonliving beings. Smoke Woman, associated with words, thought, and breath, as insubstantial and ethereal as the hot vapors through which men commune with her, flies high above the world. *Koipa Mangiang,* who is concerned with fertility, decay, and death, swims in its depths. If Smoke Woman, who is above the world and who provides to the world the words by which it is ordered, is supernatural, *Koipa Mangiang,* who swims beneath the world, is infranatural, for the world rests upon the processes over which he presides. Between them and the living, dwelling in trees in the low ground and burning on the high ground, are the spirits of those who once lived, the Spirits of Rot, and the Red Spirits. "Primitive society," says Douglas (1966: 4), "is an energized structure at the center of its universe." At the center of the Maring universe, in the world of life, these two sets come together in the relationship between men and women. Society is possible only in their union, a union represented in the planting of *rumbim* and *amame* in and around the oven. Avoidance and taboo facilitate their union, for they are not only mutually dependent, but also in some degree inimical. At least the spiritual and cultural order, embodied in men particularly, is in danger of being engulfed by the natural processes necessary to its perpetuation. In this view, Maring beliefs concerning female pollution are not simply an outcome or aspect of an opposition between nature and culture, an opposition that is virtually explicit in the dichotomy Maring make between *t'p wombi* and *t'p demi.* It is an aspect of their union as well.

*   *   *

Absolution from the taboos assumed when the fighting stones were hung requires reductions in the debt owed by the living to the dead, and all adult and adolescent animals owned by members of a group are offered to spirits when the *rumbim* is planted. Only juveniles escape the slaughter. The dead are said to devour the spirits of the pigs, while the flesh of the animals is consumed by the living. It is of interest that although the Red Spirits are more important in warfare, most of the sacrificed pigs are offered to the spirits of the low ground because the flesh of pigs dedicated to them can be presented to allies, and allies as well as spirits must be repaid for their assistance. Only agnates may consume the flesh of pigs offered to the Red Spirits.

The pork presented to ancestors and allies with the planting of *rumbim* constitutes no more than a first payment to them. A large debt remains outstanding, and therefore many taboos, including those on marsupials and eels and those dealing with the enemy and forbidding trespass upon enemy territory, remain. Since the Maring believe that warfare can be successful only with the assistance of spirits, and since the aid of spirits will not be forthcoming if debts to them remain outstanding, a group cannot initiate a new round of warfare until it has fully repaid its debts from the last. A sanctified truce thus comes into effect with the planting of *rumbim*. This prevails until there are sufficient pigs to repay the spirits.

The question of how many pigs are sufficient and how long it may take to acquire them has been dealt with in detail elsewhere (Rappaport 1968). Here I would only note that whereas the goal or motive for raising pigs is to repay debts owed to spirits and to allies, the number of pigs required to discharge those debts is not specified. Honor sets a lower limit: to give prestations that seem stingy shames the donor (and may lose him the support of the beneficiary). In complement, the attractions of prestige urge donors to give as lavishly as possible. Nevertheless, the fact of debts to ancestors and allies and the size of those debts are to be distinguished or, to put it differently, the social obligations themselves do not establish what is required to discharge them. To gain an insight into the number of animals required we must consider some objective aspects of Tsembaga pig husbandry.

Aside from the rituals associated with warfare and festivals, the Tsembaga usually kill and consume pigs only during rituals associated with illness and injury.* It may be nutritionally sound to reserve the limited quantity of pigs for consumption when their masters are experiencing physiological stress and thus are in need of high quality protein, but whether or not this is the case, the rate of increase of the pig population is obviously related to the health of the human population. It might also be noted that since all male pigs are castrated (to increase their size and decrease their fierceness), sows can be impregnated only by feral boars, and the herd grows more slowly than it would if domestic boars were kept.

When the pig population is of moderate size it can be fed upon substandard tubers obtained while harvesting for humans. However, when the pig herd grows it becomes necessary to plant gardens especially for them. The amount of acreage and work can be substantial. When the Tsembaga herd was at maximum (170 animals), 36 percent of the gardens were devoted to the support of pigs. The additional labor entailed by these gardens falls mainly upon women, who eventually begin to complain of overwork. Moreover, as they become more numerous, pigs

---

*There is some evidence that there was some variation in this respect, even prior to contact by agents of the Australian government. Jimi Valley Maring seem to have kept more pigs than Simbai Valley Maring, possibly because they relied more heavily upon sweet potato and less upon taro, in turn a possible consequence of the conversion of a substantial portion of their forests to grassland. With more pigs there may have been more occasions for killing and consuming them. Jimi Valley Maring seem to have made prestations of pork to affines outside of festival contexts. The Tsembaga did not.

become nuisances, often invading gardens, and garden invasions cause trouble between pig owners and garden owners. In short, a large number of pigs becomes either a burden or a nuisance, and when the pigs have become intolerable to a sufficient number of people to affect the consensus, there are sufficient pigs to repay the ancestors. It takes anywhere from six or seven to twenty years to accumulate this number.

When there are sufficient pigs, stakes marking the boundaries of the local population's territory are ritually planted. If the enemy remains on his territory, they are planted at the old border. If the enemy was driven out, however, the taboo on entering his land is abrogated and the stakes may be planted at new locations incorporating some or all of his land. It is assumed that by this time even the spirits of the enemy's ancestors have departed to take up residence with their living descendants, who, after they were routed, sought refuge with kinsmen living elsewhere. Erstwhile enemy land is thus considered unoccupied, and as such may be annexed.

Also abrogated at this time is the taboo on trapping marsupials, and a ritual trapping period, lasting for one or two months (until a certain variety of pandanus fruit ripens) commences. This culminates in an important ritual in which the *rumbim* planted after the last fight is uprooted. During this ritual there is further debt reduction and important reintegration of the cosmos. The beneficiaries of the slaughter of pigs at this time are mainly the Red Spirits. The pigs offered them are, in part, payment for their past assistance and in part in exchange for the marsupials (their pigs) that have recently been trapped and smoked and are now consumed. A relationship of equality with the Red Spirits, replacing the former indebtedness, is now being approached by the living. Correlated with this, the communion entered into years before by men when they took the Red Spirits into their heads is now concluded. The Red Spirits are asked to take the pig being offered them and leave.

It has already been mentioned that the cassowary is associated with the spirits of the high ground, the pandanus with the low, and from the point of view of reintegration perhaps the most interesting act in this elaborate ritual is the piercing, by a man dancing on hot stones, of a pandanus fruit with a cassowary bone. Then the pandanus is cooked with marsupials, and the mixture consumed. The spirits of the high and the low, long separated, are being drawn closer together, and the congregation, gradually absolving its debts, is drawing closer to both.

With the uprooting of the *rumbim* the taboo on beating drums is abrogated, and a *kaiko*, a year-long festival, culminating the entire ritual cycle, commences. During this festival other local populations are entertained from time to time at elaborate dances, and about six months after the uprooting of the *rumbim,* when the taro has begun to open in the gardens, the fighting stones are finally lowered during a ritual called *kaiko nde.* With the lowering of the fighting stones, it becomes possible to trap eels, and one to three months later eel traps are placed in special places in various streams. In the meantime friendly groups continue to be entertained, but taro is now the focus of the food presentations to the visitors. Taro is to the Maring the most important of foods; even sacrificial pig is called "taro" in addresses to spirits, and ritual presentations of taro to guests symbolize the ability of the hosts to maintain gardens on the one hand and social relations on the other. Among the Maring food sharing is synonymous with friendship; people will not eat food grown by enemies, and to eat a man's taro is to say that he is your friend.

The festival concludes in a series of rituals occurring on successive days. On the first day a few pigs are slaughtered and dedicated to the Red Spirits in ritual abrogating some residual taboos on relations with other groups arising out of warfare in earlier generations. At this time, too, inter-dining taboos among members of the local population assumed with respect to each other in moments of anger are abrogated. The renunciation of these taboos permits the locals to conduct, usually on the next day, the rituals that are the climax of the entire ritual climax. Performed at sacred places in the middle altitudes, and accompanied by the slaughter of great numbers of pigs, these rituals suggest a cosmic procreative act.

The trapped eels, kept in cages in nearby streams, are carried by young men to the sacred sacrificial places (*raku*) up newly cut pathways, through frond-bedecked arches, where they are joined by the women and young girls. The young men, women, and girls proceed together to the center of the *raku* where the eels are removed from their cages and, grasped by their tails, flailed to death on the flank of a female pig, just slaughtered. The eel and the pig are then cooked together in the *tmbi ying,* a small circular house with a pole projecting through its roof. It is a house, moreover, into which on the previous night both *Koipa Mangiang* and Smoke Woman had been called and in which both had been present at the same time. Penetration, ejaculation, and gestation—or processes formally similar to them—seem to be represented, and the universe is finally reintegrated by them.

The next day on the dance ground there is a massive distribution of pork to members of friendly groups through a window in a ceremonial fence (*pabe*) especially constructed for the occasion. When the pork has been distributed, the hosts, who have assembled behind the fence, crash through to join the throng dancing on the dance ground. Yesterday they reunited the high with the low and themselves with both in what might appear to the observer to have been a great procreative act. Today, in what may be a rebirth, they have broken through the restrictions separating them from their neighbors. Their debts to both the living and the dead have been repaid, and if the central government had not recently pacified the area they would have been again free to initiate warfare, for the sanctified truce had ended.

III

This account of the Maring ritual cycle points to certain of the inadequacies of the formulation of the relationship between cognized and operational models reviewed at the beginning of this essay. For one thing, few if any societies break the world into the more or less distinct systems distinguished by Western science. Not all of them, surely, distinguish environmental from social relations. Among the Maring, it is clear, ecological, political, and social relations (most notably the relations between the sexes) are not separately conceived and their regulation proceeds in terms of an integrated set of understandings and principles. Moreover, these understandings and principles, which, in the Maring view, both account for the structure and state of the world and invest the world and actions in it with meaning, are not confined to the particular material and social relations regulated. They include as well metaphysical abstractions of great generality. If representations of cognized models in accordance with which ecosystems are regulated were to be confined to folk accounts of ecosystemic elements and processes *per se* little more than sets of folk taxonomies and gardening and hunting lore would be included in them. I do not wish to denigrate the ethnoscientific enterprise, nor the taxonomies and "cultural grammars" that it is capable of discovering or constructing. I would simply suggest that these and other representations of both the material elements of which ecosystems are composed and the processes relating these elements to each other should be conceptualized in the larger metaphysical and epistemological contexts which, as far as the actors are concerned, give them value and significance. They should not be alienated from other processes, social, political, or spiritual, from which they are not separated in the actors' understandings.

Another point follows. Although the Maring ritual cycle surely does regulate social, political, and ecosystemic relations, regulatory operations just as surely cannot account for the entire cycle in all its aspects and with all of the understanding it embodies. Maring liturgical order, and liturgical orders generally, seem far richer in understanding and meaning than social, political, or ecological regulation obviously requires. An examination of the structure of these understandings and meanings will reinforce such an impression.

Our description of the Maring ritual cycle surely has indicated that the cognized models expressed in liturgy are not mere heaps of disparate understandings. Liturgical orders impose structure upon understanding or, perhaps it is better to say, provide the structure without which understanding can only be fragmented and contradictory. I have argued elsewhere (see "The Obvious Aspects of Ritual" in this volume) that liturgical orders possess several dimensions, and it is in terms of these dimensions that the concepts and notions represented in ritual are organized. The most apparent is the sequential dimension. One representation follows another, usually in fixed order, in the enactment of a ritual, and one ritual follows another in the progress of a ritual cycle or series. Each representation in such sequences may, however, signify many things at one and the same time, binding its varied significata together in chordlike fashion. This second aspect of ritual may be called its "simultaneous dimension." Less immediately apparent and more difficult to grasp is liturgy's hierarchical dimension. It is sufficient to observe here that some rituals seem fundamental or constitutive (e.g., the Mass) whereas others seem to be contingent upon the fundamental rituals (e.g, crowning a king in the name of God), or instrumental (e.g., a marriage service). The fundamental components of liturgical orders, or even of particular rituals, moreover, seem to be more sacred, enduring, invariant, and authoritative than those which are contingent or instrumental. We may compare here the creeds and the eucharist to the substance of sermons. A concomitant of the hierarchical structure of liturgical orders is the hierarchical organization of the understandings encoded in those orders. I shall treat this dimension of Maring understanding first.

At the apex, so to speak, of the conceptual structure embodied in the Maring liturgical order are understandings, formal expression of which is largely confined to ritual, concerning the existence of spirits and the relations prevailing among them. These understandings, the significations of which are not material and are beyond the reach of logical refutation, are neither verifiable nor falsifiable, but are nevertheless taken to be unquestionable. They are of the class that elsewhere I have called "ultimate sacred propositions," but which might better be called "ultimate sacred postulates" (see "The Obvious Aspects of Ritual"). This class includes, for example, the Jewish declaration of faith called the *Shema* ("Hear, O Israel, the Lord our God, the Lord is One") and the creeds of Christians. No such creed or declaration is made explicit by the Maring, but postulates concerning the existence of sentient and puissant spirits are surely implicit in the highly stylized addresses to those spirits which occur in all Maring rituals.

A second class of understandings, a class composed of cosmological axioms, is closely associated with ultimate sacred postulates. I include in this category Maring notions of the world as constituted by a set of oppositions between certain qualities which are, on the one hand, associated with the two general classes of spirits and, on the other hand, manifested in the social and physical world. Thus, the hot, hard, dry, strong, cultural, spiritual, and immortal are associated with the Red Spirits on the one hand and substantiated in men, patrilineages, territoriality, warfare, and high land on the other. In opposition, the low, soft, cold, moist, fecund, natural, and mortal are associated with the Spirits of the Low Ground on the one hand and substantiated in women, gardening, pig husbandry, and the lower portion of the body on the other. I further include among Maring cosmological axioms their conceptions concerning the mediation of these oppositions through ritual. Whereas the oppositions *per se* are irreducible the relationship of the opposed terms is transformed, through the course of the cycle, from inimical to complementary.

Whereas cosmological axioms concerning fundamental oppositions and their mediation are explicit in Maring exegeses of their liturgical cycle, other cosmological axioms are implicit in its formal actions, in the transformations achieved by these actions, and in their order and progress (to which I shall return). First among these implicit principles is that of reciprocity. All assistance must be reciprocated, all trespasses compensated or avenged. A second assumption concerns the relationship of humans to spirits. All important human understandings require the acquiescence of spirits and for many activities, particularly warfare, their active assistance is crucial. Like the principle of reciprocity, this understanding is seldom, if ever, explicitly articulated, but is implicit in virtually all invocations of spirits. A corollary of both of these axioms taken together is that spirits must be repaid for their help in past warfare if they are to provide the help needed for success in the future.

It should be clear that I have been using the term "cosmological axioms" to refer to assumptions concerning the fundamental structure of the universe or, to put it differently, to refer to the paradigmatic relationships in accordance with which the cosmos is constructed. I do not include within this class what are generally called "values." Some values may, however, be implicit in them, be entailed by them, or even be derived as theorems from them. For instance, the high value that Maring place upon unity or integrity is at least implicit in the progress in the ritual cycle from a condition of maximum segregation of parts of the universe from each other to one in which segregation is radically reduced. The negative value placed upon the failure to fulfill reciprocal obligations follows from the assumption that reciprocity is fundamental to cosmic structure. Given this assumption, lapses in reciprocity are violations of the order constituting the world.

I have distinguished cosmological axioms as a class from ultimate sacred postulates on several grounds. First and most obviously, ultimate sacred postulates are typically devoid of material significata, whereas cosmological axioms are concerned with relationships among qualities that may themselves be sensible (e.g., hot and cold) and that are manifested in physical and social phenomena (e.g., the relationship between men and women). It follows, second, that if cosmological axioms are manifested in social and physical phenomena the occasions for their expression are more general and varied than those in which it is appropriate to express ultimate sacred postulates. The proprietous expression of the latter is largely confined to ritual whereas the expression of the former is implicit in much of daily life. Third, and related to the first and second, whereas ultimate sacred postulates, by themselves, are either devoid of explicit social content or very vague in this regard, cosmological axioms are more specific and often do have direct, explicit, and substantial political, social, and ecological import. Fourth, cosmological axioms serve as the logical basis from which both specific rules of conduct and the proprieties of social life can be derived. Ultimate sacred postulates are more remote from social life. They do not themselves provide a logical foundation for it, nor even for cosmological structure (which, I have asserted, is axiomatic). But they are not otiose. They sanctify, which is to say certify, the entire system of understandings in accordance with which people conduct their lives. Without sanctification the axioms of cosmology would remain arbitrary, constituting nothing more than speculative conceptual structures, amounting to nothing more than attempts at explanation. When a cosmology is sanctified it is no longer merely conceptual nor simply explanatory nor even speculative. It becomes something like an assertion, statement, description, or report of the way the world in fact *is*. To invert the hierarchical metaphor, whereas ultimate sacred postulates do not themselves provide the *logical* ground upon which the usages and rules of social life are established, they provide the ground, deeper than logic and beyond logic's reach, upon which cosmological structure can be founded. It follows that cosmological structures can change—expand, contract, or even be radically altered structurally—in response to changes in environmental or historical conditions without changes in, or even challenge to, ultimate sacred postulates. Being devoid of material terms, ultimate sacred postulates are not fully of this mortal world and can be regarded as eternal verities. Being devoid of explicit social content they can sanctify everything, including change, while remaining irrevocably committed to nothing.

A third and yet "lower" level in hierarchies of understanding is composed of the yet more specific rules (to which I have already alluded in discussing cosmological axioms) governing the conduct of relations among the persons, qualities, conditions, and states of affairs whose oppositions are decreed by cosmological axioms (e.g., between men and women, men and cold foods, etc.). These rules are, of course, expressed in the performance of rituals, a matter to which I shall return, but they also govern the behavior of everyday life. Among the Maring taboos of all sorts are prominent among such rules.

The oppositions of the cosmological level, including as they do terms that may be materially manifested, are more concrete and have more direct social import than do the ultimate sacred postulates sanctifying them. So, in turn, are the rules of conduct more concrete than the cosmological oppositions they express. They are, therefore, able both to "realize" or substantiate those oppositions and to provide them with a specific social import that they, by themselves, do not clearly and un-ambiguously possess. It is one thing to establish cosmologically men and women as members of opposing sets. It is quite another to exclude women on such grounds from participating in ritual.

The rules of the third level, then, transform cosmology into conduct. It is important to note that as the cosmological structure of the second level can be modified without challenge to ultimate sacred postulates so can these rules be changed without affecting the oppositions they make material. I shall later cite an instance of such a change in discussing the sequential dimension of liturgical order and its understandings.

Our account so far may seem to suggest that liturgical orders somehow create understandings that are then exported to the world outside of ritual (although I have indicated in passing that cosmological axioms and the rules that make them concrete may change in response to historical or environmental change). It is important to make clear, however, that this is not the whole of the matter. Liturgical orders also import information from the external world in the form of formal indications of currently prevailing conditions. These importations form a fourth level in hierarchies of understandings.

Among the Maring indications of the states of ecological relations are prominent among the understandings imported. The uprooting of *rum-bim*, for instance, indicates that relations among such phenomena external to ritual as the size and rate of increase of the pig population, the amount of land in cultivation, the intensity of women's labor, the patience and health of women, the frequency of garden invasions by pigs and other factors as well, have reached a certain complex composite state which, in material terms, can be described as "all the pigs the group can maintain or tolerate." When imported into the liturgical order, however, this description of a material condition is invested with cosmological meaning and transformed into "sufficient pigs to repay the ancestors."

The Maring ritual cycle provides opportunities for signifying states of affairs other than ecological, of course. For a resident alien to join in planting *rumbim* indicates his naturalization into the local group, the size of a visiting contingent of dancers at a *kaiko* indicates to the hosts the amount of military support they may expect to receive from that group in future rounds of warfare (see *Pigs for the Ancestors*). Liturgical orders differ in what conditions prevailing in the external world their performance, or aspects of their performance, may signify, but intrinsic to all rituals is indication of some aspect of the contemporary social, psychic, or physical state of the performers and, possibly, of aspects of their environmental relations as well (Leach 1965: 11).

I shall only note what I shall call a fifth level of understandings, more or less completely external to the liturgical order but investing domains over which the liturgical order ultimately presides. I refer here to secular understandings of the everyday world, its people, its animals, its plants, its places, its activities. It is on this "level" (surely more complex than the notion of a single level suggests) that classification seems to be most highly elaborated.

A hierarchy of understandings is, then, represented in the Maring liturgical order. At the apogee stand postulates concerning spirits. Ultimately sacred, these understandings are not open to material refutation, for their significata are not material, nor are they vulnerable to logical refutation. Yet they are taken to be unquestionable, immutable, and eternal. Cosmological structure is elaborated in a second class, a class of axioms by or through which the spirits postulated are associated with elements and relations of the material and social world in a set of abstract structural oppositions that apply to both: as the Red Spirits are hot, hard, dry, and strong, so are men; as the Spirits of the Low Ground are cold, soft, wet, and fertile, so are women. These relations are given concreteness and specificity in yet a third level of understandings constituted of rules and taboos concerning action appropriate or inappropriate in terms of the understandings of the cosmological structure that informs them. Indications of material and social conditions immediately prevailing in the everyday world are imported into ritual, where they constitute a fourth level of understandings, and are translated there into the terms of cosmology. Secular knowledge of the everyday world constitutes a fifth level of understanding that, for the most part, remains external to ritual. The hierarchy of understanding organized by ritual is, thus, one of sanctity, mutability, concreteness, specificity, and immediacy. Further aspects of such hierarchies and how their features may be related to adaptive processes are discussed in "Adaptive Structure and Its Disorders" and "Sanctity and Lies in Evolution."

*　　*　　*

The second dimension of liturgical order is the sequential. The succession of elements in ritual is usually fixed and so are the successions of rituals composing liturgical calendars and cycles of other sorts. It should be kept in mind, however, that all components of ritual are likely to have their places in the liturgical order defined by all dimensions simultaneously. Thus, the sanctified succession that proceeds from the maximal segregation of categories of spirits, persons, foods, and lands from each other when the fighting stones are hung to their maximal integration at the end of the *kaiko* has sacred, cosmic, social, and ecological significance. It is a rule-governed succession through the actions of which the oppositions explicit in cosmological structure are transformed from an antagonistic to complementary state in response to indications of ecosystemic conditions and changes in them. The actions transforming cosmic relations also transform social and ecological relations in the Maring case.

It is important to note that the specific rules in accordance with which these transformations are effected—those stipulating how and when to repay spirits and what it takes to repay them—are flexible. The quantity of pigs required is not a specific number but is the function of relations among a number of variables, and the length of intervals between rituals is elastic. Furthermore, the rules are not only flexible, but mutable as well. For example, in 1955 envoys from the Kauwassi, the largest of the Maring groups, invited the Tukmenga to join them in a concerted attack upon the Monamban, whose lands lay between their territories. The Tukmenga at first refused, protesting that their *rumbim* remained in the ground, for they had not yet fully repaid the spirits for their help in the last war. After prolonged discussion they were persuaded that the spirits could be satisfied by a different procedure requiring fewer pigs and no delay. A few pigs were, accordingly, immediately killed and laid on the roofs of *ringi ying,* no doubt as offerings to Red Spirits, and the Tukmenga stormed off to join the Kauwassi in the rout of the Monamban. Informants told Vayda that this procedure had always been acceptable, but could not, or at least would not, cite any precedents, although pressed to do so (Rappaport 1968: 152).

We may note here than in our accounts of the hierarchical and sequential dimensions of liturgical orders we have touched upon their adaptive characteristics. The sequential dimension of non-calendrical liturgical orders are able to expand and contract, as it were, in response to fluctuations in indications of material conditions. The flexibility and elasticity inherent in the Maring ritual cycle as constituted by its rules is further enhanced by the mutability of the rules themselves. If pressure is great enough they may be changed. It is of interest that when the Kauwassi were persuading the Tukmenga to change their rules concerning the repayment of spirits they were the largest of the Maring local groups in their own right, their numbers were further swollen by refugees, and their land was the most degraded in Maringdom.

It may be suggested that the elasticity of sequence in response to fluctuations in indications of material conditions and the flexibility and mutability of rules for realizing cosmological transformations not only maintains cosmological and sacred understandings unchanged in the face of perturbation, but also tends to do so within environmental limits. This is to say that the fit between the cognized and operational models among the Maring is to be accounted for, at least in part, by formal characteristics of the liturgical order in which the cognized model is encoded; in particular, those characteristics that make it flexible.

To speak of the sequential dimension of ritual and its ordering of understandings, it should be clear from this account, is not to speak of elements distinct or separate from those encompassed in hierarchies of understanding. It is, rather, to consider the temporal relations of the same postulates, axiomatic oppositions, rules, and indications. The sequential dimension of liturgical order adds understandings of transformation, process, and possibly even of cause and time, to the hierarchy of understanding.

It is not the concern of this essay to pursue the causal and temporal significance of liturgical orders *per se.* Suffice it to note that to effect a transformation must be, in some sense, to cause it. As far as time is concerned I will only mention that ritual's ability to distinguish before from after with perfect clarity permits it to impose upon nature discontinuities much sharper than nature's own. Not only may it distinguish one period from the next unambiguously, but it may thereby fashion time itself out of mere duration. In distinguishing one period from the next, furthermore, it distinguishes both before and after, as periods, from the non-periodic times between them—the times between times occupied by ritual itself—and thus it separates mundane time from sacred time which, being time out of time, may be associated in ritual with the eternal (see Turner 1967b).

Finally, I may mention briefly the simultaneous or chordlike dimension of liturgical order. The representations of ritual follow one another, but each may have multiple significations (Campbell 1959: 461ff.; Ortner 1973; Turner 1967a). Thus, *rumbim* and its planting signify at one and the same time Red Spirits, spirituality, immortality, maleness, patrilineality, patrilocality, territoriality, particular patriclans, membership in particular patriclans, hotness, hardness, ferocity, strength, the domination of nature by culture and women by men. It is, in Ortner's terms, a key symbol representing at one and the same time all, or virtually all, of the terms making up one of the two sets party to the oppositions stipulated by Maring cosmological axioms. As such, it binds together the different realms in which the qualities composing the set are manifested—gender relations, political relations, ecological processes. They are not only regulated by the same rules sequentially applied but become icons of each other and of relations among spirits. I shall touch upon these matters in another context later.

*   *   *

Several general points are to be made in concluding this discussion of the structure of the understandings encoded in the Maring liturgical order. First, the analytic framework sketched here may help to relate the insights of some other more particular approaches to understanding to each other. The notion of structure as organized sets of oppositions and their mediation (Lévi-Strauss, 1955) is manifest in what I have called "cosmological axioms" and in the transformation of the nature of the oppositions they specify through the progress of the ritual cycle. Such a conception of structure also invests the taboos and other rules of "the third level" that realize the oppositions of the second. The comprehension of signs indicating material and social conditions, an area of understanding emphasized in systemic and ecological analyses, is accommodated on "the fourth level," and folk taxonomies, the domain of linguistic-cognitive anthropologists, dominate "the fifth," and "lower" secular levels, although they are not confined to them. The multivocalic and bipolar symbolic meanings (Campbell 1959; Turner 1967a) infusing the symbols appearing in ritual are manifested in what I have called the "simultaneous dimension" of liturgical order.

Second, it is important to emphasize that the temporal entailments of the structure I have sketched are not limited to its sequential dimension but are intrinsic to its hierarchical dimension as well. We may consider differences in the longevity of the understandings assigned to the several levels of such hierarchies. Ultimate sacred postulates are taken to be eternal verities and seem, in fact, to persist for long periods. The *Shema* of the Jews has endured for at least three thousand years. Cosmological axioms may be taken by those accepting them to be as enduring as ultimate sacred postulates, but are probably less so, and the specific rules that realize those axioms and govern social behavior are likely to be yet shorter-lived. Signs indicating contemporary states in an ever-fluctuating world are ephemeral. Differences in the longevity of understandings may or may not be recognized by those entertaining them, but whether or not they are, we can observe in the ascent from the understandings of everyday life to those of ultimate sacred postulates a progression from the quick to the eternal.

Systematic disparities in the longevity of understandings imply a dynamic beyond the invariant series of transformations effected by rituals and sequences of rituals. The relationship between the quick and the eternal is also a relationship between the ever-changing and the never-changing. It is of importance that the most labile of values are both the most specific and the most concrete. For example, the number of pigs sufficient to repay spirits varies from one festival to the next in response to changes in demographic, social, political, and ecological circumstances. Such variation is, of course, in accordance with highly flexible rules, rules that are maintained unchanged through changes in the magnitudes of the reference values which they set. But, as we have seen, such rules can themselves change while higher-order cosmological understandings remain unchanged, and, similarly, these cosmological understandings can change without affecting ultimate sacred postulates. These, taken to be immutable, can remain unchanged as all understandings of "lower order" change. Indeed, they are likely to be changed only in response to, or as an effect of, fundamental social or political change. In "Adaptive Structure and Its Disorders" the adaptive significance of concordance between temporal qualities and transmutative capacity will be considered at some length. It is necessary here only to emphasize that it is change in concrete material values (e.g., the number of pigs that is "sufficient") that maintains high-order understandings unchanged.

This relationship of the concrete to the conceptual leads to a third general point of great importance. As the understandings of the Maring ritual cycle guide and regulate the social, political, and ecological processes in which the Maring participate, so do these material and social processes support or maintain the understandings that guide them. This view accords with the nature of cybernetic and other forms of self-regulation generally and, for that matter, with our account of them as an aspect of cognized and operational models. Cybernetic and other self-regulating processes equilibrate systems around reference values which stipulate or define the satisfactory, if not ideal. To put this in Bateson's (1972) terms, they operate to preserve the truth value of propositions about the systems in which they occur in the face of continuous threats to falsify them. It is, thus, value and meaning that define the teleology of such systems; it is value and meaning, and not biological and ecological integrity, that they tend, in the first instance, to preserve. Recognition of this characteristic of the cybernetic operation of sociocultural systems, it should be made clear, does not in and of itself invalidate the proposal reviewed at the beginning of this essay—that cognized models may be *assessed* in terms of the ecological and biological effects of the behavior they elicit. We shall return to this matter.

Although our concern is not so much with ritual as it is with the understandings that, in the Maring case as in the cases of many tribal peoples, are expressed, embodied, or encoded in ritual, it is nevertheless worth noting that to encompass in a single liturgical order understandings that include ultimate sacred postulates, cosmological axioms concerning relations among spirits, qualities, persons, things and processes, rules for transforming these relations, and indications of prevailing states of society and nature, is to establish a unity or integrity of understanding that may seem highly meaningful to those grasping it and that may be tenuous or lacking in societies poor in ritual. It is well to make clear, however, that I do not propose that the sanctified liturgical ordering of understandings into more of less consistent structures guarantees that everyone's view of the world will duplicate the views of everyone else. The understandings of which I have spoken, and the relations among them, not only leave room for some individual interpretation, but demand it. The liturgical representation of a public order of understandings does, however, ensure the persistence of a common corpus for interpretation and sets limits upon the private interpretations possible.

I would suggest, finally, that the understandings embodied by a liturgical order may seem particularly meaningful not only because of their relatively high degree of coherence, consistency, and integrity, but also because rituals are constituted of *acts* as well as concepts. By participating in a liturgical order—by becoming part of it—an actor radically reduces or even annihilates disparities between his conduct and his understanding of what is true and correct. Ritual action thus has a special significance for the actors, for it realizes conceptions of the moral in the very postures and movements of the body (see "The Obvious Aspects of Ritual" for a discussion of the entailments of ritual participation).

IV

To say that understandings may be more or less meaningful is to distinguish meaning and meaningfulness from understanding. My use of the term "understanding" has, I think, been clear, but what I mean by the terms "meaning" and "meaningful" may be obscure.

I suggest that three types or levels of meaning may be distinguished. First, there is the notion of meaning in its simple, everyday semantic sense. The meaning of the word "dog" is *dog, dog* being distinct from *cat*, which is signified by the distinct term "cat." Meaning in this low-order sense is closely related to what information theorists mean by "information." In this technical sense information is that which reduces uncertainty. The minimal unit is the "bit," which can be understood as a binary distinction, or as that which eliminates the uncertainty between the two alternatives in a binary choice, or, to put it slightly differently, as the answer to a yes/no question when "yes" and "no" are equally probable.

Taxonomies are the typical but, of course, not the only forms within which low-order meaning is organized.

When, however, we begin to consider not only simple meaning but *meaningfulness,* we become concerned not only with rationally drawn distinctions, but with emotionally charged values as well. Low-order meaning is founded upon distinction, but higher-order meaning is of another sort. The sense of meaning to which the question "What does it all mean?" points when asked by one confronted by a complex mass of information is surely not that of simple distinction. In answering such a question we do not attempt to increase distinction but, on the contrary, to decrease it by discovering similarities among apparently disparate phenomena, namely, that which we seek to understand on the one hand, and that which we already know, or at least think we know, on the other. In higher-order meaning these similarities among obviously distinctive phenomena become more significant than the distinctions themselves. The paradigmatic vehicle of higher-order meaning is metaphor. Metaphor, we may note, enriches the world's meaning, for the significance of every term that participates in a metaphor is transformed into more than itself, that is, into an icon of other things as well. It is significant that art and poetry rely heavily upon metaphor, a mode of representation that, because of its connotative resonance, is affectively more powerful than straightforward didactic forms.

Whereas low-order meaning is based upon distinction and higher-order meaning is based on similarity, highest-order meaning is grounded in identity or unity, the radical identification of self with other. It is not so much intellectual as experiential and is perhaps most often grasped in ritual and other religions devotions. Those who have known it in its highest form may refer to it by such obscure phrases as the "Experience of Being," or "Being Itself," or "Pure Being." They report that, although it is nonreferential, it seems enormously or even ultimately meaningful. It signifies only itself, but it itself seems comprehensive. All distinctions seem to disappear into an immediate and undeniable sense of union with others or even with the cosmos as a whole. Highest-order meaning, it is of interest to note, not only stands beyond language—it is non-discursive—but, being devoid of distinction, is also devoid of information. The meaning of informationlessness is discussed further in "The Obvious Aspects of Ritual" later in this volume.

We note, then, three bases of meaningfulness: distinction, similarity, and identity. Each of these stipulates a different relationship of significata to those for whom they are meaningful. The semantic distinctions that constitute low-order meaning are properties of the messages or texts themselves and as such are distinct from those for whom they are meaningful. Higher-order meaning is based upon the structural similarity of a text to the experience of those for whom it is meaningful. Persons and significata are, as it were, drawn closer together than they are by low-order meaning. In highest-order meaning the distance between significata and those for whom they are significant is annihilated, for the latter participates in, or becomes united or identified with, the former. Meaning becomes a state of being.

It is worth remarking that each level of meaning seems to be roughly associated with a different class of Peirce's tripartite classification of signs (1960: 143ff.). There is an approximate correlation of low-order meaning, which relies most heavily upon the semantic distinctions of language, with symbols in Peirce's sense, that is, with signs "associated by law," as he put it, with their significata. Higher-order meanings are conveyed iconically, and highest-order meaning, founded upon identity, seems close to indexical representation, in which signs are either effects of, or aspects of, what they signify. It is of interest that it is low-order meaning, which is elaborated by language, that is the *sine qua non* of humanity. The ultimately meaningful, being largely non-discursive and almost free of language altogether, may triumph, at least from time to time, over the experiences of fragmentation and alienation that are, possibly, the concomitants of language's objectifying powers (Van Baal 1971).

To distinguish three levels of meaning is not, of course, to separate them. It is unfortunate that the students of each tend to be different people, for surely these levels must be related to each other in systematic ways. It would seem that association with, or subsumption by, higher-order meaning invests meanings of lower order with significance and value; that is, makes mere information "meaningful." Conversely, low-order meanings provide the distinctions upon which those of higher order operate. It is not possible to illuminate similarities among distinct phenomena through metaphor until the distinctions among those phenomena have been drawn. Similarly, it would not be possible to dissolve all distinctions into a transcendent unity if there were no distinctions to dissolve.

V

Cognized models may differ in meaningfulness. Some may be rich in low-order meaning but poor in meaningfulness because higher-order meanings, those of similarity, integration, and unity, remain undeveloped or, more likely, because they have been damaged or become diluted. A long line of theologians, philosophers, and social scientists precedes me in proposing that modern society is rather worse off with respect to meaningfulness than traditional society. It is nevertheless worth considering this matter briefly, noting particularly that destruction of meaning may be intrinsic to developments we have taken to be advances in epistemology, computation, and social structure.

We are led here to consider differences in the ways in which knowledge—the medium of meaning—is conceived and organized in traditional and modern societies. Generalizations concerning such matters can be no more than approximate, but our discussion has suggested that among tribal peoples and in archaic civilizations, sacred knowledge was ultimate. I have already indicated that by "sacred knowledge" I refer to postulates in their nature neither verifiable nor falsifiable but nevertheless taken to be unquestionable because mystically known or because ritually accepted (Rappaport 1971b; and "The Obvious Aspects of Ritual"). Concerned with gods and the like, they are typically devoid of terms having material signification and are thus without sociological specificity. Such postulates do, however, sanctify, which is to say certify, other sentences. As we have seen, these include axioms concerning the structure of the cosmos, rules for behavior, and values entailed by these axioms and rules. If, as I have suggested, high-order meaning is derived from the perception of deep similarities underlying apparent distinctions, the result of such an ordering of knowledge is a world laden with high-order meaning. If, further, highest-order meaning is an outcome of identification with the meaningful by those for whom it is meaningful, the ritual representation of such an ordering of knowledge also invests the world with highest-order meaning, for to perform a ritual is to participate in it. Finally, there is knowledge of ordinary material facts, the facts of farming, hunting, cooking. The Maring are as aware as any other cultivators of, for instance, the special characteristics of particular plants (in which soils they will grow, how long they take to mature, the special treatment they require), but they consider such knowledge to be obvious, transient, and hardly fundamental. Of "greater meaning" to them is the subsumption of material facts by cosmological oppositions and the elaboration of taboos and other rules on the foundation those oppositions provide.

The coherence, orderliness, and meaningfulness of the conceptual structures liturgy organizes stand in striking contrast to those of modern society, for it would seem that the order of knowledge has been inverted in the course of history. Ultimate knowledge has become knowledge of fact. To be sure, facts are ordered within limited domains by subsumption under more or less specific scientific taxonomies and laws, but these are perpetually subject to modification, or even overthrow, by the discovery of further facts. Attempts to apply general ordering principles to disparate domains are often regarded as improper, and thus "respectable" generalizations are of limited scope. Those that apply to physical or organic phenomena, for instance, are said not to apply to the social domain. Indeed, attempts to subsume substantively distinctive phenomena under common generalizations are likely to be dismissed as "merely analogic" or even "reductionistic." Thus, as we come to know more and more about ever more limited domains, the domains themselves become ever more isolated, and ever less meaningful to whatever lies outside of them. Nothing is any longer an icon of anything else, and if higher-order meaning lies in the perception of deep similarities underlying apparent distinctions, then, paradoxically, meaning has been diminished as knowledge of fact—empirical knowledge—has increased. The position of that which in earlier times was taken to be ultimate knowledge—the unquestionable religious postulate—becomes anomalous in a world subordinated to the fact, and so do the values it sanctifies. The empirical and logical rationality that not only discovers and ascertains facts but that defines knowledge as knowledge of fact is not hospitable to the authority of either sanctity or value. Ultimate sacred postulates are no longer even counted as knowledge but are mere beliefs, if not superstitions. Values are defined by preference and as such become no more than matters of taste or of the arithmetic of economizing. If high-order meanings are not destroyed they are demeaned and their influence upon human affairs minimized by "serious" and "practical" men who give to rationality itself an ever-narrower construction. It is a rationality reduced to the syllogism, the experiment, and those self-serving mental processes denoted by the economists' use of the term. It is a rationality that has no room for the insights of art, religion, fantasy, or dream. The evaluational capacities of such a dispassionate but impoverished reason are limited, to say the least, and hardly trustworthy.

It is of considerable interest that money is an important component of evaluational procedures in societies in which facts have been apotheosized. If meaning is fragmented by fact it is dissolved by money. It may seem that money, which makes it possible to assign commensurable "values" to things that are radically distinctive, represents similarities underlying apparent disparities with unparalleled precision and facility. As such money would seem to enrich meaning. In fact it does not. Rather than finding or emphasizing similarities among the distinctive phenomena to which it is applied, it renders the distinctions among them irrelevant, which is to say meaningless, from the beginning. The application of a common monetary metric to dissimilar things reduces their *qualitative distinctiveness* to the status of mere *quantitative difference*. The most appropriate answer to questions of the type "What is the difference between a forest and a parking lot?" becomes so many dollars per acre. Evaluation becomes nothing more than what is called "the bottom line," the result of the operations of addition and subtraction. Right and wrong, correct and erroneous, perhaps even true and false, are reduced to, or displaced by, more and less. Low-order meaning is demeaned as distinctions are dissolved into differences and, of course, higher- and highest-order meanings are debilitated by the dissolution of significant distinctions underneath which similarities are to be discovered or in the transcendence of which unity is to be experienced.

Money degrades meaning, but not only meaning. It also, and by the same token, degrades the objective world. It is obvious that the nature upon which the simple metric of money is imposed is not as simple as that metric. It is perhaps less obvious that it must not be. Living systems require a great variety of distinct and incommensurable substances to remain viable. Monetization, however, forces the great range of things and processes to which it is applied into a specious commensurability. As such, at the same time that it impoverishes the meaningfulness of experience, it threatens life itself. Decisions made in terms of simple-minded monetary considerations, freed from the surveillance of higher-order meanings, are in their very nature unmindful of the uniqueness and incommensurability of elements in the objective world upon which life depends, and the deployment of large amounts of mindless energy under the guidance of money is almost bound to be brutal and destructive. More generally, it may be suggested that the meaningful and material aspects of living processes are systematically related. That which damages one damages the other, and it may be further suggested that danger to them is greater in societies in which technological development, monetization, and the dissolution of high-order meaning have proceeded furthest.

VI

Concern with the coherence of cognized models, with their fragmentation, their meaningfulness, and adaptiveness, cannot be limited to considerations of the structure of understanding *per se.* The differing ways in which societies distribute knowledge among their members must also be taken into account. The subject is a complex one, and has not been well studied. It does, nevertheless, seem safe enough to say that some gross differences among societies are related to equally gross differences in social complexity. That, in tribal societies, substantially similar knowledge is available to persons of similar age and sex, and that the members of a category generally entertain similar if not identical values, may follow from the common circumstances of their lives and from joint participation in ritual. High redundancy in the distribution of knowledge, a general feature of societies characterized by mechanical solidarity (Durkheim 1933 [1893]) confers a high degree of autonomy upon individuals and small local groups, enhancing their ability to survive in isolation, reducing the degree to which they are perturbed by events abroad, increasing their ability to settle new and distant lands. Polynesia, for example, seems to have been explored and settled by small groups of voyagers who, isolated from their homelands, were able to reproduce the general forms of the societies from which they had emigrated.

The redundancy of knowledge associated with the segmentary organization of tribal societies is sharply reduced in contemporary nation-states. As social organization has become increasingly differentiated and solidarity "organic," so have the understandings of individuals become increasingly specialized. As redundancy has its adaptive virtues so does differentiation and specialization. The society in which specialized knowledge is differentially distributed among its membership can, in its entirety, "know more" than a society in which redundancy is high. But, as societies as wholes become able to gain, process, and store ever larger amounts of knowledge, each individual and the specialized groups into which they are organized may come to know less, to become ever more narrow in their orientation, to lose awareness of the whole and their place in it. Specialization of knowledge entails loss of autonomy and the increasingly obligatory nature of interdependence may reach dangerous proportions. This problem is exacerbated by the attenuation of generally accepted higher-order meanings, itself a concomitant of specialization, for such meanings stand opposed to the parochialism of specialized understandings and interests. We touch here upon aspects of the social malaise discussed in recent years by "Death of God" theologians (see Buber 1952; Alitzer and Hamilton 1966; Murchland 1967) and in debates concerning "the end of ideology."

The redundancy of knowledge in tribal societies suggests that they are not only like to be *dominated* by one more or less integrated set of understandings, but to be *pervaded* by one. We may, therefore, speak with some degree of confidence of "the cognized model" of a tribal society. In contrast, the differentiated condition of modern society may be so extreme as to make it bootless to search for pervasive and integrated sets of understandings. But to say that a society is not pervaded by any coherent set of understandings is not to say that it is not dominated by such a set. We are led here to questions concerning the relationship of knowledge and meaning to power. At least three classes of questions are to be considered.

The first, and most obvious, is concerned with the degree to which sets of understandings are differentially influential as a function of relations of domination and subordination among those who hold them. It is obvious that not all of the knowledge and understandings possessed by all of the members of any contemporary society enter into the conduct of that society's affairs in degrees commensurate with relevance, accuracy, or wisdom. A great deal of knowledge concerning the effects of various modes of intervention upon ecosystems is diffused throughout contemporary society, but analyses based upon this information usually fail to prevail over economic considerations in plans for using what are called "natural resources" (itself an economic term) because, among other things, those avowing economic interests are politically more powerful than those articulating ecological concerns. I do not claim that there is anything mysterious about this aspect of the politics of understanding, but would nevertheless suggest that the elucidation of the ways in which economic understandings have come to prevail over ecological and humanistic understandings in particular instances would not only be theoretically rewarding but could contribute to attempts to correct those symptoms of systemic disorder and of the disorder of meaning that we label "ecological problems" and, for that matter, a host of other social, political, and economic "problems" as well.

That some understandings prevail over others because they are held by the powerful may be obvious, but hardly sufficient to account for the power of some ideas. We are led here to a second class of questions and considerations. Some understandings may be inherently more coercive than others. It may be, for instance, that the individual living in a contemporary capitalist society is virtually forced to act in a manner conforming in considerable degree to the model of *Homo economicus,* regardless of his own convictions concerning the nature of humanity and its proper goals and purposes. In a world in which "nice guys finish last," he probably had better not be a nice guy. Other alternative sets of understandings, because less punitive, may be less coercive and as such they may not be acted upon even by those who "believe in" them.

Questions of a third class concerning the relationship of knowledge and meaning to power are the inverse of those of the first. Whereas questions of the first class are concerned with relationships among sets of understandings as consequences of the social and political relations of those holding them, questions of the third class are concerned with relations of domination and subordination among persons as a consequence of the distribution of knowledge and the control of meaning.

We may return here to the matter of redundancy. Redundancy of knowledge implies equivalence and the egalitarian nature of tribal societies is surely related to high redundancy. It must not be imagined, however, that the understandings of all members of any tribal society are uniform. That some variation within common frameworks is usual, even among people of similar age and sex, is demonstrated by variations in the folk taxonomies commonly provided by different informants in the same community (see, for example, Messer 1978, especially chapter 4). Distinctions of much greater magnitude are likely to distinguish different categories of persons. Such distinctions do not necessarily imply inequality. Among Australian aborigines sacred knowledge is typically distributed among men according to their section, subsection, moiety, and totemic affiliations, and sometimes by locality as well. The *Gadjari* cycle of the Walbiri, for instance, re-enacts or celebrates the dream-time journey of the Mamandabari Men along a path meandering for fifteen hundred miles across the desert (Meggitt 1965). No one knows the myth in its entirety, let alone all of the *Gadjari* songs and rituals, but in each of the four major Walbiri "countries" there are men who know the portion of the cycle pertaining to their own region. The *Gadjari* thus creates a set of understandings that no individual fully possesses but in which many individuals participate. Interdependence is intrinsic to the ways in which sacred knowledge is distributed among Australian aborigines, and it may be that the dependence of local groups upon each other for the performance of the rituals understood to be necessary to maintain the world counteracts the social fragmentation likely to attend hunting and gathering in vast deserts (Yengoyan 1972, 1976). Each group's knowledge is sacred, and it is also deemed to be as necessary to others as it is to those possessing it. The *Gadjari* thus seems to establish equivalence, and thus equality, as it establishes interdependence among those whom it differentiates. We are, however, led here to the relationship of knowledge to subordination.

The "distinctive equals" related to each other by the *Gadjari* are men. The Walbiri, like many other tribal peoples, deny detailed sacred knowledge to women. Women are excluded from their rituals; indeed, that a woman has laid eyes on certain religious objects provides grounds for her execution. Inasmuch as the domain of the sacred is a domain of high-order meaning, to exclude women from ritual is to deny them full and direct access to higher-order meaning. Such meanings are given to them, or rather imposed upon them, by men.

Whether or not the men consciously manipulate these meanings to their own advantage, they are, among the Walbiri, organized in ways that favor men over women, and other tribal societies generally resemble the Walbiri in this respect. For example, among the Maring we have seen that a series of abstract oppositions—hot/cold, high/low, hard/soft, dry/wet, strong/fecund—pervade the world. The term "male" is associated with the series high-hot-hard-dry-strong, "female" with the opposing series, low-cold-soft-wet-fecund. The qualities composing each of these series are considered to be inimical to those they oppose under certain circumstances, and when those circumstances prevail objects and persons in which they are manifest must be insulated from each other. (Most Maring taboos can be understood in this light. See Douglas 1966.) It is important to note, however, that although the sets associated with "male" on the one hand and "female" on the other are opposed, and although their opposition implies that things in which their qualities are manifest may be dangerous to each other, inequality is not intrinsic to the *logic* of their relations. That which is "cold" may be inimical to that which is "hot," but neither hot nor cold is necessarily superior. And yet, although some Maring do say that under certain circumstances contact with men may "burn" women, it is pollution of the pure men by impure women that is feared, and it is to the well-being of men that Maring taboos are dedicated. Moreover, two further oppositions identify the spiritual and immortal with male and the mortal and natural with female. It is possible that whatever is spiritual and immortal is inherently superior to whatever is natural and mortal, but the association of the superior terms with male and the inferior with female is not logically entailed by either the opposition of the two sets or the nature of the other members composing each of them. It would, rather, seem to be grounded in the simple fact that women are excluded from the rituals in which men, through their participation, partake of the sacred.

Whether or not Maring men manipulate the meanings intrinsic to these oppositions, they accept them and act in accordance with them. Their women may, from time to time, flout them, but in the main they too accept both them and the radical inequality that they entail. As Buchbinder and I (1976: 31), following Read (1952: 16), have observed, sanctified pollution beliefs elaborated among the Maring (and other New Guinea Highlanders) raise the justification of male dominance from that of arbitrary material advantage to that of inexorable spiritual principle. The subordinated as well as the subordinating can accept spiritual principle with resignation if not with equanimity.

The subordination of women in the New Guinea Highlands, the Australian desert, and elsewhere indicates that even in the absence of material grounds for stratification, differential control of meaning may serve as a basis for social inequality. Indeed, differential control of meaning may have constituted the primordial ground for the subordination of some persons by others—probably women by men. It has, of course, remained crucial to the maintenance of stable relations of subordination throughout history.

VII

To observe that the subordinated acquiesce to, or even participate in, their own oppression because of the meanings provided them by those who are the masters of meaning does not, perhaps, adequately convey the nature of this meaningfulness. Discussion of it will elucidate the capacity of cognized models not merely to describe a cosmos, but to constitute it.

It should be clear that we are not primarily concerned here with low-order meaning, or the meaningfulness that informs adequate explanation. Acceptance of subordination does not follow from the situation being well explained. We are concerned, rather, with meaning of a very high order—not the meaning of explanation but of identification. The matter may be illustrated by continuing our consideration of the subordination of Maring women to men.

The male/female distinction is universal, simple, obvious, and, if anything at all is, it is naturally significant as well. As such, it is "easy to think," and as such it has been invoked by many societies to order other phenomena. Buchbinder and I have argued that among the Maring it is not simply another opposition in the set of oppositions with which it is associated but that set's living summary and representation. It stands, in other words, in a metaphoric relationship to the sum of distinctions that the opposition of the two sets include. Male : female :: high-hot-hard-dry-strong-spiritual-immortal : low-cold-soft-wet-fecund-natural-mortal.

It is important to note that, unlike some oppositions, male/female is not simply a figure of speech. It is not merely a verbal metaphor but a material one, and thus it substantiates or realizes the abstract or even abstruse qualities and concepts with which it is associated. Yet even the recognition that male/female is not simply a metaphor but a material metaphor does not do full justice to its peculiar properties of signification, for it is not simply a material metaphor either. After all, contrasting objects manipulated in ritual—let us say *rumbim* and *amame*—can also substantiate or realize the opposition of the same abstractions. *Amame* and *rumbim,* however, and the distinction between them, differ in an important way from male, female, and the distinction between them. Whereas *amame* and *rumbim* are separate from those who make distinctions by manipulating them, "male" and "female" are not. The terms of this opposition are inseparable aspects of those who use it metaphorically to make other distinctions. The actors themselves become terms in their own logic of the concrete.

The use in metaphor of one's person and the persons of others from whom one is distinguished by gender is surely a powerful aid to understanding. The remote, abstract, ethereal, and unfamiliar is thereby brought into the grasp of the immediate, material, concrete, and apparently absolutely unknown. But the consequences may be grave. Brief reference to the role of metaphor in predication will be useful here.

The predication of nominals is one of language's fundamental processes. Perception is organized into comprehension when we say that a subject either *is,* or *has,* or *does* something. Subjects, that is, are defined, specified, identified, or invested with the qualities of predicates. Predication can be either literal or metaphoric (Thomas 1969: 59), and Fernandez has even argued that "the elementary definition of the metaphor . . . is the predication of a sign-image upon an inchoate subject. The first mission of metaphor is to provide identity for such subjects" (1974: 120). Subjects, this is to say, by employing metaphors that include self-referential or subjective terms, are open to predication by those metaphors. Thus the Maring, in taking the gender distinction to be a metaphor for the conventional oppositions they impose upon the world, not only make those oppositions comprehensible but establish them in their own bodies and in whatever distinguishes the bodies of men from those of women. The conceptual cleavages dividing or fragmenting the world are not only made substantial but, being established in the flesh, become as apparently natural as the sexual difference itself. As such they become inescapable, unchallengeable, and ever-present, and so, of course, do the dangers and antagonisms they entail.

It may be that male/female is "easy to think" and "likely to be thought," providing as it does an intuitively comprehensible metaphor in terms of which many aspects of the world may be ordered. But to say that it is "easy to think" is not to say that it is "good to think," and its cost may be high. Metaphors may work in both directions: as the proximal terms and the relations between them illuminate the distal terms and the relations between them, so may the distal terms predicate the proximal. The Maring use of male/female to order obscure or abstract oppositions may illuminate those oppositions but it also permits the horrors attending them to storm back across the metaphoric bridge, so to speak, to invade the bodies of those who thought them into being. Thus we can see that the concept of female pollution among the Maring does not derive from the properties of substances, such as menstrual blood, nor from the metaphoric imposition of any of women's other physical characteristics upon the world. Women are polluting because they are predicated by the abstractions they have come to embody, and because these abstractions are opposed to, and therefore dangerous to, the abstractions embodied by men.

VIII

More germane to the concerns of this essay than a theory of female pollution *per se* is the light cast by this instance of predication on the force of cognized models generally. It may be that those whose actions are guided by any cognized model assume, if they think about the matter at all, that it is composed of descriptive, evaluative, and metaphysical statements concerning orders existing independently of those statements.

If, however, cognized models can predicate those who are guided by them, they are not simply complex statements. They are in effect, although not by conscious intention, at least partly performative in character.

"Performatives," or "illocutionary acts," are conventional acts or utterances through which conventional effects are achieved (Austin 1962). Verbal performatives—and all performatives are either fully or partially verbal or at least have been provided meaning by words—may be lexically and grammatically indistinguishable from reports or descriptions, but the relationship of a performative to the states of affairs with which it is concerned is very different from that of a statement. For instance, when a priest pronounces the couple standing before him to be man and wife he is not reporting or describing the act of marriage to them. He is making them man and wife. The utterance itself is part of the act of marriage and the conventional state of marriage is not only subsequent to but contingent upon the utterance because the utterance brings it into being. This is the inverse of the relationship prevailing between reports or descriptions and states of affairs. For a report or description to be a report or description, and not a lie, myth, or fiction, the state of affairs to which it supposedly corresponds must exist independent of and prior to the report or description.

The importance of performatives in human affairs is obviously enormous. Conventional states of affairs are achieved and conventions themselves are established performatively and perhaps only performatively (see "The Obvious Aspects of Ritual"), and thus human social life is, in considerable degree, performatively constituted. As the myths of many peoples have told us, our conventional worlds have been uttered into being.

Performative creation is, however, almost always mystified. Public affairs in contemporary Western society, for instance, are guided more by the assumptions of formal economics than by those of any other discipline. Indeed, the institutions dominating our society are founded upon its understandings, central to which is that of man as *Homo economicus*. This conception is an invention of market economics and formal economics, but it is presented to us by formal economics as that discipline's discovery of quintessential human nature. This is to say that formal economics and the cognized models that it dominates are not, as economists would have us believe, descriptions of processes constituted by a precultural and quintessential human nature (see Sahlins 1972: 13 passim). They are not maps but, as it were, blueprints and operating instructions for establishing and maintaining conditions that will reproduce *Homo economicus*.

That cognized models dominated by formal economics are covertly performative while advertised as descriptive does not distinguish them from other cognized models, of course. It would be a mistake, moreover, to consider this form of masquerade to be nothing more than epistemological error or exploitative lie, for such mystification is an inevitable cultural process. "Models for" become "models of" instantaneously (Geertz 1965: 34). That which has been established performatively can subsequently be described, often in words identical to those of the performative and, in being described, may come to seem as real as trees or rocks, as natural as respiration or photosynthesis or digestion. Having become natural it may seem to be necessary and inevitable, and as such less vulnerable to subversion, dissolution, or rebellion than that which is nakedly conventional (see "The Obvious Aspects of Ritual").

It may well be that the continuity of all cultures requires the naturalization of their fundamental conventions, but as necessary as such naturalization might be, problems are likely to be generated in its course. Whereas the *conventions* of the worlds inhabited by humans are performatively established these worlds are, of course, not entirely conventional. Some of their components are constituted by what are called "the laws of nature."

The lawful and the meaningful are *never* coextensive, and they are differently known. If the laws of nature are to be known they must be discovered. In contrast, the understandings and meanings of humankind must be constructed. Natural processes are described by laws; conventions are performatively established through understandings and meanings. Discovered laws may provide some of the material out of which understandings and meanings are constructed, but they do not in and of themselves provide, constitute, or maintain meaning or meaningfulness. Indeed, by apotheosizing fact, I earlier argued, the search for natural law may violate the structure of meaning. Such searches may also abet the subversion of nature, for to know nature starkly and coldly may be to encourage attempts to subordinate it to narrow, short-run, and short-sighted purposes.

Discovered law does not constitute meaning, nor can it do meaning's work. If the natural processes that statements of law describe are to be preserved they must be comprehended by understandings more encompassing than those laws. They must, this is to say, be "made meaningful."

As law cannot do the work of meaning neither can meaning do the work of law. The lawful operation of natural processes is neither constituted nor transformed by understanding, and the laws of nature prevail in their domains whether or not they are understood or meaningful.

Relations between that which is performatively established and that which has been naturally constituted through the workings of the sun, the wind, the waves, the motions of continents, and the coevolution of organisms, are both intimate and complicated. It is surely not the case, as some recent writers would perhaps have us believe, that the natural merely provides material to the convention which then shapes the world to its will as if it were clay in the hand of God. Nature is not simply the source of the human world's substance but, with culture, a source of its form as well. Indeed, the formative effects of nature and culture are inseparable. Nor is the relationship one of simple limitation, as the old possibilists proposed. The briefest glance at the present condition of the world must indicate that the establishment of convention is not constrained by ecosystemic characteristics, that it is possible to establish systems of conventions that persistently violate and continually degrade naturally constituted ecosystemic processes. Ecosystemic limitations of conventional processes might operate, finally, only apocalyptically. We return here to the matter of contingency. Whereas it is surely the case that no conventional system can long persist if it destroys the natural processes sustaining it, it is equally the case that the persistence of humanity, albeit a species constituted by natural evolutionary processes, is itself contingent upon conventions. To say, however, that human society is contingent upon conventions is not to say that it is contingent upon any particular set of them, and sets of conventions may differ in their appropriateness to particular sets of circumstances.

We are concerned with a species that must construct the understandings and meanings by which it lives in a world whose laws it can neither change nor fully comprehend. In contradiction of the doctrine of cultural relativism it may be asserted that some of the understandings that societies may construct for themselves are false because they lead those for whom they are meaningful to act in ways that are so at variance with the natural constitution of the world as to make damage to it and to themselves inevitable. The lawful order of nature—through which the processes of understanding and convention emerged—continues to provide criteria in terms of which the appropriateness of understandings and conventions can be assessed. Such criteria suggest to us that, for instance, the conventional orders of industrialized capitalism, which must expand to remain stable, have become, if they were not always, inappropriate, infelicitous, and maladaptive, because they must sooner or later degrade or violate the finite ecosystemic processes over which they exercise domination but upon which they depend. It should be clear that I do not propose here the sovereignty of the material. Earlier in this essay a systemic relationship between the meaningful and material aspects of the living processes constituting humanity was explicitly recognized in a discussion of the material consequences of the impoverished understandings of monetary semantics. It was suggested then that that which damages meaning damages the world as a whole.

But, as the impoverishment of meaning deadens life and threatens its continuity, so may the richness of life be enhanced and its continuity abetted by cognized models that permit distinctions to multiply, metaphors to prosper, and the experience of unity to flourish. A cognized model that is "true," or in Austin's (1962) usage "felicitous," is not one that simply corresponds to natural laws, but one that provides an order of understandings that leads those for whom it is meaningful to act in ways that are in harmony with natural processes. Such models always recognize, more or less crudely or precisely, some natural laws—at least some empirical generalizations from experience. But they are never exhausted by such laws, for the relevance of natural law to human experience is always a matter of meaning and understanding, and not itself a matter of law.

It may seem that, at the end, we come to a simple and straightforward reiteration of the formulation that, at the beginning, was said to be inadequate. In fact, we have not. The earlier formulation proposed that material desiderata should, as it were, sit in judgment of meanings and understandings. Meanings and understandings were, in that view, mere instruments in the service of material ends. In the course of the essay it has been demonstrated that this view of meanings and understandings not only will not account for them but does not even do justice to their role in the adaptations of human societies. It now may be added that serious problems beset the use of biological criteria themselves. First, despite their apparent materiality, ecological and other biological criteria (the invocation of which, it was hoped, would permit us to assess objectively the "truth" of cognized models) are ambiguous. Slobodkin and Rapoport (1974) have observed, for one thing, that it may not be possible to specify any particular feature of biological structure or operation that will always and everywhere abet the persistence of all of the systems in which it occurs. Whether or not this is the case, it is indubitable that the complexity of living systems is of such an order that their responses to particular perturbations may be counter-intuitive. It is often, therefore, difficult to predict even the more or less immediate outcomes, biological or otherwise, of actions undertaken in them, let alone effects which may be distant in time or space. This difficulty does not call into question the validity of a concern with the biological and ecological consequences of actions proposed by cognized models. It does, however, call into question the validity of invoking *specific* biological or ecological standards as *ultimate* criteria of the adequacy of cognized models.

The rejection of specific biological criteria might seem to leave the notion of the "truth" or "falsity" of cognized models so vague as to be meaningless, but reference to discussions of the structure of understanding and meaning appearing earlier in this essay save us from exchanging specious precision for pious vacuity. Our observations concerning the dissolution of qualitative distinctions into quantitative differences as an entailment of the monetization of evaluation points in this direction. Even more fundamentally, in the accounts of the structure of understanding and meaning offered in this essay, and in subsequent proposals concerning the mutual dependence of meaningful and material processes, it has been implicitly assumed that it is possible to stipulate the formal characteristics of orders of understanding that preserve meaning and meaningfulness and, in preserving them, preserve other living processes as well. This proposal is less mysterious than it may seem at first, and is elaborated in essays appearing later in this volume. It is well, however, to recall there the discussion earlier in this essay of the hierarchical structure of orders of understanding. It was proposed that the understandings of which cognized models are made are not simply heaps, but are organized hierarchically with respect to sanctity, mutability, temporality, specificity, and concreteness. Thus, ultimate sacred postulates, the most sacred of concepts, are also, typically, understood to be immutable and eternal. They do not have concrete or material referents and are devoid of social specificity. In contrast, rules of conduct, which are high in specificity, are much less sacred than ultimate sacred postulates, are not taken to be eternal verities, and are regarded as mutable. I also suggested that it may be in the very nature of the ritual form to preserve hierarchical order among the ultimate sacred postulates, cosmological axioms, rules of conduct, and social and environmental states of affairs represented in them. This would suggest that the degradation and abandonment of ritual, widespread in the contemporary world, is contributing significantly to social and environmental problems, as well as to failures of meaning. Be this as it may, to make explicit a proposal that has been implicit throughout much of this essay, *disorderings of hierarchical relations among understandings differing in the qualities of sanctity, mutability, temporality, specificity, and concreteness* (for instance, the investment of highly specific rules of conduct with a degree of sanctity appropriate to a cosmological axiom or even an ultimate sacred postulate) *lead not only to the destruction of meaning but of the material world as well.*

The formal characteristics of adaptive systems, of which both meaningful and material processes are inextricably interrelated components or aspects, are explored in "Adaptive Structure and Its Disorders," where it is further argued that anomalies in, or disorderings of, such structures are to be regarded as maladaptive. Like "Adaptive Structure and Its Disorders," the other essays that follow were written earlier than this one and do have themes of their own, but in developing their own themes they develop and elaborate discussions broached here. "The Obvious Aspects of Ritual" discusses neither adaptation nor maladaptations but is, rather, an attempt to elucidate the construction of meaning and convention in and by liturgy. It is concerned, in particular, with the concepts and notions intrinsic to the very form, structure, or order that is definitive of ritual. These include not only social contract, morality, creation, and those which ultimate sacred postulates express, but the very concept of the sacred. "Sanctity and Lies in Evolution" returns to problems of the falsification of meaning, understandings, and ultimately, of sanctity itself.

REFERENCES CITED

Alitzer, Thomas, and William Hamilton
  1966   *Radical theology and the death of God.* Indianapolis: Bobbs-Merrill.
Austin, J. L.
  1962   *How to do things with words,* ed. J. O. Ormson. Oxford: Oxford University Press.
Bateson, G.
  1951   Conventions of communication: where validity depends upon belief. In J. Ruesch and G. Bateson, *Communication: the social matrix of psychiatry,* pp. 212-227. New York: Norton.
  1967   Cybernetic explanation. *American Behavioral Scientist* 10:29-32.
Buber, Martin
  1952   *Eclipse of God.* New York: Harper & Brother.
Buchbinder, G., and R. A. Rappaport
  1976   Fertility and death among the Maring. In *Man and woman in the New Guinea Highlands,* ed. Paula Brown and G. Buchbinder. American Anthropological Association Special Publication Number 8.
Campbell, Joseph
  1959   *The masks of God.* Vol. 1, *Primitive mythology.* New York: Viking.
Douglas, Mary
  1966   *Purity and danger.* New York: Praeger.
Durkheim, Emile
  1933   *On the division of labor in society. Being a translation of "De la division du travail social" [2nd edition 1902] with an estimate of his work.* George Simpson, translator. New York: Macmillan.
Fernandez, James
  1974   The mission of metaphor in expressive culture. *Current Anthropology* 15:119-146.
Geertz, Clifford
  1965   Religion as a cultural system. In *Anthropological approaches to the study of religion,* ed. Michael Banton. ASA Monograph 3. London: Tavistock.
Harris, Marvin
  1976   History and significance of the emic/etic distinction. *Annual Review of Anthropology* 5:329-350.
Lévi-Strauss, Claude
  1955   The structural study of myth. *Journal of American Folklore* 67-428-444.

Meggitt, M. J.
    1965   *Gadjari among the Walbiri aborigines of Central Australia.* Oceania
           Monographs.
Messer, Ellen
    1978   *Zapotec plant knowledge: classification, uses, and communication about
           plants in Mitla, Oaxaca, Mexico.* Vol. 5, part 2 of *Prehistory and human
           ecology of the Valley of Oaxaca,* Kent V. Flannery and Richard E.
           Blanton, general editors. Memoirs of the Museum of Anthropology
           of the University of Michigan, no. 10.
Murchland, Bernard, ed.
    1967   *The meaning of the death of God.* New York: Random House, Vintage
           Books.
Ortner, Sherry
    1973   On key symbols. *American Anthropologist* 75:1338–1346.
Peirce, Charles Sanders
    1960   *Collected papers of Charles Sanders Peirce,* vol. 2, *Elements of Logic,* ed.
           Charles Harthorne and Paul Weiss. Cambridge: Harvard University
           Press.
Rappaport, Roy A.
    1963   Aspects of man's influence on island ecosystems: alteration and con-
           trol. In *Man's place in the island ecosystem,* ed. F. R. Fosberg. Hono-
           lulu: Bishop Museum Press.
    1968   *Pigs for the ancestors.* New Haven: Yale University Press.
    1971   Nature, culture, and ecological anthropology. In *Man, culture, and
           society,* 2nd ed., ed. Harry Shapiro. New York: Oxford University
           Press.
Read, Kenneth
    1952   The Nama cult of the Central Highlands, New Guinea. *Oceania*
           23:1–25.
Sahlins, Marshall
    1972   *Stone age economics.* Chicago and New York: Aldine, Atherton.
Slobodkin, L., and A. Rapoport
    1974   An optimal strategy of evolution. *Quarterly Review of Biology* 49–
           181–200.
Thomas, Owen
    1969   *Metaphor and related subjects.* New York: Random House.
Turner, Victor
    1967a Symbols in Ndembu ritual. In *The forest of symbols.* Ithaca: Cornell
           University Press.
    1967b Betwixt and between: the liminal period in rites de passage. In *The
           forest of symbols.* Ithaca: Cornell University Press.
Van Baal, J.
    1971   *Symbols for communication: an introduction to the anthropological study of
           religion.* Assen: Van Goracum.
Yengoyan, Aram
    1972   Ritual and exchange in aboriginal Australia: an adaptive interpreta-
           tion of male initiation rites. In *Social exchange and interaction,* ed.
           E. N. Wilmsen. Anthropological Papers No. 46, University of Michi-
           gan Museum of Anthropology.
    1976   Structure, event, and ecology in aboriginal Australia: a comparative
           viewpoint. In *Tribes and boundaries in Australia,* ed. N. Peterson.
           Canberra: Australian Institute of Aboriginal Studies.

Adaptive Structure

and Its Disorders

I shall be concerned in this essay with the structure of adaptation and with its maladaptive disordering. The concept of adaptation is central to much of biological and anthropological thought but, like most central concepts, it is not entirely clear. Perhaps it shouldn't be. In remaining vague it itself remains adaptive. Be that as it may, because usage and understanding vary it is necessary for me to make my understanding of adaptation explicit at the beginning, even at the risk of rehearsing elementary matters.

I

I take the term "adaptation" to refer to the processes through which living systems maintain homeostasis in the face of both short-term environmental fluctuations and, by transformations in their own structures, through long-term nonreversing changes in their environments as well. It would be well to comment upon certain features of this characterization before exploring its implications.

First, I include with the class "living systems" both organisms and associations of organisms. The latter may include such social groups as families, clans, tribes, states, and even societies and ecosystems—any association that can be shown to have inhering in it as a unit distinct processes initiated in response to and as response to perturbation.

This essay is an expansion of the second half of the essay "Ecology, Adaptation, and the Ills of Functionalism (Being, among Other Things, a Response to Jonathan Fried-man)" originally published in *Michigan Discussions in Anthropology* 2:139-190, 1977.

The application of a common set of concepts to organisms and to associations of organisms, some of which are culturally governed, is likely to attract charges of organic analogizing. Such charges would be, in my view, misplaced. To say that organisms and associations of organisms are loci of adaptive processes is to recognize that they are both subclasses of a larger class, namely living or adaptive systems, and not to propose that social systems are detailed icons of organisms (or vice versa). To recognize general similarities among systems differing in obvious respects is not to deny their differences or the significance of their differences, but to contextualize them. We shall return to certain of these differences shortly. It may be noted in passing, however, that the organic analogy doesn't even apply very well to organisms, which turn out to be more like ecosystems than is generally thought (Thomas 1974).

Adaptation is a process, or category of processes, universal to life. It is to be observed in simple animals and elaborate empires, and its application to human affairs may provide supracultural criteria in terms of which the operations of particular societies may be assessed. Although it may be acceptable to speak of adaptive processes "inhering in" living systems, it is more accurate and therefore preferable to propose the converse: that adaptive processes define (and bound) living systems. The scope of an adaptive process distinguishes a living system (which may, of course, include others and be included by others of greater scope) from its environment.

Relatively autonomous adaptive systems are what have sometimes been called "general purpose systems." The term is ugly but it does convey the notion that such systems to not have special goals. They cannot be defined, as can the special-purpose systems which they include, by the production of some special product, like petroleum or pituitrin, of by some special activity, as can hearts, lungs, or fire departments. Their ultimate goal is so low in specificity as to seem a virtual nongoal. It is simply to persist. As Slobodkin (1968) has put it in a discussion of the difficulties of applying game theory to evolution, general purpose systems are players of the existential game, a game that is peculiar in that the only reward for successful play is to be allowed to continue to play, a game in which the phrase "cashing in your chips" is a euphemism for losing. Individual humans and societies may, of course, mystify such goals (or non-goals) while maintaining their low specificity (e.g., "It is the goal of society to serve God."), but for them to set for themselves enduring goals as specific as those appropriate for their subsystems is likely to reduce their chances of staying in the existential game by reducing their flexibility. Central to adaptation is the maintenance of systemic flexibility, the maintenance of an ability to keep responding homeostatically to perturbations the magnitude and nature of which usually cannot be predicted, given the complexity of the universe.

A second feature of our definition of adaptation bearing brief comment is its inclusion of the term "environment." "Environment" and "ecosystem" are not synonymous, and "environment" here is meant to embrace cultural and social as well as physical and biotic phenomena. Whereas both individuals and ecosystems are to be included within the class "living systems," social and cultural anthropologists may be expected to take human social units or formations to be the adaptive systems with which they are *primarily* concerned.

Third, the term "homeostasis" appears in the definition. Systemic homeostasis may be given specific, if not always precise, meaning if it is conceived as a set of ranges of viability on a corresponding set of variables abstracted from what, for independently established empirical or theoretical reasons, are taken to be conditions vital to the persistence of the system. This is to say that any process, physiological, behavioral, cultural, or genetic, that tends to keep the states of crucial variables (e.g., body temperature, population size, protein intake, energy flux) within ranges of viability or tends to return them to such ranges should they depart from them may be taken, other things being equal, to be adaptive. Later it will be necessary to consider difficulties in the association of adaptiveness with particular variables, but this preliminary formulation may stand for the present, because it underlines certain features of adaptive process and structure.

Fourth, it is important to note that the terms "homeostasis" and "dynamic equilibrium" *do not* imply changelessness. Indeed, the opposite is the case. In an ever-changing world the maintenance of homeostasis requires constant change of state and, for most systems at least, occasional change in structure. We shall return to this.

*   *   *

The definition of adaptation offered here implies, or even entails, self-regulation. Self-regulation depends upon a limited family of mechanisms. These include, first, *immutability,* in which some aspect or component of the system is held in what seems to be an absolutely invariant state. The clearest cases are probably religious propositions, such as creeds, taken by those adhering to them to be eternally true. These have considerable importance in the self-regulation of human societies. Second, there are what Piaget (1971: 14) calls *operations.* These are perfectly reversible processes, best exemplified by mathematical and logical formulations. As such they are of considerable importance in thought. Although they do not apply directly to matter and energy transactions, within which inexactitude prevails and entropy is ubiquitous, they may be important in the regulation of such transactions. In the essay "On Cognized Models" elsewhere in this volume Maring ritual procedures for reversing damage done to the cosmos are described. *Time-dependent regulation,* exemplified by circadian rhythms, traffic lights, and some seasonal festivals form a third class of regulatory mechanisms of considerable importance in social and physical processes, but perhaps most important is the *variable-dependent* or *cybernetic* mode.

It is, perhaps, obvious that the various regulatory modes may be embodied or, in social systems, institutionalized in a variety of ways. Discrete regulators (e.g., chiefs, big men, kings) are important in some systems, but regulation may be the outcome of unmediated interactions among components, as in hypothetical "perfect markets" and in dynamic interactions among distinct species populations. Regulation in human societies and ecological systems dominated by humans may also reside in tradition, in ritual cycles, or in the entailments of social structure.

Self-regulation entails corrective responses, and corrective responses may have several effects. In some instances the stressing factor is eliminated. In others, compensatory adjustments are made within the existing structure of the system. In yet others, however, changes—genetic, constitutional, structural—in the very organization of the responding systems themselves are, and must be, made. The *self-regulating* processes through which living systems *maintain* themselves thus entail or subsume the *self-organizing* processes through which they transform themselves.

These two classes of processes, self-regulation and self-organization, have generally been distinguished in the social sciences, forming the foci of two distinct modes of analysis, "functional" on the one hand and "evolutionary" on the other. The distinction has been overdrawn because the maintenance ("persistence," "adequate functioning," "survival") of systems in a changing world requires constant change. The connecting generalization is what Hockett and Ascher (1964) have called "Romer's Rule," after Alfred S. Romer, the zoologist who first enunciated it in a discussion of the emergence of the amphibia (1954; originally published 1933). The lobe-finned fish, Romer argues, did not come onto dry land to take advantage of its previously unexploited opportunities. Rather, relatively minor modification of their fins and other subsystems made it possible for these creatures to migrate from one drying-up stream or pond to another still containing water during the intermittent droughts presumed to have been frequent during the Devonian period. Such structural changes thus made it possible for them to maintain their general aquatic organization during a period of marked environmental change. In slightly different terms, *self-organizing or evolutionary changes in components of systems are functions in the self-regulatory process of the more inclusive and enduring systems of which they are parts.* Structural or evolutionary changes, such as fin to leg, may be distinguished from "functional" changes or "systemic adjustments" on some grounds, but they are not separated from them in the larger more inclusive scheme of adaptive process. Together they form ordered series of responses to perturbations. Several comments are in order before discussing adaptive response sequence.

First, it is worth reiteration, because there seems to be considerable confusion surrounding this matter, that the view of adaptation proposed here suggests that there is no contradiction between the maintenance of homeostasis and evolutionary change. Indeed, Romer's parable—it may be no more than that—suggests that the most salient question to ask concerning any structural change is "What does this change maintain unchanged?"

Second, earlier I proposed that the goal of an adaptive system, as a player of Slobodkin's existential game, is simply to persist. Our account suggests that that which persists is not necessarily any particular feature or component of the adapting system, but simply an organized set of adaptive processes. Even structure may change. It follows that the frequently asked question, "When does a system stop being what it has been and become something else?" a question that is generally deemed impossible to answer and thus devastating to systemic approaches to evolutionary transformation, is close to nonsensical. There has been, for instance, an unbroken continuity in English society from the days of the heptarchy until today despite enormous changes in both structure and cultural content. In the course of their unbroken successions ecosystems may replace all, or almost all, of their constituent species several times. That we distinguish and name the phases following each other in these successions, just as we may distinguish and name and periods following each other in the history of societies, or, for that matter, in the ontogeny of individuals, and that these phases and period differ in important ways, does not mean that they are discontinuous. Slobodkin and Rapoport (1974) have noted two distinct ways in which distinctive associations of conspecifics can cease to exist, and they have admonished us not to confuse them. On the one hand, there can come a time when no descendants of that association remain alive. At such time we can say that the adaptive processes that it embodied have come to an end. We can further say in such cases that the evolutionary process has ended in failure. On the other hand, such an association may apparently cease to exist because its descendants have been so transformed as to warrant being called by a new species name. In this instance the adaptive processes continue and the evolutionary process continues to be successful.

A third major point is that insofar as adaptive processes are cybernetic they are possessed of a characteristic structure, because cybernetic systems have a characteristic structure, namely that of the closed causal loop: in a cybernetic system a deviation from a reference value itself initiates the process that attempts to correct it.

Fourth, although adaptive processes may have cybernetic characteristics, all that is cybernetic is *not* adaptive in the sense outlined in the first paragraphs of this essay. In the most general terms, cybernetic systems attempt to maintain the truth value of propositions about themselves in the face of perturbations tending to falsify them (Bateson 1972). In systems dominated by humans, at least, the propositions so maintained (and the physical states represented by such propositions) may not correspond to, or may even contradict, homeostasis biologically or even socially defined.

II

Adaptation is not constituted of a class of isolated responses. Orderly adaptive processes are, rather, organized into ordered sequences of responses, and these sequences *as sequences* have certain interesting structural properties (Bateson 1963; Frisancho 1975; Rappaport 1976a; Slobodkin and Rapoport 1974; Vayda and McKay 1975). The responses most quickly mobilized are likely to be energetically and behaviorally expensive, but easily and quickly reversible following the cessation of stress. Should a perturbation or stress continue, however, the earlier responses are eventually relieved by slower-acting, less energetically expensive, less easily reversible changes. Responses earlier in the sequence are likely to be gross behavioral and physiological state changes. Changes later in the sequence are likely to be structural (constitutional in social systems, irreversible somatic change, and ultimately genetic change, in organisms and populations of organisms; formally similar sequences can possibly be observed in various psychological processes). While the earlier responses operate, the system may well be deprived of some behavioral flexibility, but while these earlier easily reversible responses continue, the structure of the system in which they occur remains unchanged. Later responses, although they may be more efficient energetically than the earlier, and although they do restore some immediate behavioral flexibility to the system, are less easily reversible or even irreversible. This is to say that later responses may entail structural change. Both Bateson, and Slobodkin and Rapoport, have suggested that the *probable* effect of structural change in response to *specific problems* is the reduction of long-term flexibility. There is likely to be trade-off, then, in adaptive response sequences, of long-term systemic flexibility for immediate efficiency (or other advantage). In an unpredictably changing universe it is good evolutionary strategy, they say, to give up as little flexibility as possible, to change no more than is necessary. (To put the matter in more familiar terms, structural change in response to particular stresses is likely to lead to increased specialization, and increased specialization to earlier loss in the existential game, a game in which even the rules change from time to time.) This argument was presaged in *Evolution and Culture,* edited by Sahlins and Service in 1960.

* * *

Evolutionary wisdom seems to be intrinsic to the graduated structure of the adaptive response sequences of organisms, but may not be as well founded in social systems. In human social systems, at least, adaptive response sequences can, and do, become disordered, a matter to which I shall return in the next section. First, however, we must consider the structure of adaptive systems, to consider, that is, how systems must be constructed if they are to maintain continuing homeostatis through the mobilization of orderly sequences of responses to perturbation.

We have already noted that adaptive systems are self-regulating, and that self-regulating processes have characteristic structures. The causal structure of the cybernetic mode, probably the most important, takes the form of a closed circuit. Adaptive processes are not only cybernetic, sequential, and graduated, however. The adaptive structure of any living system is not merely a collection of more or less distinct feedback loops. Particular or specific adaptations must be related to each other in structured ways, and general adaptations, human or otherwise, biological or cultural, must take the form of enormously complex sets of interlocking corrective loops, roughly and generally hierarchically arranged, and including not only mechanisms regulating material variables, but regulators regulating relations between regulators and so on (Kalmus 1966; Miller 1965a, 1965b; Pattee 1973: Rappaport 1969, 1971a; Simon 1969). Adaptive structures are *structured sets of processes,* and regulatory hierarchies, whether or not they are embodied in particular organs or institutions, are found in *all* biological and social systems. It is important, however, to issue a caveat here: to say that regulatory structure is hierarchical is not to say that it is centralized, nor that it entails social stratification. For instance, among some egalitarian societies, components of regulatory hierarchies are embedded in ritual cycles; in others in segmentary kinship organization (Brookfield and Brown 1963; Meggitt 1965, 1972; Ortiz 1969; Rappaport 1968; Sahlins 1961).

The hierarchical organization of adaptive processes is manifested not only in the relationship of regulators to each other but also in the relationships of parts to the systems in which they are included. This relationship is, of course, implicit in the parable of the emerging amphibia. Transformations in one or several subsystems made it possible for the general structure of those organisms to remain unchanged during the initial stage of the terrestrial adaptation. It may be possible to distinguish transformations of differing degrees of profundity. "Low order" transformations, transformations of the internal structure of specific subsystems, may be occurring more or less continuously, but because complex living systems are, to use Simon's (1969) phrase, "loosely coupled," their effects may be confined to the subsystems in which they occur. High-order transformations, transformations in the structures of more inclusive systems, are rarer, and, of course, their effects are more profound. To speak, simply, of structural transformation is not sufficient, but there are possibilities for identifying transformations of different order and to consider relations—temporal, causal, and formal—among these transformations.

Whereas the adaptive structure of all living systems must share certain fundamental features—hierarchical organization and both self-regulating and self-transforming properties (see Piaget 1971), those of different classes surely differ in important respects that may be most significantly related to differences in their characteristic coherence and in the relative autonomy of their subsystems. There are also, and perhaps related, differences among hierarchies in the extent to which they are organized in accordance with segmentary or sectorial principles (in the former, subsystems at each level are similar, in the latter differentiated).

The increasing differentiation, in the course of evolution, of discrete special-purpose subsystems in organisms, societies, and ecosystems has been called "progressive segregation," and it is often accompanied in organisms and social systems, but not ecosystems, by increasing centralization of regulatory operation, or "progressive centralization." In organisms we note the elaboration of central nervous systems, in societies the development of administrative structures. This contrast between the development of ecological and other systems may rest upon their contrasting bases for order maintenance. The basis of orderliness in ecosystems seems to shift, in the course of their development from "pioneer" to "mature" stages, from a reliance upon the resilience of individual organisms to a reliance upon the increasing redundance of matter and energy pathways resulting from increasing species diversity. These contrasting bases of order maintenance may, in turn, reflect differences in the degrees of coherence that different classes of systems require and can tolerate. Whereas anthropologists traditionally have been concerned with the ways in which the various components of sociocultural systems are bound together—the jargon is "integrated"—they have generally ignored the ways in which the parts and processes of such systems are buffered from each other and each other's disruptions. I further suggest that organisms are, and in their nature must be, more coherent than social systems, and social systems more coherent than ecosystems. As a rule of thumb, the more inclusive the system, the less coherent it is and must be. The less inclusive the system, the more its internal orderliness and the effectiveness of its activities depends upon the fine coordination of its parts. An organism requires and can tolerate closer coordination of the activities of its parts than societies, and societies more (at least from time to time) than ecosystems. Coordination depends upon centralization, hence progressive centralization in organisms and societies, but not ecosystems.

The relative autonomy of a system is a function of the degree to which the regulatory mechanisms upon which its persistence depends are intrinsic to itself. To put it a little differently, "relative autonomy" refers to the extent to which systems are themselves more or less distinct adaptive units. Organs, for instance, have very little autonomy, for they cannot function in the absence of the organisms of which they are parts. Whole organisms have a much higher degree of relative autonomy; they are distinct adaptive units. It should be kept in mind, however, that no system less inclusive than the solar system is absolutely autonomous. To repeat, whereas the adaptive structures of all living systems share certain fundamental features, they also differ in certain ways, probably related most importantly to differences in their coherence and in the relative autonomy of their subsystems.

III

Much conceptual and empirical work remains to be done, but it may be tentatively suggested that in orderly adaptive systems, relations between subsystems and regulators at different levels should be hierarchical along a number of dimensions. The simplest of these, entailed by the characteristics of response sequences, to which reference has already been made, include: specificity of goals (highly specific at lowest levels to highly general at highest levels), response time (very fast and continuously operating at low levels, slower and tending toward sporadic operation at higher levels), and reversibility (easily and quickly reversible at lowest levels to irreversible only at the highest levels).

It follows from the ordering of the simple dimensions that higher-order regulators are not so much engaged in the regulation of specific material and behavioral processes as they are in the regulation of relations among these processes. They become involved in the details of the systems subordinate to them only when lower-order regulation experiences difficulty. In contrast to regulators of low order, each of which may respond to fluctuations in a number of distinct and specific processes, higher-order regulators operate in terms of simplified and highly aggregated variables, like monetary values. This implies that higher-order regulators do not "know" or need to know all that is known by their subordinates; that they needn't be any more complex, and may be simpler, than those of lower order; that they may operate less continuously than those of lower order; and that they include within their repertoires programs for changing structurally, or even replacing, lower-order regulators or subsystems.

In sum, there is an ordering in adaptive hierarchies from a range of highly specific concerns at lowest levels to increasingly more aggregated and general concerns at higher levels, and characteristic relationships of reversibility and time are associated with this order. The temporal dimension requires further brief discussion, for it is rather complex and we have considered only one of its aspects, the speed of response. There is also the matter of duration. First, the concerns of lower-order systems are likely to be transitory, while those of higher order systems are enduring. This is reflected in differences in the temporal qualities of the sentences typically concerned with regulation of lower and higher order. Low-order directives are typically commands, and as such are situation-specific and therefore ephemeral. Rules, which are more or less enduring, being category- rather than situation-specific, are typical of middle-range regulation. Principles, characteristic of yet higher order regulators, may be taken by those accepting them to reflect enduring or even timeless aspects of morality or nature, and highest-order regulation is likely to be associated with propositions concerning gods conceived to be altogether outside of time and man's reach. We move from the quick to the eternal. Adaptive structures include processes, experienced by those participating in them as continuously changing in the flux of time, and components, understood as immutable and thus not subject to time's vicissitudes. Adaptive structures not only include both temporal and atemporal features; they are constituted by relationships among these features; and, it may be suggested, evolution and history are to be understood in terms of the dynamic relationship between the ever-changing and what is understood as never-changing.

The correlation of the dimensions of time, specificity, and reversibility, a correlation that may be intrinsic to adaptive systems of all classes, leads to, or perhaps even entails, other dimensions of hierarchy that may be unique to human social systems. These dimensions may be related both to the low degree to which patterns of behavior are specified genetically among humans and to the *relative* autonomy of higher-order regulatory goals and conventions from environmental constraint. In proceeding from lower, more goal-specific regulation to regulation of higher order, the degree to which operation is determined or limited by environmental and other factors decreases. Regulation of increasingly higher order is increasingly informed by conventional rather than material considerations. To put this into a different terminology, relations of production are less determined by environmental factors than are means of production. Environments place tighter constraints upon the way crops are grown than they do upon claims to the product.

Possibly associated with the increasing arbitrariness of higher-order regulation is increase in the value-laden terms employed in regulatory discourse. For instance, discourse concerning wheat farming is highly concrete, and the fundamental agricultural assumptions of Soviet and American wheat farmers are probably close. But when economics is discussed, phrases like "free enterprise" and "from each what he can give, to each what he needs" begin to appear. The difference between what is connoted by these phrases is not technical, but ideological. Both are taken by those subscribing to them to be highly moral. Yet higher-order regulation is bolstered by such notions as honor, freedom, righteousness, and patriotism. Moreover, highest-order regulation may be explicitly concerned with the preservation of notions taken to be naturally or self-evidently moral, like "Life, Liberty, and the Pursuit of Happiness." These are explicitly stated to be principles or values for the preservation of which governments and other institutions are mere instruments. Regulatory hierarchies are *always* hierarchies of values, and even of sanctity. At the highest levels of regulation, divinity is often invoked. Pharaoh was the living Horus; Elizabeth is by Grace of God Queen; and even the United States is One Nation under a God in whom we trust* and by whom our highest principles, Life, Liberty, and the Pursuit of Happiness, are said to be given.

The hierarchical arrangement of values in adaptive structures is worth emphasizing. In well-ordered adaptive systems values are ordered such that they proceed from instrumental values at the lower levels to what may be called "ultimate" or "basic" values at the highest levels. Whereas instrumental values are highly specific, ultimate values are not only very general, they are also very vague. What, after all, is "Liberty," and what is "Happiness"? And who or what is the God endorsing them?

Vagueness is not a flaw but an adaptive characteristic of the ultimate. Propositions about God typically are devoid of material terms and therefore in themselves specify no particular social arrangements or institutions. Being devoid of, or at least low in, social specificity, they are well suited to be associated with the general goals of societies, namely their own perpetuation, for they can sanctify changing social arrangements while they themselves, remaining unchanged, provide continuity and meaning through those changes. Their typically cryptic nature is also important, for if they are vague the association of the ultimate and

---

*I refer doubters to our currency.

eternal with the immediate realities of history requires continual interpretation. Interpretation and reinterpretation do not challenge ultimate
sacred postulates, but only previous interpretations of them. If postulates are to be taken to be unquestionable, it is important that they be
incomprehensible. The very qualities of such propositions that lead
positivists to take them to be without sense, or even nonsensical, are
those that make them adaptively valid.

To summarize, I have argued so far that the persistence of living
systems is founded upon ordered sequences of responses to perturbations. If such sequences are to remain orderly the systems in which they
occur must possess certain structural characteristics. More specifically,
they must be both cybernetic and hierarchical, with their hierarchical
dimensions including specificity, concreteness, reversibility, arbitrariness, response time, duration, value, sanctity, and authority.

IV

A hierarchy of values is, *ipso facto,* a hierarchy of meaning, for values are
a category of meaning. In ascending hierarchies of values we proceed, as
I have already noted, from highly specific and often precise instrumental
values to more general, vague, and even cryptic ultimate values. There
are corresponding changes in the nature of their meanings and in meaning in general. Low-order meanings, in particular the meanings of words
per se, are those of definition and distinction, and as such are virtually
synonymous with information in the technical sense. Low-order instrumental values can be specified adequately in words and numbers.

Higher-order meaning is of a different sort. The sense of meaning to
which the question "What does it all mean?" points is really no longer
that of simple distinction or definition when asked by one confronted by
a complex mass of information. Indeed, in answering such a question,
information is radically reduced: "It all means that the world is good," or
that "the world is evil," or that "Life is like a fountain." But as information is decreased, meaningfulness is increased; for similarities, substantive or structural, between that which we seek to understand and that
which we already "know," are made explicit. Metaphors are constructed.
The application of a rule, principle, or classificatory device to a wide
range of phenomena (such as the application of the hot/cold dichotomy
to gender, other social relations, plants, and conditions of the body)
invests the world with meaning, for everything is not only itself but also
an icon of other things.

Higher-order meaning is, then, not information in the digital sense
but, rather, metaphoric. Although the discursive content of higher-order
meanings may be less than that of lower-order meanings, higher-order

meanings may well be affectively more powerful, which is to say more meaningful. It is significant that representations of art, poetry, and ritual rely heavily upon metaphor, and that primary process thought is largely metaphoric.

The meaningfulness of highest-order meaning, that which lies around —and beyond—ultimate sacred postulates, is again different. The discursive content of ultimate sacred postulates is low, and beyond such sentences the meanings of language may evaporate completely. Even metaphor's grasp is exceeded. Just as meaningfulness does not vanish with information, neither is it limited to that which metaphor may reach. Meaning may be nondiscursive. All distinction and all likeness may dissolve into a sense of no-distinction, or unity. Ultimate meaning is without reference, signifying only itself. It is a state of being, and is sometimes called by such names as "pure being" and "Being-Itself." It is of interest that the meanings that seem peculiar to humans, those we associate with what we are wont to call their "highest faculties," predominate at lowest levels. The meanings prevailing at higher and highest levels are diminishingly discursive, increasingly affective, and, perhaps, increasingly archaic and decreasingly distinctive of humanity. Be this as it may, the objectification of self and the world, and the concomitant alienation of self from the self and the world that is intrinsic to the use of language, may be overcome for the nonce by the sense of identity with self and the world (see Van Baal 1971) that constitutes highest-level meaning. This is mystical. It should not be forgotten, however, that mystical experiences (in a broad sense) do occur, particularly in religious rituals, the characteristics of which tend to encourage them. Elsewhere (1967b; "Sanctity and Lies in Evolution" in this volume) I have argued that such experience may provide deeper and more compelling understandings of perfectly natural and extremely important aspects of the physical and social world than can be provided by discursive reason alone. They may make palpable to us the reality of the larger systems of which we are parts, but which are ordinarily hidden from us by the evidence of our senses, which inform us of our autonomy and separation. Highest-order meaning has an important place in the adaptive structure of humanity, and so does the order of meaning in general.

I commenced with adaptation, a notion derived from biological disciplines, but find myself discussing meaning and meaningfulness, notions more obviously associated with the disciplines of mind. Two enterprises have proceeded in anthropology since its earliest days. One, objective in its aspirations and inspired by biological disciplines, seeks explanation and is concerned to discover laws and causes. The other, subjective in its orientation and influenced by philosophy, linguistics, and the humanities, attempts interpretation and seeks to elucidate meanings. I take any radical separation of the two to be misguided, for the relationship between them, with all of its difficulty, ambiguity, and tension, is a reflection of, or metaphor for, the condition of a species that lives in terms of meanings in a physical world devoid of intrinsic meaning but subject to causal law. The concept of adaptation when applied to human society must take account of meaning as well as cause and of the complex dynamic of their relationship.

It could, perhaps, be argued that all organisms behave in terms of meanings, but it is obvious that meaning must be implicated in unique ways in the adaptive organization of a species whose constituent groups not only conduct themselves in accordance with meanings, but must themselves construct those meanings. My earlier attempts (1963, 1968, 1971b) to deal with the place of meaning in adaptive structure by proposing that "cognized" as well as "operational" models are requisite to analyses of the ecological relations of human groups were inadequate on several grounds. In a more recent essay ("On Cognized Models," in this volume) I have tried to rectify some of the earlier problems, among which was too great a readiness to take the relationship of meaning to biology to be, simply, instrumental and contingent, instrumental in that understandings could be taken to be parts of the survival mechanisms of organisms and populations of organisms, and not themselves the objects of homeostatic processes. Relations of contingency take a little more spelling out in this context.

I have suggested that the proper goal of adaptive systems is merely to persist, but have said nothing about what persistence entails. We may be reminded here that the term "adaptation" is biological in origin and that the cultural systems with which we are concerned are founded upon living organisms. Cultural systems are living systems, and it is obvious that no living system (cultural or otherwise) could persist if the population of organisms realizing it did not persist. No particular convention is indispensable to the persistence of any human social system, but human organisms, in contrast, are obviously indispensable to the persistence of all such systems and, of course, the maintenance of ecosystemic function is indispensable to the survival and well-being of humans.

We note here that contingency may be regarded as another dimension of the hierarchical structure of adaptive systems. The cultural is ultimately contingent upon the organic, but consideration of relations of contingency leads beyond dimensions of hierarchy to consideration of the shape, as it were, of hierarchy itself; "the organic" is, of course, realized in individuals, and, in the end, contingency turns the adaptive hierarchies of human societies back upon themselves. They become circular. That is, although humans are subordinate to the regulatory structures of the societies in which they participate, their persistence is the *sine qua non* of the persistence of those societies. The highest and lowest levels of the hierarchy thus meet in the individual.

To say, however, that persistence is nothing if not biological is not to say that it is only biological. We have already noted that in the most general terms, cybernetic and other self-regulating mechanisms can be understood to operate in a manner that preserves the truth value of propositions concerning the systems in which they occur in the face of perturbations tending to falsify them (Bateson 1972). Although the effect of such mechanisms may be, and often is, the regulation of matter and energy processes, they operate in terms of information in a broad sense, including meanings. Whether or not we wish to argue that meanings are guiding for all creatures, there are special problems for humans. The "truths" maintained in organic processes are, in large measure, genetically established, and no doubt correspond closely to organic requisites. The same may be asserted, to a greater or lesser degree, for the behavioral and social processes of infrahuman species. Humans, however, must construct the meanings they maintain, and considerable disparity may develop between those meanings on the one hand and, on the other, the organic requisites of individuals and the requirements of the ecosystems in which they participate. We shall discuss such disparities later in the course of discussing maladaptive forms. Here I shall merely reiterate two obvious points. First, adaptive systems must maintain meanings as well as organic function because the self-regulatory processes upon which organic function depends (and is in some degree ordered) operate in terms of information and meaning. The relationship, in fact, between meaning and information on the one hand, and matter and energy on the other, is so intimate and interdependent that it is an error to take either to be ultimate. And just as the organic is realized in individuals, so are the processes of meaning and information. Although symbols and other forms of collective representation may be the vehicles of meaning, *meaningfulness* is *experienced,* and experience has its locus in individuals. The hierarchical structure of adaptive systems turns back upon itself, or is circular with respect to meaning as well as, and partially as corollary of, the circularity following from contingency relations. In the conjunction of the highest and lowest levels of the hierarchy in the individual, I have argued elsewhere (see "Sanctity and Lies in Evolution" in this volume), the ambitions of separate men may be subordinated to common interest *while, at the same time,* the operations of societies are reviewed and tempered by the psychic and physical needs of the humans constituting them.

Second, and also obvious, disagreements between the meanings maintained by a society and the requisites, organic, populational, and ecosystemic, of its persistence may be likely to develop in all human societies not only because of the opportunity and need to invent meanings but also because the increased information processing capacity provided by language increases opportunities for error. The likelihood of such disparities may, furthermore, increase in the course of cultural evolution because, among other things, cultural evolution produces, as a concomitant of social differentiation, what are called "special interests." In orderly adaptive structures, however, the meanings maintained are not in conflict with the persistence of organic and ecosystemic processes. This does not mean that biological variables are explicitly denominated as ultimate. They never seem to be in the religious systems of living societies, and it would probably be adaptively ineffective for them to be thus elevated. I have already argued that sacred postulates, themselves specifying nothing, appropriately occupy the status of ultimate. The implication of my argument is that the maintenance of organic and ecosystemic function is intrinsic to orderly adaptive structure, to a certain ordering of processual and systemic components with respect to time, specificity, reversibility, sanctity, value, contingency, and meaning.

At the beginning of this essay I associated systemic homeostasis with the maintenance of sets of vital variables within ranges of viability, but immediately noted that difficulties attend such a conception. As far as biological variables are concerned, given the counter-intuitive nature of complex systems, it is difficult or impossible to assess the long-run effects of any aspect of culture on particular biological variables. For a second, it does not seem possible to specify any particular feature of biological structure or function that will always contribute to survival chances (Slobodkin and Rapoport 1974). Although particular variables are, and must be, maintained within ranges of viability at particular times, these ranges, and even the systemic components of which they are states, may be changed by evolution. As there may be no particular biological variables that under all circumstances must be maintained, neither are there specific meanings that must always and everywhere be taken as true. Adaptiveness, therefore, is not to be identified with specific variables, but with a *general,* or *systemic, homeostasis* that is *structural* in nature. *If orderly adaptive structure is maintained, organic function, meaning, and meaningfulness will be maintained.* This is to propose that the *formal* or *structural* characteristics of adaptive processes have *substantive* implications. This proposal will become clearer in the course of a discussion of maladaptive forms, particularly that called "usurpation."

V

If adaptive processes are those tending to maintain homeostasis in the face of perturbation, maladaptations are factors internal to systems interfering with their homeostatic responses. They reduce the likelihood of a system's persistence, not so much by subjecting the system to stress as by impeding its ability to respond effectively to stress. Maladaptations are not to be confused with exogenous stressors or perturbing factors, although they themselves can, of course, produce stress. This view of maladaptation is similar to the concept of disease (dis-ease) proposed by Young and Rowley (1967).

If the maintenance of homeostasis depends upon hierarchically ordered sequences of responses, and the mobilization and ordering of such responses depends upon a structure of a characteristic sort, then it should be possible to describe or define maladaptation, or maladaptations, structurally. Maladaptations may be conceived as anomalies in the hierarchical and self-regulatory features we have taken to be characteristic of orderly adaptive structure. That is, relations along the several dimensions of adaptive order—response time, duration, reversibility, specificity, sanctity, meaning, value—can become disordered, producing interlevel contradictions or conflicts. These disorders are what I mean the term "maladaptation" to designate. Although maladaptation may be conceived in structural terms, these structural anomalies have material consequences that we recognize as substantive problems—the ecological problem, the energy problem, the problems of oppression and imperialism. We may now turn briefly to a few of the many possible maladaptive forms.

The simplest of these forms are such cybernetic difficulties as impedances to the detection of changes in the states of variables; the delay, loss, or distortion of information transmitted to system regulators; and the inability of regulators to interpret the signals they receive. These structural problems may produce inappropriate responses, or errors in scale of response, like "too little, too late." These difficulties are exacerbated by increased size. For instance, the more nodes through which information must pass, the more subject it is to distortion or loss. Thus, the higher the administrator, the less accurate and adequate his information is likely to be, and the more likely the production of an erroneous or inappropriate regulatory response.

The likelihood of hierarchical anomaly also increases with scale. For instance, the deeper the regulatory hierarchy, the more likely are time aberrations. Whereas excessive lag may be a problem, so may be *premature responses* of high-order regulators, for if they constantly override those of lower order they will destroy them, throwing additional burdens on themselves, perhaps to the point of overload and breakdown. Moreover, premature responses of higher-order regulators may well be *over-responses*—"too much too soon," resulting in more or less irreversible changes when less drastic adjustments would not only have been sufficient but conservative of long-term flexibility. The contribution of high-energy technology to premature override and over-response is patent. We may note that premature override is facilitated by high-speed communication, a product of high-energy technology, and magnitude of response is freed by high-energy technology from the limitations set by the energy available from local and contemporary biological processes.

Several other related trends seem to flow from the increased scale of social and economic organization. First, there is what may be called *over-segregation.* Whole regions or even countries come to specialize in one crop or product. But increasing regional specialization is usually, if not always, accompanied by decreased ecological stability. High-yield varieties of staples planted in monocrop fields are in themselves delicate; moreover, their successful growth depends upon fuel, machinery, and chemicals delivered from great distances through extensive and complicated networks. Remote as well as nearby difficulties can thus disrupt agriculture anywhere. With the loss of local self-sufficiency that follows from geographical specialization, there is also loss of local regulatory autonomy. The homeostatic capacity lost from local systems is not adequately replaced by increasingly remote centralized regulators responding to increasingly aggregated and simplified variables, like monetary values, through operations increasingly subject to cybernetic impedances and time aberrations. Moreover, the responses of distant regulators are often to factors extraneous to some of the local systems affected by them. For instance, changes in oil prices threaten to cause increased starvation in India by reducing the production of Japanese fertilizer upon which Indian agriculture in some degree depends. We recognize here yet another maladaptive form which has elsewhere been called *hyper-coherence* (Flannery 1972; Rappaport 1969, 1967a, 1977a). The coherence of the world system increases to dangerous levels as the self-sufficiency of local systems is reduced and their autonomy destroyed and replaced by more centralized agencies whose operations are inadequate to the regulation of the complex systems over which they preside.

Oversegregation and *overcentralization* taken together are complementary aspects of a more general structural anomaly which may be called the *hierarchical maldistribution of organization.* An increasingly complex world organization is based upon decreasingly organized local, regional, and even national social and ecological systems. It seems doubtful that a worldwide human organization can elaborate itself indefinitely at the expense of its local infrastructures, and it may be suggested that the ability of the world system to withstand perturbation would be increased by returning to its local subsystems some of the autonomy and diversity they have lost, as China seems to be doing. This is not to advocate fracturing the world into smaller, autonomous self-sufficient systems, as undesirable as impossible, but to suggest that redistribution of organization among the levels of the world system would serve well the world system as a whole.

Another class of maladaptations combines with those discussed so far. The basic form has elsewhere been called *usurpation, escalation,* and *over-specification* (Flannery 1972; Rappaport 1969, 1976a, 1977a). I speak here of special-purpose subsystems coming to dominate the larger, general-purpose systems of which they are parts. When particular individuals become identified with special-purpose systems they tend to identify the special purposes of those subsystems with their own general purposes; that is, with their own survival and betterment. Their own general purposes become highly specialized, and they attempt to promote these purposes to positions of predominance in the larger systems of which they are parts. As they become increasingly powerful, they are increasingly able to succeed. Needless to say, power is not equally distributed among the various components of highly differentiated "developed" societies such as our own, but is, rather, concentrated in their industrial and financial sectors. These sectors are frequently able to dominate the agencies charged with regulating them, and the logical end is for the interests of groups of industrial firms, financial institutions, and related military establishments to come to dominate the societies of which they are merely specialized parts. This eventuality is nicely summed up in the phrase "What's good for General Motors is good for America." But no matter how public-spirited or benign General Motors might be, what is good for it cannot in the long run be good for America. For a society like the United States to commit itself to what may be good for one of its special-purpose subsystems, such as General Motors, or even the entire set of industries devoted to the manufacture, maintenance, and operation of automobiles, is for it to overspecify or narrow the range of conditions under which it can persist—that is, it reduces its evolutionary flexibility.

Loss of evolutionary flexibility is disguised by what seem to be the characteristics of progress, and is therefore difficult to discern. Other more obvious concomitants of the elevation of low-order goals and values to positions of predominance in higher-order systems may be related to loss of flexibility, but have other implications as well. First, as industrial subsystems become increasingly large and powerful, the quality or utility of their products, or both, are likely to deteriorate, for the subsystem's contribution to the society becomes less its product and more its mere operation, providing wages to some, profits to others, and a market for yet others. Arms, which are both expensive and immediately obsolete, and automobiles into which obsolescence is built, are ideal products, and there is nothing wrong with products that serve no useful purpose whatsoever. The product tends to become a by- or even waste-product of what might be called the "industrial metabolism" which is, ultimately, simply the operation of machines. Neither competition nor an independently established demand serves to regulate or limit "industrial metabolism" effectively because large industries are usually not very competitive and they can exercise considerable control over the demand to which they are supposed to be subject.

Second and more serious, with the escalation of low-order goals to dominating positions in society, it becomes increasingly possible for ancient and complex systems, particularly ecological systems, to be disrupted by ever smaller groups with ever more narrowly defined interests. For instance, there is some evidence to support the contention that certain fluorocarbons used in propellants in spray cans dispensing shaving cream, deodorants, and the like are destroying atmospheric ozone that shields life from lethal intensities of ultraviolet radiation. Yet these aerosols are still manufactured and sold. That the putative effects of these chemicals upon the atmosphere have not yet been "proven" hardly justifies their continued use, given the trivial nature of their advantages and the catastrophic nature of the risks their use may entail. We note in this and many other instances—the clear-cutting of forests in areas in which they are unlikely to regenerate, offshore oil drilling in unstable geological zones, the dumping of undegradable poisons into fresh waters—the violation of orderly time relations, relations of contingency, and relations between the instrumental and the fundamental. Short-run, narrow, and instrumental interests have usurped the places of, or subordinated, long-run, general, and fundamental needs and values. These instances suggest that the facilitation of disruption for the sake of narrowly defined special interests is not the whole of the ecological or indeed human problem following from the promotion of the low-order goals of industrialized subsystems to predominant positions in societies. The ultimate consequence is not merely that the short-run interests of a few powerful men or institutions come to prevail, but that the "interests" of machines—which even powerful men serve—become dominant. Needless to say, the interests of machines and organisms do not coincide. They do not have the same needs for pure air or water, and being blind and deaf, machines have no need for quiet or for landscapes that refresh the eye. Whereas organisms have need of uncounted numbers of subtle compounds, the needs of machines are few, simple, and voracious. It is in accordance with the logic of a world dominated by machines to rip the tops off complex systems like West Virginia and Colorado to extract a single substance, coal.

Usurpation is, in formal terms, to be regarded as an anomaly in the structure of values. It is an error of logical typing: short-term instrumental goals of high specificity are elevated to the status of enduring

fundamental principles. Their predominance becomes more encompassing than their specificity warrants and, as a consequence, regulation
comes to maintain the trivial at the possible expense of the necessary.
That is, under such circumstances it is likely that reference values—the
values around which the system equilibrates itself or, to put it differently,
the values the truth of which is cybernetically maintained—will be set
outside of goal ranges, the ranges of conditions under which the system
remains viable.

I have been emphasizing the material effects of this logical-moral-
adaptive aberration, having discussed elsewhere (in slightly different
terms) the dissolution of meaning and meaningfulness entailed by it (see
"On Cognized Models"). Two points should be made here in this regard,
however, First, to observe that as a consequence of this anomaly the
trivial is maintained at the expense of the necessary or fundamental is not
only to point to the preservation of spray cans at the expense of atmospheric ozone, but to the preservation of interests at the expense of
principles. It is as much a statement about the processes of meaning as it
is about the state of the biosphere.

Finally, there is the degradation of sanctity itself. As the material goals
of lower-order systems usurp the places properly belonging to values of
greater generality, they may lay claim to their sanctity. What is highly
sanctified is resistant to change, and to oversanctify the specific and
material is to reduce adaptive flexibility. It is of interest that the theologian Paul Tillich (1957: 11) called the absolutizing of the relative and the
relativizing of the absolute "idolatry" and took it to be an evil. I am
proosing that it is maladaptive, but it may be that in this instance, at least,
the two coin~ide. The social effects of what we, following Tillich, may call
"idolatry" are, of course, not limited to the reduction of adaptive flexibility. At least as serious is the degradation of basic values, not usually
through their explicit replacement by those of lower order, but by their
conflation with them. The pursuit of "happiness," a term which in the
eighteenth century seems to have denoted felicity, becomes the pursuit
of pleasure and the accumulation of goods. Liberty becomes little more
than the right to serve oneself. Materialism and selfishness become
honored as highest ideals. We hardly need dwell upon the unacceptable
demands that the sanctification of these values makes upon undeveloped
countries and upon ecosystems, for they are obvious.

VI

Earlier I suggested that what we take to be substantive problems—
ecological problems, problems of poverty, oppression, imperialism, and
others that we might name—are social and material consequences of

structural anomaly. It may now be suggested, however, that structural anomaly and material problems stand in relationships of mutual causation. Moreover, the brief account I have offered of maladaptive forms and of some of the substantive difficulties associated with them implies that maladaptive trends are nourished by, or may even inhere in, cultural evolution itself. In the world of events cause is seldom simple, and I can do no more, at the end, than to discuss, briefly and tentatively, a few of the evolutionary advances that seem to have contributed both to the structural deformities I have called maladaptations and to the material problems associated with them.

Some suggestions have already been made about increases in the amounts of energy captured. It is important to keep in mind, however, that energy capture has sometimes been taken to be the metric of cultural evolution. Over a quarter of a century ago, Leslie White, following Ostwald, proclaimed what he called "The Basic Law of Cultural Evolution" as follows:

Other factors remaining constant, culture evolves as the amount of energy harnessed per capita per year is increased, or as the efficiency of the instrumental means of putting energy to work is increased. [1949: 368-369]

There can be no denying the first clause of this formulation. Large technologically developed states appearing late in history surely do harness more energy per capita per day or year than do the small "primitive" societies which appeared earlier. One recent estimate would place daily energy consumption in the contemporary United States at 230,000 kilocalories, and in hunting and gathering societies as 2,000-3,000 (Cook 1971).

The contemporary United States has a population of 200,000,000 people; the bushman bands seldom include more than a score or two of people; and increases in energy capture have made possible much larger and more sedentary social systems. But some, if not all, of the maladaptive trends I have suggested here are related to increased scale. Moreover, high-energy technology itself frees those operating in local ecosystems from the limits imposed upon them by the need to derive energy from the contemporary biological processes of those systems. Gasoline, pipelines, bulldozers, high-voltage electrical transmission permit virtually unlimited amounts of energy to be focused upon very small systems, and the ecological disruption of those systems can be tolerated—at least for a time—because of the increased specialization of other local systems. I have argued, however, that in the long run the increasing specialization of larger and larger regions—itself made possible by a technology that provides means for moving even bulky commodities long distances inexpensively, and for transmitting information long distances instantaneously—is unstable.

The increasing specialization of increasingly large geographical regions is simply one aspect of increasing internal differentiation of social systems. Progressive segregation and progressive centralization were, of course, encouraged by the emergence of plant and animal cultivation ten thousand or so years ago, for plant and animal cultivation provided significant opportunities for full-time division of labor. By 4000 B.C., if not earlier, subsistence, craft, religious, and administrative specialization was well developed. But the emergence of high-energy technology based upon fossil fuels has accelerated and exaggerated this trend and the maladaptations associated with it. These include not only oversegregation and overcentralization, with their concomitants of ecological instability and hypercoherence; high-energy technology is differentially distributed among the subsystems of societies and it permits or encourages the promotion of the special purposes of the more powerful to positions of greater dominance in systems of higher order than their degree of specialization warrants.

High-energy technology is, of course, not alone in impelling maladaptive trends. All-purpose money has also played a part. In addition to its obvious contribution to the concentration of real wealth and regulatory prerogative, it flows through virtually all barriers, increasing the coherence of the world system enormously. Its ability to penetrate whatever barriers may have protected previously autonomous systems against outside disruption rests upon its most peculiar and interesting property: it annihilates distinctions. It tends to dissolve the differences between all things by providing a simple metric against which virtually all things can be assessed, and in terms of which decisions concerning them can be made. But the world upon which this metric is imposed is not as simple as this metric. Living systems—plants, animals, societies, ecosystems—are very diverse and each requires a great variety of particular materials to remain healthy. Monetization, however, forces the great ranges of unique and distinct materials and processes that together sustain or even constitute life into an arbitrary and specious equivalence and decisions informed by these terms are likely to simplify, that is, to degrade and to disrupt the ecological systems in which they are effective. Needless to say the application of large amounts of mindless energy under the guidance of the simplified or even simple-minded and often selfish considerations that all-purpose money makes virtually omnipotent and, when united with a capitalist ideology, even sacred, is in its nature stupid, brutal, and almost bound to be destructive.

With increases in the amounts of energy harnessed, with increases in the internal differentiation of social systems, with the monetization of even larger portions of life, the contradiction between the direction of cultural evolution on the one hand and the maintenance of living processes, both meaningful and material, has become increasingly profound. We are led to ask whether civilization, the elaborate stage of culture with which are associated money and banking, high-energy technology, and social stratification and specialization, is not maladaptive. It is, after all, in civilized societies that we can observe most clearly oversegregation, overcentralization, oversanctification, hypercoherence, the domination of higher- by lower-order systems, and the destruction of ecosystems. Civilization has emerged only recently—in the past six thousand or so years—and it may yet prove to be an unsuccessful experiment.

What are taken to be evolutionary advances institutionalize new contradictions and set new problems as they solve or resolve older problems or overcome earlier limitations, and social systems may eventually become paralyzed by accumulating structural anomalies at the same time that they are increasingly perturbed by mounting substantive difficulties. It may be recalled that both Bateson and Slobodkin have argued that it is good evolutionary strategy for evolving systems to change no more than persistence requires, but increasing systemic deformity may require radical correction. Revolution has historically been an ultimate corrective response of systems so afflicted by maladaptation as to be unable to respond homeostatically to the events continually perturbing them. Flannery has argued that the radical correction of structural anomaly has been an important factor in the evolution of civilization (1972), and inquiry into the dynamic relationship among structural anomaly, substantive problem, and profound corrective processes is, in other terms, central to the thought of Marx.

Bateson (1972), however, has located the problem at a level that may be beyond the reach of revolutionary correction—in the characteristics of human intelligence. He argues that purposefulness is the dominant characteristic of human reason, a plausible suggestion, for purposefulness, encompassing both foresight and concentration, must have been strongly selected for during man's two or three million years on earth (and even earlier among man's prehuman forebears and other animals). But, located in the conscious minds of individuals and serving in the first instance their separate survivals, purposefulness must incline toward self-interest or even selfishness. (Indeed the philosopher Bergson in recognizing this problem took religion to be society's defense against the "dissolving power" of the human mind.)

That some human purposes are selfish cannot be gainsaid. But Bateson suggests that the problem of purposefulness is more profound. Purposefulness, he argues, has a linear structure. A man at point A with goal D takes actions B and C, and with the achievement of D considers the process to be completed. Thus, the structure of purposeful action is linear: A → B → C → D. But the world is not constructed in linear fashion. We have already discussed the circular structure of cybernetic, that is, self-correcting, systems, and it is well known that ecosystems are roughly circular in plan, with materials being cycled and recycled through the soil, the air, and organisms of many species. Moreover, the circularity of both cybernetic and ecosystemic structure blurs the distinction between cause and effect, or rather suggests to us that simple linear notions of causality, which lead us to think of actors, objects upon which they act, and the transformation of such objects, are inadequate, for purposeful behavior seldom affects only a single object, here designated D, but usually many other objects as well, often in complex and ramifying ways. Among those being affected in unforeseen and possibly unpleasant ways may be the actor himself.

It may be suggested, however, that linear, purposeful thought is adequate to the needs of simple hunters and gatherers, and not very destructive to the ecological systems in which they live, because both the scope and power of their activities are limited. It is when linear thought comes to guide the operations of an increasingly powerful technology over domains of ever increasing scope that disruption may become inevitable.

Bateson argues that the problem is not only to make men aware of the ramifying and circular structure of the universe, but to make the imperatives of this structure more compelling than their own linearly defined goals. He believes that this requires that more of their minds than their conscious reason be engaged. It is also necessary to engage the non-discursive aspects of their processes of comprehension, and he suggests that this is achieved through art and religion. I would agree, and elsewhere in this volume ("Sanctity and Lies in Evolution") I discuss the place of religious experience in adaptive structure.

To argue that more than reason may be required to maintain adaptive structure in human social systems, or to restore adaptiveness to systems beset by maladaptations, is not to argue for the banishment of reason nor for its replacement by blind commitment or mystic insight. Conscious reason has entered into the evolutionary process, cannot be ignored, and should, obviously, be put to the task of rectifying adaptive difficulties. An apparent paradox may be that attempts to solve problems of adaptation are likely to cause further problems, perhaps because "problem solving" is in its nature linear. Moreover, the systems in which men participate are so complex that we cannot now, and probably never shall be able to, analyze them in sufficient detail to predict with precision the outcome of many of our own actions within them. We must, therefore, investigate the possibilities for developing theories of action that, although based upon incomplete knowledge, will permit us to participate in systems without destroying them and ourselves along with them. This task is not hopeless. To say that the complexity of living systems is so great as to confound prediction is not to say that we cannot apprehend the salient characteristics of their structures.

The account of adaptive structure and of maladaptation offered here is abbreviated, tentative, and, I am certain, erroneous in many respects. It does, however, represent an attempt to relate structure and process, the historical and the changeless, meaning and cause within an *"ordre des ordres"* in a manner permitting the identification of disorder as well as of order. I offer it for discussion, but it would be well to make explicit, although it is probably obvious, that it has not been my intention to develop a descriptive model the verisimilitude of which might be substantiated by even a single case. It has been, rather, to propose a *normative* model no instances of which exist, but in terms of which historical systems may be assessed and their difficulties comprehended (Rappaport 1977b).

There has recently been much concern, and rightly so, about the relationship of anthropology to the peoples traditionally constituting its most immediate and obvious subject matter. Awareness of the services anthropology, or anthropologists, have rendered to colonialism is growing and so is sophistication concerning the dangers of applied anthropology. Less thought has been given to the relationship of anthropology to the society that has spawned it and may constitute its less apparent but ultimate subject matter. It may be suggested, however, that in its very existence anthropology constitutes a tacit critique of that society. Criticism implies correction, but our culture is without an adequate theory of correction. What is called "problem-solving" is problematic, making as many problems as it solves, and revolutions are destructive, often institutionalizing conventions as maladaptive as those they overthrow. The suggestions concerning adaptive structure offered here may, perhaps, make a contribution to a theory of correction, a theory, that is, for restoring adaptiveness to systems vexed by maladaptation. Whether or not these suggestions have such a value, anthropology, I think, has much to offer to the development of such a theory and, possibly, to its application to public affairs. If this seems presumptuous and dangerous we should keep in mind that social policy is, at present, frequently informed by views of the world, its ills, and ways to cure its ills provided by other, narrower disciplines no better founded and considerably less humane than our own.

REFERENCES CITED

Bateson, Gregory
    1963   The role of somatic change in evolution. *Evolution* 17:529-539.
    1972   Effects of conscious purpose on human adaptation. In *Steps to an ecology of mind.* New York: Ballantine.
Brookfield, H., and P. Brown
    1963   *Struggle for land: agriculture and group territories among the Chimbu of the New Guinea Highlands.* Melbourne: Oxford University Press.
Cook, Earl
    1971   The flow of energy in an industrial society. *Scientific American,* Sept.
Flannery, Kent
    1972   The cultural evolution of civilizations. *Annual Review of Ecology and Systematics* 3:399-426.
Frisancho, Roberto
    1975   Functional adaptation to high altitude hypoxia. *Science* 187:313-319.
Hockett, C. F., and R. Ascher
    1964   The human revolution. *Current Anthropology* 5:135-168.
Kalmus, Hans
    1966   Control hierarchies. in *Regulation and control of living systems,* ed. H. Kalmus. New York: Wiley.
Meggitt, Mervyn
    1965   *The lineage system of the Mae-Enga of New Guinea.* Edinburgh: Oliver & Boyd.
Miller, James
    1965a   Living systems: basic concepts. *Behavioral Science* 10:193-257.
    1965b   Living systems: structure and process. *Behavioral Science* 10:337-379.
Ortiz, Alphonso
    1969   *The Tewa World: space, time, being and becoming in a Pueblo society.* Chicago: University of Chicago Press.
Pattee, H. H., ed.
    1973   *Hierarchy theory.* New York: Braziller, International Library of Systems Theory and Philosophy.
Piaget, Jean
    1971   *Structuralism.* London: Routledge and Kegan Paul.
Rappaport, R. A.
    1963   Aspects of man's influence upon island ecosystems: alteration and control. In *Man's place in the island ecosystem,* ed. F. R. Fosberg, pp. 155-174. Honolulu: Bishop Museum Press.
    1968   *Pigs for the ancestors.* New Haven: Yale University Press.
    1969   Sanctity and adaptation. *Io* 7(1970):46-71. (Paper prepared for Wenner-Gren Conference on the Moral and Aesthetic Structure of Human Adaptation, 1969).
    1971a   The sacred in human evolution. *Annual Review of Ecology and Systematics* 2:23-44.
    1971b   Nature, culture, and ecological anthropology. In *Man, culture, and society,* rev. ed., ed. H. Shapiro, pp. 237-268. New York: Oxford University Press.
    1976a   Adaptation and maladaptation in social systems. In *The ethical basis of economic freedom,* ed. Ivan Hill, pp. 39-82. Chapel Hill, N.C.: American Viewpoint.

(Rappaport, R. A.)

1976b Liturgies and lies. *International Yearbook for the Sociology of Knowledge and Religion* 10:75–104.

1977a Maladaptation in social systems. In *Evolution in social systems,* ed. J. Friedman and M. Rowlands. London: Duckworth.

1977b Normative models of adaptive process: a response to Anne Whyte. In *Evolution in social systems,* ed. J. Friedman and M. Rowlands. London: Duckworth.

Romer, Alfred S.

1954 *Man and the vertebrates.* London: Penguin. First published 1933.

Sahlins, Marshall

1961 The segmentary lineage: an organization of predatory expansion. *American Anthropologist* 63:322–345.

1969 Economic anthropology and anthropological economics. *Social Science Information* 8:13–33.

Sahlins, Marshall, and E. Service

1960 *Evolution and culture.* Ann Arbor: University of Michigan Press.

Simon, Herbert

1969 *The Sciences of the artificial.* Cambridge: MIT Press.

Slobodkin, L.

1968 Toward a predictive theory of evolution. In *Population biology and evolution,* ed. R. Lewontin. Syracuse, N.Y.: Syracuse University Press.

Slobodkin, L., and A. Rapoport

1974 An optimal strategy of evolution. *Quarterly Review of Biology* 49:181–200.

Thomas, Lewis

1974 *The lives of a cell.* New York: Viking Press.

Tillich, Paul

1957 *The dynamics of faith.* New York: Harper & Row.

Van Baal, J.

1971 *Symbols for communication.* Assen: Van Goracum & Co.

Vayda, A. P. and B. McKay

1975 New directions in ecology and ecological anthropology. *Annual Review of Anthropology* 4:293–306.

White, Leslie

1949 *The science of culture.* New York: Grove Press.

Young, I. J., and W. F. Rowley

1967 The logic of disease. *International Journal of Neuropsychiatry.*

The Obvious Aspects

of Ritual

I

This essay is not about the symbols of which human rituals are made, nor yet about the entities, ideas, or processes—physical, psychic, social, natural, or cosmic—that these symbols may represent. It is concerned with the obvious rather than the hidden aspects of ritual, those of its features that, being most apparent, lead us to identify events as instances of ritual.

Some difficulties beset presentation. For one thing, it is necessary to state the obvious—that which is immediately apparent and generally accepted—before discussing it, and it will be necessary, for the sake of clarity and continuity, to connect what I take to be non-obvious observations about the obvious with remarks that may themselves be obvious. Moreover, the argument is in part concerned with what seems to be logically necessary. When arguments are based upon logical necessity rather than empirical demonstration social scientists are inclined to take them to be trivial or tautologous. One of the points that I shall try to make, however, is that there is at the heart of ritual a relationship that has certain logically necessary entailments. Certain meanings and effects are intrinsic to the very structure of ritual, and ritual thus may impose, or seem to impose, logical necessity upon the vagrant affairs of the world. This may sound like a functional observation. In fact it is not, and it may be well to make clear at the outset that the argument developed in this

This essay expands an earlier version, published in *Cambridge Anthropology* 2(1):3-69, 1974.

essay is formal- rather than final-causal in nature. Because I have discussed this distinction in some detail in "Ecology, Adaptation, and the Ills of Functionalism" (in this volume), it will suffice to note here that functional formulations, which are properly system-specific, account for "items" in respect of the contributions they make to the systems of which they are elements. Here, however, I shall not be concerned with specific contributions rituals make to the systems in which they occur but with entailments of the *ritual form* wherever it appears.

If an expedition into the obvious calls for justification, it may be suggested that in their eagerness to plumb ritual's dark symbolic or functional depths, to find in ritual more than meets the eye, anthropologists have, perhaps increasingly, tended to overlook ritual's surface, that which does meet the eye. Yet it is on its surfaces, in its form, that we may discern whatever may be peculiar to ritual. It is in its depths that ritual meets other symbolic forms—myth, poetry, graphic art, architecture. Indeed, it is in respect to its symbolic content that ritual is *least* distinctive. It is in respect to its symbolism that myth and ritual are "one and the same," to recall Leach's famous dictum of a quarter-century ago (1954: 13ff.), an identity more recently expressed by La Fontaine in the introduction to a volume of essays on the interpretation of ritual. "In this book ritual actions are seen as exemplifying in another medium the cultural values that find expression in . . . statements which we call beliefs and which are elaborated in narratives or myths" (1972: xvii).

It would be well to make clear that I am raising no objections whatsoever to symbolic analyses of rituals as a class or to functional and adaptive analyses of ritual as a class. Both surely may increase our understanding of the world. I am only asserting that to view ritual as simply a way to fulfill certain functions that may as well or better be fulfilled by other means, or as an alternative symbolic medium for expressing what may just as well—or perhaps better—be expressed in other ways is, obviously, to ignore that which is distinctive of ritual itself. Moreover, it becomes apparent through consideration of ritual's form that ritual is not simply an alternative way to express certain things, but that certain things can be expressed only in ritual. This is to reiterate that certain meanings and effects are intrinsic to the ritual form, which is further to suggest that ritual is without equivalents or even alternatives. This would account for its widespread occurrence and remarkable persistence. I do not wish to press this point and will only assert that that which can be expressed only in ritual is not trivial. It is, I think, crucial, and because of it I take ritual to be *the* basic social act. I will argue, in fact, that social contract, morality, the concept of the sacred, the notion of the divine, and even a paradigm of creation are intrinsic to ritual's structure.

It should be clear that the phrase "the structure of ritual" refers here to relations among ritual's general features or components and not to relations among the symbols that may appear in rituals, for I have contrasted the depth of ritual with ritual's surfaces, those of its obvious, distinctive features that ae immediately available to the senses. In contrast to its depths, in which mutually dependent symbols propitiate the obscure understanding of the faithful or await the exegesis of holy man or anthropologist, the surfaces of ritual are *not* symbolic, or at least not entirely so. Indeed, that ritual is not entirely symbolic seems to me to be one of its most interesting and important characteristics, for through ritual some of the embarrassments and difficulties of symbolic communication are overcome.

There is more to be said about the structure of ritual than that social contract and morality are intrinsic to it, and that it is not altogether symbolic, of course, and I shall proceed as follows: First, I must make explicit what I take to be ritual's obvious features. This will lead to a discussion of the two classes of message expressed in ritual and of the nonsymbolic way in which one of these classes may be transmitted. Next, the representation of analogical processes by digital signals will be noted, and then we shall approach what J. L. Austin (1962) would call the "performativeness" of ritual. This will lead to what I take to be distinctive of ritual, namely the social contract and morality intrinsic to its structure. The fact that rituals generally include physical acts as well as words will be considered, and I shall suggest that in including both word and act ritual may hold within itself a paradigm of creation. Some suggestions concerning liturgical orders will then be advanced, and it will be further suggested that the concept of the sacred may emerge from ritual's structure. Finally, the numinous emotions generated in some rituals will be discussed briefly, and some suggestions will be offered concerning possible grounds in ritual for the notion of the divine.

II

I take ritual to be a form or structure, defining it as the performance of more or less invariant sequences of formal acts and utterances not encoded by the performers. I shall be concerned to unpack the implications of this definition, noting first that no single feature of ritual is peculiar to it. It is in the conjunction of its features that it is unique. It is, nevertheless, convenient to consider its simple features at the beginning. The unique implications of their concatenation will emerge later.

First there is formality. Formality is an obvious aspect of all rituals: both observers and actors identify acts as ritual in part by their formality. Rituals tend to be stylized, repetitive, stereotyped, often but not always decorous, and they also tend to occur at special places and at times fixed by the clock, calendar, or specified circumstances.

There are problems in distinguishing some events from others by the criterion of formality because events are not easily discriminated into those that are formal and those that are not. There is, as Roger Abrahams (1973) has pointed out, a continuum of behavioral formality from (*a*) the formal words and gestures that intersperse ordinary conversation and acts, through (*b*) that of the "everyday ceremoniousness" of greeting behavior and formal expressions of deference and demeanor, through (*c*) the rather invariant procedures of, say, the courtroom within which the variant substance of litigation is contained, and through which it is presented in orderly fashion, through, next, (*d*) such events as coronations, in which the invariant aspects of the event begin to predominate over the variant, to, finally, (*e*) highly invariant events, like those of certain religious liturgies in which almost all of the performance is specified, and opportunities for variation are both few and narrowly defined.

Two points are to be noted. First, invariance emerges out of, or is an aspect of, increasing formality. Second, it may be useful to make a distinction between *ritual,* the formal, stereotyped *aspect* of all events, and *rituals,* relatively invariant *events* dominated by formality. Be this as it may, there is little value in separating rituals from other events by imposing an arbitrary discontinuity upon the continuum of formality at any particular point. I will simply note that the phenomena with which this essay is largely concerned lie toward the more formal, less variant end of the continuum. We shall be mainly concerned with rituals sufficiently elaborate to include what may be called "liturgical orders," more or less invariant sequences of formal acts and utterances repeated in specified contexts. The term "liturgical order" will, however, be extended here to include not only the fixed sequences of words and acts providing form to individual ritual events, but also, following Van Gennep (1909), to the fixed sequences of rituals that lead men around circles of seasons, along the straight paths that depart from birth and arrive at death, through the alterations of war and peace or along the dream tracks that cross Australian deserts.

While ritual is characterized by its formality, all that is formal, stereotyped, repetitive, or decorous is not ritual. Certain decorative art is similarly formal, and so are many buildings. It is of importance to recognize, although it seems banal, that performance as well as formality is necessary to ritual. Performance is the second *sine qua non* of ritual, for if there is no performance there is no ritual. This is not simply to say that a ritual is not a book or myth or television set, but to emphasize that performance is not merely a way to express something, but is itself an aspect of that which it is expressing.

Of course, not all formal performance is ritual. Ordinary usage would not so have it, and there is no analytic advantage here in violating ordinary usage. For instance, although they bear some resemblance to each other, ritual and drama, at least in their polar forms, are best distinguished. For one thing, dramas have audiences, rituals have congregations. An audience watches a drama, a congregation participates in a ritual. This participation often if not always requires more than the entertainment of a certain attitude. Participation is frequently active, and is likely to require of the members of a congregation that they sing, dance, stand, kneel, or respond in litanies at particular times. For another thing, those who act in drama are "only acting," which is precisely to say that they are not acting in earnest, and it is perhaps significant that drama's synonym in English is "play." Ritual in contrast, is in earnest, even when it is playful, entertaining, blasphemous, humorous, or ludicrous.

To say that ritual is in earnest is not to say that the formal action of ritual is instrumental in any ordinary physical sense. Indeed, another of ritual's criterial attributes—at least one proposed by many people—is that it is not. There seem to be two main lines of thought concerning this.

The first, clearly enunciated by Leach long ago (1954: 12ff.), implies the distinction already made between ritual and rituals. Ritual in this view is the non-instrumental aspect or component of events that may also include an instrumental component, "technique." Ritual is that frill or decoration that communicates something about the performance or the performer.

The other general view, which initially appears to be more different from the first than it actually is, would hold that ritual not only communicates something but is taken by those performing it to be "doing something" as well. There would seem to be support for this position from some of the words designating ritual in various languages. The Greek "dromenon" means "thing done," "liturgy" comes from the Greek for "public work," the English term "service" connotes more than talk; the Tewa Indians (Ortiz 1969: 98ff.), as well as the Tikopians (Firth 1940) refer to some rituals as "spirit work." Howver, that which is done by ritual is not done by operating with matter and energy on matter and energy in accordance with the laws of physics, chemistry, or biology. The efficacy of ritual derives, to use a term that Fortes (1966) favors in a rather general way, from "the occult." The occult differs from "the patent" in that the patent can be known in the last resort by sensory experience, and it conforms to the regularities of material cause. The occult cannot be so known and does not so conform. Goody (1961) similarly characterizes ritual as "a category of standardized behaviour (custom) in which the relationship between means and ends is not intrinsic."

We have neither the time nor the need to examine in any detail either what anthropologists claim to be folk theories of the basis of occult efficacy, or what they claim to be the occult's foundation "in reality." Suffice it to say that one large and heterogeneous set of analytic theories would derive the occult from the affective force and persuasiveness of ritual performance, and we may note in passing that some students would take some sort of systematic relationship to the emotions to be an aspect of virtually all ritual. Other analytic theories would see the occult to be founded upon certain characteristics of language, a view that accords with the widespread, almost universal belief in the magical power of words (Tambiah 1968). The two views are neither mutually exclusive nor exhaustive. The point that is of importance here is that if the efficacy of liturgical rituals rests in whole or in part upon words (both in native theory and in the theory of the anthropologist) then the distinction between ritual as communication and as efficacious action breaks down. This is not to claim that all rituals, even those for which efficacy is claimed, are deemed to possess occult efficacy, but simply to take efficacious ritual to be a subclass of the larger class, ritual, itself one of many modes of communication. Leach stated—or perhaps overstated—this or a similar point when he asserted that the distinction between communication behavior and behavior potent in terms of cultural convention is trivial (1966).

It may be objected that a view of ritual as communication comes up against the fact that many rituals are conducted in solitude. But the subjective experience of, say, private prayer, is one of communication. Moreover, given the extent to which in solitary rituals various parts of the psyche may be brought in touch with each other it is reasonable to take ritual to be auto-communicative as well as allo-communicative (Wallace 1966: 237ff.). Auto-communication is important even in public rituals. In fact, the transmitters of ritual messages are often, if not always, their most significant receivers.

Although we may recognize that ritual, even efficacious ritual, is a mode of communication, we must also sympathize with the concern that Fortes expressed when he observed that "it is but a short step from the notion of ritual as communication to the non-existence of ritual *per se*" (1966). It is simply not enough to say that ritual is a mode of communication. But to say that ritual is a mode of communication is surely not to say that it is interchangeable with other modes of communication nor, necessarily, to denigrate its uniqueness. It is, rather, to accept an expanded notion of communication, one that includes the achievement of effects through the transmission of information rather than through the application of matter and energy. Communication, this is to say, not only includes "saying," but certain sorts of "doing" as well, sorts of doing in which the efficacious principle is informative rather than powerful.

III

There seem to be two broad classes of messages transmitted in ritual. First, whatever else may happen in some human rituals, in all rituals, both human and animal, the participants transmit information concerning their own current physical, psychic, or sometimes social states to themselves and to other participants. As Leach put it, ritual "serves to express the individual's status in the structural system in which he finds himself for the time being" (1954: 11). I shall, with some misgiving, follow Lyons (1970: 73) and refer to these transmissions as "indexical" transmissions, and to this information as "indexical."

In perhaps all animal rituals, and in some human rituals too, this is all there is. When one baboon presents his rump to another he is signaling submission; when the other mounts he signals dominance. The information content of the ritual is exhausted by the messages concerning their current states being transmitted by the participants. The ritual is only indexical.

But some human rituals are different, for in them the sum of the messages originating among and transmitted among the participants concerning their own contemporary states is not coextensive with the information content (using the term information in a broad sense) of the ritual. Additional messages, although transmitted by the participants, are not encoded by them. They are found by participants already encoded in the liturgy. Since these messages are more or less invariant obviously they cannot in themselves reflect the transmitter's contemporary state. For instance, the order of the Roman mass does not, in itself, express anything about the current states of those performing it. In recognition of the regularity, propriety, and apparent durability and immutability of these messages I shall refer to them as "canonical." Whereas that which is signified by the indexical is confined to the here and now, the referents of the canonical are not. They always make references to processes or entities, material or putative, outside the ritual, in words and acts that have, by definition, been spoken or performed before. Whereas the indexical is concerned with the immediate the canonical is concerned with the enduring. Indeed, its quality of perdurance is perhaps signified—its sense is surely conveyed—by the apparent invariance of the liturgy in which it is expressed.

Earlier I claimed that one of ritual's most salient characteristics is that it is not entirely symbolic. Since the term "symbol" is used in several ways in the literature it is important that I make clear that I am conforming to Peirce's (1960: 143ff.) tripartite classification of signs into *symbols, icons,* and *indices.* In this usage a symbol is merely "associated by law" or convention with that which it signifies. The word "dog" is a symbol designating a certain sort or class of creatures. Words are the fundamental, but not the only, symbols; for objects, marks, nonverbal sounds, gestures, movements may be assigned symbolic meaning by words. The virtues of symbolic communication are patent. With symbols discourse can escape from the here and now to dwell upon the past, future, distant, hypothetical, and imaginary, and with a complex symbolic system, such as a natural language, an unlimited variety of messages may be encoded through the orderly recombination of a small number of basic units. Although a few other species may make very limited use of symbols, symbolic communication is characteristic of the human species, and has made possible for men a way of life so different from that of other animals that some anthropologists would compare the emergence of the symbol in importance and novelty only to the emergence of life itself.

In contrast to symbols, *icons* by definition share sensible formal characteristics with that which they signify. A map is an icon of the area to which it corresponds, and many of what are called symbols in other usages are, in this terminology, iconic. A "phallic symbol," for instance, is an icon. In contrast to both symbols and icons, *indices* are, to use Peirce's phrase, "really affected by" that which they signify. A rash is an index of measles, a dark cloud of rain. An index is caused by, or is part of, that which it indicates; in the extreme case it is identical with it.

Canonical messages, which are concerned with things not present and often not even material, are, and *can only be,* founded upon symbols, although they can employ, secondarily, icons and may even make limited use of indices. On the other hand, information concerning the current state of the transmitter may transcend mere symbolic designation and be signified indexically. It is for this reason that I refer to such information as "indexical."

To say that indexical transmission may "transcend" "mere" symbolic transmission is to suggest that it may overcome a certain problem, to which I have called attention elsewhere (1969, 1971a, 1971b), that is intrinsic to the symbolic relationship. When a sign is only arbitrarily or conventionally related to the signified it is possible for it to occur in the absence of the signified and for it not to occur in the presence of the signified. Thus, the very freedom of sign from signified that permits discourse to transcend the here and now, if it does not actually make lying possible, facilitates it enormously and may encourage it as well.

The indexical situation does offer some opportunities for deception (see "Sanctity and Lies in Evolution" in this volume), but such opportunities are multiplied by magnitudes by the symbol. The reliability of information becomes a problem for symbol-using man: if the communication system upon which a social order depends accommodates lies, how may the recipients of information be assured that the information transmitted to them is sufficiently reliable for them to act upon? In ritual this problem is in some degree overcome by eschewing the use of the symbol and transmitting information concerning the current states of the performers indexically.

I am not sure that all messages concerning the current states of the performers transmitted in ritual are indexical in Peirce's sense, hence my misgivings in using the term "indexical" to refer to them. That such signals are indexical is clear in some cases, however. For instance, when a Goodenough Islander (Young 1971) or a Siuai (Oliver 1955) transmits the message that he is a man of importance, influence, or prestige by giving away large numbers of yams and substantial numbers of pigs he is not simply claiming to be a big man. He is *displaying* the *fact* that he is. The amount that he gives away is an index of his "bigness" because it is "really affected by" that which it signifies—his influence, prestige, authority, or whatever.

It may be noted that in this example there has been an inversion of the more familiar qualities of the sign and the signified. We are more accustomed to the sign being insubstantial, and the signified substantial, as, for instance, in the relationship in which the word "dog" stands to the animal that it designates. It may be that in cases in which claims are made concerning states that are themselves without physical properties (e.g., prestige, worth, valor), the sign must be substantial if it is to be heeded. If the sign were insubstantial it would be mere words, vaporous, "hot air." Be this as it may, ritual signs are frequently substantial, a matter to which we shall return.

The indexicality of other cases is less patent but more interesting. Let us consider the Maring man who, by dancing at the festival of another group, signifies to his hosts that he will help them in warfare (Rappaport 1968).

There is surely no intrinsic or causal relationship between dancing and fighting, particularly between fighting in the *future* and dancing in the *present*. However, the *contemporary* state tht the transmitter is signaling in this instance is a *conventional* state or act, namely one of promising or undertaking obligation. The conventional signal, dancing, is taken to be intrinsic to that conventional state, which is to say that to dance is to promise. The connection between dancing and promising is, of course, conventional. But promising is itself a convention and conventions can only be signified conventionally. I am claiming, however, that the relation between two conventions, here dancing and promising, can be, and in this instance is, indexical because they are identical. Dancing at a *kaiko* and pledging support in future rounds of warfare are one and the same.

The case of the Maring dancer not only illustrates indexicality but also suggests indexicality's limitations. While it may be that to dance is to pledge support, to pledge support does not in itself honor that pledge. The undertaking of the pledge is in the present, and can be signaled indexically, but the fulfillment of the pledge is in the future, and that which does not yet exist cannot be signified indexically. What may make the hosts confident that their guests will honor in the future the pledges they are undertaking in the present is another matter relating to other aspects of the ritual. We shall return to this question later, noting now only that this confidence—such as it is—is contingent upon the association of the indexically transmitted pledge with the canonical messages borne by the liturgy.

*   *   *

Two classes of information, then, are transmitted in ritual. All rituals, both animal and human, carry indexical information, information concerning the current states of the participants, often if not always transmitted indexically rather than symbolically. The second class, the canonical, is concerned with enduring aspects of nature, society, or cosmos, and is encoded in apparently invariant aspects of liturgical orders. The invariance of a liturgy may be an icon of the seeming changelessness of the canonical information that it incorporates, or even an index of its actual changelessness, but canonical information itself rests ultimately upon symbols.

While there is an indexical component in all rituals it might seem that in some rituals the significance of the indexical is so far outweighed by the canonical that it appears trivial, as, for instance, in the Mass. Consideration of this matter must be delayed until later but it may be well to assert—or reassert—now that in *all* liturgical rituals, and most clearly in all religious rituals, there is transmitted an indexical message that cannot be transmitted in any other way and, far from being trivial, it is one without which canonical messages are without force, or may even seem nonsensical.

To say, as it was said at the end of the last subsection, that some indexical messages are dependent for their acceptability on their association with the canonical, and to say that canonical messages are without force, or even sense, unless accompanied by certain indexical messages is to say that ritual is not merely a mode of communication in which two sorts of information may be transmitted, but a very complex form in which the two sorts of information are dependent upon each other.

IV

Certain further aspects of indexical transmission itself should be discussed before we turn to the interrelation of the indexical and canonical. Consideration of these aspects of the indexical will, in fact, lead naturally to the canonical, but they can claim some interest in their own right.

Canonical messages, it has been emphasized, are carried by that which is invariant in the liturgy. In contrast, indexical transmission must rely upon whatever opportunities more or less invariant liturgy offers for variation. There are always some. First of all, there is, in the case of noncalendrical rituals, variation in occurrence, in whether or not to conduct the ritual at a particular time. Second, there is, for the individual, the matter of whether or not to participate in a ritual that is occurring. There is, at least theoretically, always the possibility of choice. This is a matter of great importance to which we shall return later. Third, there are many opportunities for variation in the content of ritual. I shall mention one kind of possibility very briefly before moving on to occurrence, about which I shall also be brief, since I have written about both content and occurrence elsewhere (1971a, 1971b), justifying their reiteration here on grounds of coherence.

*   *   *

As far as contents are concerned, there are, among other things, usually possibilities in even the most invariant of liturgical orders for variations of a numerical sort, either cardinal or ordinal. For instance, among the Maring there is a well-specified procedure by which principal antagonists honor men from other groups who assisted them in their last round of warfare. At a public occasion at the end of their festival the principals call out the names of their allies, who come forward to receive both plaudits and salted pork. What is not specified by liturgy, but is of great importance to all concerned, is the order in which the names of the allies are called out. He who is called first is most honored. He who is called last may well feel dishonored.

Quantity is also important—this is obvious in events like Maring *kaiko* entertainments, during which hosts assess the size of future allied military detachments by the size of dancing contingents, and in potlatches and pig feasts messages concerning worthiness and prestige are communicated by numbers of pigs, pearlshells, blankets, coppers, and similar valuables.

Such rituals are obviously operating as public counting and ordering devices. But it is important to note that their operation includes more than simple counting or ordering. Incorporeal qualities that are in their nature only vaguely quantitative and certainly non-metrical, like honor and worth, are being given a form that is not only material, but clearly metrical, like numbers of pigs or coppers. In communication terms, qualities that would seem to vary analogically, like prestige, are not only being substantiated, but are being represented digitally.

The term "analogic" refers to entities and processes in which values can change through continuous imperceptible gradations—for instance temperature, distance, velocity, influence, maturation, mood, prestige, and worthiness. Signals, like other phenomena, may be analogic. Cries of pain, for instance, can proceed through continua of imperceptibly increasing intensity that may indicate the intensity of the suffering they signify. The term "digital," in contrast, refers to entities or processes whose values change not through continuous infinitesimal gradations but by discontinuous leaps.

Examples of discontinuous phemonena that lead themselves "naturally" to digital representation are the beating of the heart, and changes in the size of populations. Some objects include both digital and analogic elements. Thus, a thermostat contains both an analogic element, a thermometer, and a digital element, a switch that fluctuates back and forth between two discontinuous positions, "on and off." As there are analogic signals, so may there be digital signals employing discontinuous terms or scales, like numbers of pigs or blankets. There may sometimes be some loss of accuracy in the representation of analogic processes or entities digitally, but the advantage of digitalization is that it increases clarity. For instance, the representation of influence, prestige, or worth in numbers of discrete units, such as pigs, reduces the vagueness of a social and political situation by facilitating comparison. This reduction in vagueness is in part a function of substantiation, in part of digitalization. Thirty-two pigs thrown into a feasting competition are, simply and obviously, more than twenty-five. (To claim that digitalization increases clarity and facilitates comparison is not, of course, to claim that the clear is always to be preferred to the vague.)

*   *   *

Whereas vagueness is reduced by the digitalization of some aspects of ritual's contents, ambiguity concerning the current state of the performers may be reduced or even eliminated by ritual's occurrence. Occurrence carries the digital to the extreme—or, rather, to one step away from the extreme. That is, it brings it to the binary, to the reduction of discrete units or states to two only. Any ritual included in the repertoire of a society can at any time only be occurring or not occurring. This is to say that the occurrence of a noncalendrical ritual can transmit a significant binary, or "yes-no" (or "o/1" or "on-off") signal. But although occurrence transmits only a "yes-no" signal it may have been triggered by the achievement or violation of a particular state in some continuous (or "more-less") variable. or even a complex state in a constellation of interrelated variables. For instance, a certain ritual performed by a Maring local group signifies its transition from spiritually sanctioned peacefulness to a potential belligerence that also enjoys spiritual support. The message concerning transition is entirely free of ambiguity: a group has either uprooted its *rumbim* plant or it has not. But *when* this ritual will occur depends upon a complex concatenation among the states of a large number of ecological, demographic, and social variables, including the rates of increase in the pig population, frequencies of human misfortune, the frequency and seriousness of arguments among co-residents, the number and health of a group's women, the ratio of taro to sweet potatoes in local gardens. The occurrence of the ritual, this is to say, summarizes a great mass of constantly fluctuating heterogeneous "more-less" information and transmits its summary as a simple binary signal which is in its nature unambiguous.

Reduction of the continuous and complex to the binary through ritual occurrence is also important in the transition of individuals from one state or condition to another. For instance a Tahitian lad decides sometime around the age of twelve to have himself supercised, thus making clear his transition from the status of child to that of *T'aure'area* (Levy 1973: 117ff., 368ff.). He thereby summarizes all of the obscure, continuous physical and psychic processes that in concert constitute his maturation, and transmits information concerning his decision as a simple yes-no signal.

There may appear to be a rather clumsy bit of sleight-of-hand in this abbreviated account. On the one hand I have claimed that the signal indicates a certain stage in the boy's maturational process, on the other that it represents a decision on his part to impose a change of status upon those processes. This duality is, I think, in the nature of the case. For one thing, the process of deciding to change status—a process that is terminated by the actual decision—is itself part of the complex maturational process. More important, the boy himself is the most significant receiver of the message he himself has transmitted by having himself supercised. He has, so to speak, signaled to himself that he has imposed a simple yes-no decision upon whatever ambivalence, fear, and doubt he may have been experiencing. There is nothing for him to do now but to bring his private processes into accord with the new public status that follows from his ritual act.

Two general points are to be made here. The first concerns distinction, the second the articulation of the unlike. It is obvious that the simple "yes-no" of ritual occurrence, which separates the before from the after with absolute clarity, is admirably suited to impose upon the continua of nature distinctions that are much sharper than nature's own. It may, that is, impose *unambiguous distinctions* upon *ambiguous differences* (see Wilden 1972: 177). The binary characteristic of occurrence does not, of course, limit its application to single distinctions, for rituals are often arranged in series: the rites of passage stretching from birth to death, the festivals separating the years into seasons, those leading from war to husbandry and back again. Although we are mainly concerned in this section with the indexical content of ritual we also note here that the ability to make unambiguous distinctions, which is intrinsic to the occurrence of rituals, is not limited in its application to the indexical. Annual rounds of festivals surely distinguish the seasons from each other more clearly than the weather, and reference to them may order the lives of men more effectively than the growth of plants or changes in temperature. The clarity of ritual occurrence combined with its general formality and nonutility suit ritual ideally for service in what Bateson calls "context-marking" (1972: 289ff.) generally.

It is of considerable interest that ritual occurrence resembles digital computing machines with respect to its manner of operation as well as in its effects upon continuous processes. In an introductory textbook concerned with the logical design of digital circuits C. M. Reeves writes, "The successful operation of a real machine depends upon being able to separate the time intervals at which variables have their desired values from those in which they are changing. Logically, therefore, the passage of time is discrete where physically it is continuous" (1972: 7). Modern machines usually confine the time intervals in which the values of variables are changing to microseconds which, taken to be instantaneous, are ignored. In some rituals, similarly, the values of some variables are changed during the course of a ritual or seris of rituals (Van Gennep 1909; Turner 1969). Between an act of separation and an act of re-aggregation there is a liminal period during which some aspect of the condition or state of some or all of the actors is transformed. As in the case of the digital machine, the time during which the values of variables are changing is out of ordinary time, as Eliade (1959) and others have observed. In contrast to the machine, in which the "time between times" is often virtually infinitesimal, the liminal or marginal periods demarcated ritually may last for hours, days, or even months or years. Moreover, we know that that which occurs during rituals and is instrumental in transforming some aspect of the actors' states, is not always entirely discursive or digital. In the interstices of time, in the times out of time that lie between the befores and afters that rituals distinguish so clearly, there may be a time of continuous, highly affective performance in which boundaries and distinctions are obliterated, rather than clarified. To emphasize, as I have in this section, ritual's digital aspects is not to deny its analogic aspects. At the end of this essay we shall return to the analogic heart held both safe and harmless within the digital brackets of ritual's occurrence.

The occurrence of rituals makes distinctions, but of course does not necessarily separate. While it may be that festivals distinguish the seasons one from another it is also the case that they join them into the circle of the year. The intervals between the rituals in protracted liturgical orders become, in part because they are set apart by rituals, not simply durations during which there has been more growth or the weather has grown warmer, but distinctive periods: childhood, manhood, spring, summer, autumn, war, peace. Bound together by the rituals distinguishing them, they form significant wholes: lives and histories, and the years that set lives into histories and histories into the cosmos.

*   *   *

The occurrence of ritual not only articulates what it itself distinguishes, as the seasons by festival or sacrifice, or what it itself separates, as war from peace by ritual declaration. It also aids in the transduction of information between unlike systems. For instance, in the case of the uprooting of *rumbim* by Maring local groups, signifying, as we have noted, a passage from spiritually enforced peacefulness to potential belligerence, information concerning environmental, demographic, physical, and social variables is summarized and transmitted from a *local ecological system* into a *regional political* system (see Rappaport 1968). In the case of Tahitian supercision and other puberty rites, the ritual articulates an individual psychophysical system on the one hand and a social system on the other. Despite the fact that they share components, local ecological systems and regional political systems are "unlike," and the same may be said of individual psychophysical systems on the one hand and social systems on the other. Local ecological systems are "about" trophic exchanges, energy flows, soil depletion and replenishment. Regional political systems are "about" war, women, land, and the exchange of goods. Similarly, both psychophysical and social systems are characterized by continuous quantitative processes and continuous change in such variables as emotional, cognitive, and physical states on the one hand and changes in status, role, group affiliation, and economic status, among other things, on the other. Although they are related to each other and affect each other, and although any individual is a locus of both, psychophysical processes and social processes are quasi-autonomous with respect to each other. Neither is a direct function or outcome of the other, and information concerning the two sets is not altogether commensurable. The same may be said of the relations between local ecological systems and regional political systems.

Since social and psychophysical processes are not altogether commensurable, nor are ecological and regional political processes, continuously fluctuating quantitative information concerning any of these systems is not directly meaningful in the system to which it is articulated. By "not directly meaningful" I mean that it cannot affect systematic nonrandom proportional changes in the other without first being interpreted or translated. The occurrence of ritual as a binary transducer summarizes this quantitative information into a simple statement that not only is nonambiguous but is meaningful in the system into which it is transmitted, e.g., "this boy is prepared to become, or has become, a man." It is significant that control transduction between unlike components of organic systems also relies heavily upon binary mechanisms because of the difficulty of translating continuous and often fluctuating quantitative information directly between incommensurable systems (Goldman 1960; Wilden 1972).

In some rituals local ecological systems may be articulated to regional political systems, and in many others social units of different magnitude or type may be brought together. It may be asserted, however, that in *all* rituals private psychophysical processes are articulated with public orders. This was clear in the case of the Tahitian youth. In having himself supercised the boy reaches out, so to speak, from his private processes— those of physical and psychic maturation—into a public liturgical order to grasp the category that he then imposes upon his private processes. It is no less so in the case of planting or uprooting *rumbim* among the Maring. In performing such a ritual each participant imposes upon his own private self a transformation of his public state: by uprooting *rumbim* he transforms himself from husbandman into warrior, by planting *rumbim* from warrior to husbandman.

V

In discussing the liturgical variations that may carry indexical information we have approached the canonical, for it is from the canonical content of liturgy that are drawn the categories that give meaning to whatever indexical messages are transmitted. We come, this is to say, to the relationship of the indexical to the canonical. It is a complex relationship that I wish to address at first by returning, with a somewhat different emphasis, to an indexical message considered earlier.

By dancing at a *kaiko* a Maring man signals his pledge to help his hosts in warfare. Dancing signals a pledge because it is itself a pledging. As such, it was earlier argued, it indicates rather than merely symbolizes the pledge with which it is "identified," i.e., made identical. Now I wish to emphasize that "to pledge" is not merely to say something but to do something. A pledge is an act.

Ritual is full of conventional utterances which achieve conventional effects. "I name this ship the Queen Elizabeth." "We declare war." "I dub thee to knighthood." "I swear to tell the truth." "I promise to support you." "We find the defendant guilty." "I apologize." In all of these instances, we would agree, the speaker is not simply saying something but doing something, and what he is doing—achieving a conventional effect through some sort of conventional procedure—cannot be done by the application of matter and energy to some object in accordance with the laws of physics, chemistry, or biology.

The importance of such utterances in the conduct of human affairs is so patent as to obviate any need for comment, but philosophers have, in the last two decades especially, given considerable attention to their peculiar characteristics. J. F. Austin (1962) has called them "performative utterances" and "illocutionary acts"; J. R. Searle (1969) includes them among what he calls "speech acts"; F. O'Doherty (1973a) refers to an important subclass as "factitive" acts or utterances; J. Skorupski (1976) uses the term "operative acts" for a class resembling them closely.

It is important to note that the efficacy of what I shall, following Austin's earlier and simpler terminology, call "performatives" is not in the persuasive effect of these utterances upon others. If authorized persons declare peace in a proper manner peace is *declared,* whether or not the antagonists are persuaded to act accordingly. This is not to say that performative utterances may not be persuasive. They often have, to use Austin's terms, "perlocutionary" as well as "illocutionary" force. But an action of some sort (beyond the obvious act of producing sounds, or even meaningful sounds) is completed in the performative gesture or utterance itself. Performatives of course differ in the scope of the action they complete. Thus, if I am authorized to do so and name this ship the Queen Elizabeth, this ship is so named, and that is really all there is to it. You may call it "Hortense" if you like, but its name happens to be Queen Elizabeth (Austin 1962: 99 passim). On the other hand, if I have danced at your *kaiko,* thereby promising to help you in warfare, that is not all there is to it, for it remains for me to fulfill my promise, and I may fail to do so. Following O'Doherty, we may say that the naming, which not only constitutes an action but actually brings into being the state of affairs with which it is concerned, is not simply performative, but "factitive" as well. Whereas many actions completed in ritual—dubbings, declarations of peace, marriages, purification—are factitive, it is obvious that *all* are not. Some—among them are those Austin called "commissives" (1962: 150ff.)—do not bring into being the states of affairs with which they are concerned, but merely commit those performing them to do so sometime in the future.

While many liturgies are performative, while some sort of performative act is the main point of the performance, transforming war into peace, restoring purity to that which has been polluted, joining men and women in wedlock, performativeness is not confined to ritual. There is no advantage to be gained, for instance, in taking to be ritual the publican's utterance "The bar is closed." But when he says "the bar is closed" it is thereby closed, and we may as well go home. Performatives are not confined to ritual, but it may be suggested that there is a special relationship between ritual and performativeness.

First, the formal characteristics of ritual enhance the chances of success of the performatives they include. Like any other acts performatives can fail. If, for instance, I were to dub one of my junior colleagues knight of the garter he would not thereby become a knight of the garter, even if the conduct of the ritual were letter-perfect. Conversely, if Queen Elizabeth dubbed Princess Anne's horse to knighthood it probably wouldn't make him a knight. And if a befuddled cleric recited the service for the dead rather than the marriage liturgy it is doubtful if the couple standing before him would thereby be married or become objects of mourning (Austin 1962: passim). All of these instances of faulty performatives are of ritual performatives, and ritual performatives can fail, but the ludicrous nature of these instances suggests that they are less likely to fail than other performatives. The formality of liturgical orders helps to ensure that whatever performatives they may incorporate are performed by authorized people with respect to eligible persons or entities under proper circumstances in accordance with proper procedures. Moreover, the formality of ritual makes very clear and explicit what it is that is being done. For instance, if one Maring casually said to another whom he happened to be visiting, "I'll help you when next you go to war," it would not be clear whether this was to be taken as a vague statement of intent, as a prediction of what he would be likely to do, or as a promise, nor would it necessarily be clear what might be meant by "help." To dance this message in a ritual, however, makes it clear to all concerned that a pledge to help is undertaken, and that that help entails fighting. Ritual, this is to say, not only ensures the correctness of the performative enactment; it also makes the performatives it carries explicit, and it generally makes them weighty as well. If a message is communicated by participation in ritual it is in its nature not vague. Moreover, there is no point in mobilizing the formality, decorum, and solemnity of ritual to communicate messages that are of no importance or gravity. Promises are often communicated in ritual, but vague statements of intent seldom if ever are.

I shall only mention two other closely related reasons for considering the performativeness of ritual here. First, the association of the sacred or occult (I do not take them to be synonymous) with performatives in magical and religious rituals may hide their conventional nature from the actors, and this obviously may enhance their chances of success. To take the state of affairs established by a king's enthronement to derive from the sacramental virtue of crown and chrism is perhaps more effective with respect to the maintenance of the order of which the king is a part than would be the recognition of enthronement as a naked performative. Second, as Ruth Finnigan (1969: 550) has suggested, albeit rather unspecifically, the "truth lying behind" assumptions concerning what is often called "the magical power of words" may be related to their illocutionary force or performativeness. It may be proposed, rather more specifically, that the magical power of some of the words and acts forming part of liturgies derives from the factitive relationship between them and the conventional states of affairs with which they are concerned. Magical power may be attributed to yet other words by extension of the principle of factitiveness beyond the domain of the conventional in which it is effective into the domain of the physical, in which it is not. But it behooves us to be wary about stipulating the limits of what may in fact be effected by ritual acts. The efficacy of factitiveness may, after all, be augmented by the perlocutionary force of the acts in which the factitiveness inheres, and no one yet knows how far into physical processes perlocutionary force may penetrate. It does seem safe to say, however, that the efficacy of ritual may extend beyond the purely conventional and into the organic, for people do occasionally die of witchcraft or ensorcellement, and they are sometimes healed by faith. The magical efficacy of words may rest upon their perlocutionary force or persuasiveness as well as upon their factitiveness.

VI

Perhaps the most important reason for considering the performativeness of rituals is, paradoxically, that certain rituals are not themselves obviously performative but may make performatives possible.

There seems to be more to some or even all liturgies than the performatives they incorporate, and some liturgies may not seem to include performatives in any simple sense at all. Many religious rituals do not seem to be directed toward achieving simple conventional effects through conventional procedures. Although simple performativeness is not criterial of ritual, something like it, but of higher order, is. We approach here the conjunction of formality and performance that was emphasized in the introduction. We come, this is to say, to what is implicit in the act of performing a liturgical order.

The term "liturgical order," we may be reminded here, refers both to the more or less invariant sequences of formal acts and utterances that comprise single rituals, and to the sequences of rituals and make up ritual cycles and series. "Order" is an especially appropriate term because these series of events constitute orders in several senses beyond the obvious one of sequence. They are also orders in the sense of organization, form, or regularity (synonymous with the meaning of "order" in such phrases as "the social order"). As such they constitute order, or maintain orderliness, in contrast to disorder, entropy, or chaos. They are, further, orders in that they are in some sense imperatives or directives.

Liturgical orders, it was asserted in the first section, must be performed. Without performance there is no ritual, no liturgical order. There are still extant in books outlines of liturgies performed in Ur and Luxor, but they are dead, for they are no longer given voice by men's breaths nor energy by their bodies. A liturgical order is an ordering of *acts* or *utterances,* and as such it is enlivend, realized, or established *only when* those acts are performed and those utterances voiced. We shall return to this shortly. The point to be made here is that this relationship of the act of performance to that which is being performed—that it brings it into being—cannot help but specify as well the relationship of the performer to that which he is performing. He is not merely transmitting messages he finds encoded in the liturgy. He is participating in— becoming part of—the order to which his own body and breath give life.

Since to perform a liturgical order, which is by definition a relatively *invariant* sequence of acts and utterances *encoded by someone other* than the performer himself, is to *conform* to it, authority or directive is *intrinsic* to liturgical order. However, the account just offered suggests something more intimate, and perhaps even more binding than whatever is connoted by terms like "authority" and "conformity." The notion of communication implies, minimally, transmitters, receivers, messages, and channels through which messages are carried from transmitters to receivers. Sometimes, moreover, as in the case of canonical messages, the senders or encoders of messages are separate from the transmitters. We earlier noted a peculiarity of ritual communication, namely that in ritual the transmitters and receivers are often one and the same. At least the transmitter is always among the receivers. Now we have noted another of ritual's peculiarities. In ritual the transmitter-receiver becomes fused with the message he is transmitting and receiving. In conforming to that which his performance brings into being, and which comes alive in its performance, he becomes indistinguishable from it, a part of it, for the time being. Since this is the case, for a performer to reject the canonical message encoded in a liturgical order that is being realized by his performance as he is participating in it seems to me to be a contradiction in terms, and thus impossible. This is to say that *by performing a liturgical order the performer accepts, and indicates to himself and to others that he accepts, whatever is encoded in the canons of the liturgical order in which he is participating.* This message of acceptance is the indexical message that is intrinsic to all liturgical performances, the indexical message without which liturgical orders and the canonical messages they encode are nonexistent or vacuous. It is not a trivial message because men are not bound to acceptance by their genotypes. They are often free not to participate in rituals if they do not care to, and refusal to participate is always a possibility, at least logically, conceivable by potential actors. Participation always rests in some degree upon choice.

We see here, incidentally, how myth and ritual differ in an important way: ritual specifies the relationship of the performer to what he is performing while myth does not. A myth can be recounted as an entertainment by a bard, as an edifying lesson for his children by a father, or as a set of oppositions by a structuralist, although it may be recited as doctrine by a priest to a novice. To recite a myth is not necessarily to accept it, and a myth survives as well on the printed page as it does on the tongues of living men.

*   *   *

We are led here back to the matter of performatives and to the assertion that while all ritual may not be performative, rituals make performatives possible. Austin (1962: 26ff.) listed six conditions that must be fulfilled if performatives are to come off. These include such obvious stipulations as that they be performed by proper persons under proper circumstances. Now his first and most basic condition is that for conventional states of affairs to be achieved there must *exist accepted* conventional procedures for achieving them. They cannot be achieved without such conventions. If young men are to be transformed into knights there must be a procedure for doing so, and this procedure must be acceptable to the relevant public. The acceptance of a procedure for dubbing knights also obviously presupposes the existence of an accepted convention of knighthood. This stipulation is not vacuous, for it can be violated. For instance, it is unlikely that in the contemporary United States a slap of the glove across the cheek would ever result in a duel. The conventions of honor, of which this ritual action was a part, are no longer accepted. They no longer exist except in memory or history.

Although Austin stipulated as requisite to the effectiveness of performatives that the relevant conventions exist and be accepted, he gave no attention to the matter of how this prerequisite is fulfilled. I am arguing here that it is fulfilled by ritual. The performance of ritual

establishes the existence of conventions and accepts them simultaneously and inextricably. Ritual performance is not in itself merely, nor
even necessarily, factitive. It is not always performative in a simple way,
merely bringing into being conventional states of affairs through conventional actions. It is, rather, *meta*-performative and *meta*-factitive, for it
establishes, that is, it stipulates and accepts, the conventions in respect to
which conventional states of affairs are defined and realized. The canons
accepted in their performance may, of course, represent conventional
understandings concerning nature and the cosmos, or social and moral
rules as well as simple performatives, but in any case the performance of
a liturgical order realizes or establishes the conventions that the liturgical
order embodies. It may be suggested that as the reality lying behind
notions of the magical power of words is simple performativeness mystified, so may the reality lying behind the creative power of The Word—
the Eternal Word—be meta-performativeness mystified—the establishment of conventions through participation in invariant liturgical orders.

VII

The assertion that acceptance is intrinsic to performance is on the face of
it either dubious or indubitable, and therefore requires some comment
and clarification.

First, to say that the performer accepts the authority of a liturgical
order in performing it is not to say that he is necessarily doing anything
very grave. The gravity of the act of acceptance is contingent upon
whatever the liturgical order represents. This, of course, varies.

Second, and more important, "acceptance" is not synonymous with
belief. Belief I take to be some sort of inward state knowable subjec-
tively, if at all. Acceptance, in contrast, is not a private state but a *public
act,* visible to both the witnesses and the performer himself. This is to
reiterate in a different way a point made in section III, namely that
participation in ritual marks a boundary, so to speak, between public and
private processes. Liturgical orders are public, and participation in them
constitutes a public acceptance of a public order, regardless of the private
state of belief. Acceptance is, thus, a fundamental social act, and it forms
a basis for public orders, which unknowable and volatile belief or conviction cannot.

Acceptance not only is not belief. It does not even imply belief. The
private processes of individuals may often be persuaded by their ritual
participation to come into conformity with their public acts, but this is
not always the case. This suggests that while participation in liturgical
performance may be highly visible, it is not very profound, for it neither
indicates nor does it necessarily produce an inward state conforming

to it directly. But for this very reason it is in some sense very profound, for it makes it possible for the performer to transcend his own doubt by accepting in defiance of it. Acceptance in this sense has much in common with some theological notions of faith (O'Doherty 1973b: 8ff.; Tillich 1957: 16ff.). Nevertheless, it must be recognized that when the public and the private are so loosely related, a range of what Austin (1962: 95ff.) called "infelicities"—insincerities and the like—become possible, and they include possibilities for deceit. But the alternative to the possibility of deceit might well be the certainty of non-order or disorder if public order were required to depend upon the continuing acquiescence of the private processes of those subject to it—upon their belief, sincerity, good will, conviction, for these surely must fluctuate continuously. While it is perhaps obvious it is worth reiterating that insincerity and the possibility of deceit are intrinsic to the very acts that make social life possible for organisms that relate to each other in acccordance with voluntarily accepted convention rather than in ways more narrowly defined by their genotypes. Our argument here suggests, however, that although liturgical performance does not eliminate infelicities, it does in some degree offset or ameliorate their effects by rendering them irrelevant. It is the visible, explicit, public act of acceptance, and not the invisible, ambiguous, private sentiment that is socially and morally binding.

To say, then, that a liturgical order is in its nature authoritative, or that the canons it encodes are accepted in its performance, is not to say that the performer will "believe" the cosmic order it may project or approve of the rules or norms it may incorporate. It is not even to claim that he will abide by these rules or norms. We all know that a man may participate in a liturgy in which commandments against adultery and thieving are pronounced, then pilfer from the poor box on his way out of church, or depart from communion to tryst with his neighbor's wife. But such behavior does not render his acceptance meaningless or empty. It is an entailment of liturgical performances to establish conventional understandings, rules, and norms in accordance with which everyday behavior is supposed to proceed, not to control that behavior directly. Participation in a ritual in which a prohibition against adultery is enunciated by, among others, himself may not prevent a man from committing adultery, but it does establish for him the prohibition of adultery as a rule that he himself has accepted as he enlivened it. Whether or not he abides by the rule he has obligated himself to do so. If he does not he has violated an obligation that *he himself* has avowed. The assertion here is similar to that of the philosopher John Searle, who has argued that:

When one enters an institutional activity by invoking the rules of that institution one necessarily commits oneself in such and such ways, regardless of whether one approves or disapproves of the institution. In the case of linguistic institutions like promising and accepting the serious utterance of words commits one in ways which are determined by the meaning of the words. In certain first person utterances the utterance is the undertaking of an obligation. [1969: 189]

Searle later notes that the notion of obligation is closely related to those of accepting, recognizing, acknowledging. This suggests that there is no obligation without acceptance, and perhaps that morality begins with acceptance. While the acceptance of conventional undertakings, rules, and procedures is possible outside of ritual, the formal and public nature of liturgical performance makes it very clear that an act of acceptance is taking place, that the acceptance is serious, and what it is that is being accepted. In Austin's terms (1962: passim) it is "explicitly performative." But much more is implicit in ritual acceptance than simply making clear and weighty what is being done and in respect to what it is being done. Moreover, that the obligations clearly and explicitly accepted in liturgical performance are nullified neither by disbelief nor violation has a significance transcending the problems of insincerity and deceitfulness.

It may be that some conventions, particularly those of a more or less neutral sort, such as linguistic conventions, can emerge out of ordinary usage and be maintained by ordinary usage in sufficient stability to allow meaningful and orderly social interaction. In such cases "the norm is identical with the statistical average" (Leach 1972: 320). Variation with respect to some conventions can be comfortably tolerated and usage may be allowed to establish, maintain, or change them. But statistical averages arising out of usage are not able to establish conventional understandings, rules, or proceedings, concerning some aspects of social life. For instance, ordinary usage might have difficulty concerning the establishment of conventional understandings about things without material or behavioral referents and therefore without any ordinary usage—conventions concerning gods and the like. It may also have difficulty establishing conventions concerning aspects of social life that are not only arbitrary, but highly charged emotionally, or that are dangerous, or require coordination—those concerning, for instance, sex, leadership, service to the social group. Behavioral variations may be less tolerable with respect to these matters than with respect to linguistic usage, and variation or uncertainty as to the precise nature of the convention, a somewhat different matter, may be even less tolerable than variations in the behavior it presumably directs. Ordinary usage *always* varies, and in ordinary usage rules and conventions are frequently violated. Leach was generally correct but did not put the matter strongly enough when he suggested that "if anarchy is to be avoided, the individuals who make up a society must from time to time be reminded of the underlying order that is supposed to guide their social activities. Ritual performances have this function for the group as a whole; they momentarily make explicit what is otherwise fiction" (1954: 16). Although usage may not be faithful to it, that which is represented in liturgy is not a fiction, and the performance does more than *remind* individuals of an underlying order. It *establishes* that order. Usage erodes order and it is therefore necessary to establish at least some conventions in a way that protects them from dissolution in the variations of ordinary usage and from overthrow by the violations in which usage abounds. Liturgy preserves the conventions it encodes inviolate in the face of the vagaries of usage, and in this respect it may be without functional equivalents. Conventions promulgated by decree and maintained by force may also be insulated from dissolution in usage. But the acceptance by those whom they aim to subordinate is not intrinsic to decrees. It may also be suggested in passing that the conditions permitting some men to establish conventions by issuing directives to which other men must conform may be relatively recent, for they may rest upon differential control of strategic resources, and there was probably little opportunity for such differentiation to develop before the appearance of plant and animal cultivation ten thousand or so years ago. Moreover, even after social stratification based upon resource control became well developed, authorities continued—as some still do—to stand upon their sanctity, and sanctity itself may emerge out of ritual. We shall return to this later, noting here that the performance of ritual does not require superordinate human authorities, and must have antedated forms for promulgating conventions that do. It is plausible to suggest, therefore, that ritual, in the very structure of which authority and acquiescence are implicit, was the primordial means by which men, divested of genetically determined order, established the conventions by which they order themselves.

In sum, ritual is unique in at once establishing conventions, that is to say enunciating and accepting them, and in insulating them from usage. In both enunciating conventions and accepting them, it contains within itself not simply a symbolic representation of social contract, but a consummation of social contract. As such, ritual, which also establishes a boundary between private and public processes, thereby insulating public orders from private vagaries (and vice versa)'* is *the* basic social act.

---

*Ervin Goffman, in "The Nature of Deference and Demeanor" (1956) and later works, has argued that the rituals of deference and demeanor protect the psyche from lacerations that would inevitably result from naked encounters.

VIII

To say that ritual is the basic social act must be to say that it is in some sense moral, for the social subsumes the moral. Not all rituals are explicitly moral, but it is worth making explicit that morality, like social contract, is implicit in ritual's very structure.

Moral dicta may, of course, form part of the canon that a liturgy carries, and we have already noted that it is also implied by obligation, which some philosophers, at least, would take to be entailed by the acceptance intrinsic to performance. Failure to abide by the terms of an obligation that one has accepted is generally, perhaps even universally, categorized as immoral, unethical, or wrong. It might even be argued that the violation of obligation is the fundamental immoral act. This is not our concern here, however, and morality is intrinsic to ritual's structure in a yet more subtle way. While not confined to them, the matter may be illustrated most clearly by reference to specifically factitive rituals like ordinations, dubbings, and peace declarations. It is of the essence to contrast such performative acts or utterances with ordinary descriptive statements. Austin initially tried to say that performatives are neither true nor false (1970– 233ff.) whereas statement are. Later he found this not always to be the case. However, they do differ from statements in a related way which he did not note but which does have to do with truth, and with the foundations of morality.

The adequacy of a descriptive statement is assessed by the degree to which it conforms to the state of affairs that it purports to describe. If it is in sufficient conformity we say that it is true, accurate, or correct. If it is not we say that it is false, erroneous, inaccurate, lying. The state of affairs is the criterion by which the statement is assessed. The relationship of performatives—particularly factitives and commissives—to the states of affairs with which they are concerned is *exactly* the inverse. If, for instance, a man is properly dubbed to knighthood and then proceeds to violate all of the canons of chivalry, or if peace is declared in a properly conducted ritual but soon after one of the parties to the declaration attacks the other, we would not say that the dubbing or the peace declaration were faulty, but that the states of affairs were faulty. *We judge the state of affairs by the degree to which it conforms to the stipulations of the performative ritual.* Thus, liturgical orders provide criteria in terms of which events—usage and history—may be judged. As such, liturgical orders are *intrinsically* correct or moral. Morality is inherent in the *structure* of liturgical performance *prior* to whatever its canons assert about morality itself or about whatever in particular is moral. This morality is not limited to the structure of simple factitive and commissive rituals, which seek to establish particular conventional states of affairs, but is intrinsic as well to rituals that seek to establish conventional orders. It is of interest here than ancient Persians and Indians referred to states of affairs that departed from the proper order, which was established liturgically, by a term, *anrta,* that also seems to have meant "lie" (Duchesne-Guillemin 1966: 26ff.; Brown 1972: 252ff.).

IX

That virtually all rituals include acts as well as words, and often objects and substances as well, suggests that not all messages are communicated equally well by all media. We touched upon this question earlier in noting that the indexical messages transmitted by the distribution of objects—pigs, pearlshells, blankets, and copper plaques—in competitive feasting could not have been transmitted as well—or even at all—by words, and physical acts may also have distinct communicative virtues. Formal postures and gestures may communicate something more, or communicate it better, than do the corresponding words. For instance, to kneel subordination, it is plausible to suggest, is not simply to state subordination, but to display it, and how may information concerning some state of a transmitter better be signaled than by displaying that state itself? We have returned here to the indexical status of messages concerning the state of transmitters, adding to our earlier discussion the suggestion that although words may serve as indices, and may even be necessary to stipulate the indexicality of physical acts (dancing would not be promising unless it were sometime so stipulated in words), physical acts carry indexical messages more convincingly than does language. "Actions," as the saying goes, "speak louder than words," even when the actions are ritual actions—or perhaps especially when they are ritual actions, for the acceptance of a particular order is intrinsic to a ritual act. Liturgy's acts may also speak more clearly than words. The very limitations of display may enhance its clarity. The subtlety of ordinary language is such that it can suggest, connote, hint at, or imply such delicately graded degrees of, say, subordination, respect, or contempt that it can shroud all social relations in ambiguity, vagueness, and uncertainty. But one kneels or one does not, and we may recall here the clarity that is intrinsic to binary signals.

It may be objected, however, that the language of liturgy is not ordinary language, but stylized and invariant. As one kneels or one does not, so one does or does not recite a ritual formula, and so ritual words as well as acts can—and undoubtedly do—transmit indexical messages. Acts, however, have a related virtue not possessed by either words or the objects and substances that rituals may employ. Earlier I suggested that in ritual, transmitter, receiver, and canonical message are fused in the participant, but nothing was said about what it is that constitutes the participant. Given the possibility, or even probability, of discontinuity, or even conflict, between public and private processes this is not a trivial question. Indeed, it is highly problematic.

I would now propose that the use of the body defines the self of the performer for himself and for others. In kneeling, for instance, he is not merely sending a message to the effect that he submits in ephemeral words that flutter away from his mouth. He identifies his inseparable, indispensable, and enduring body with his subordination. The subordinated self is neither a creature of insubstantial words from which he may separate himself without loss of blood, nor some insubstantial essence or soul that cannot be located in space or confined in time. It is his visible, present, living substance that he "puts on the line," that "stands up (or kneels down) to be counted." As "saying" may be "doing," "doing" may also be an especially powerful—or substantial—way of "saying."

As ritual acts and objects have special communication qualities so, of course, do words have others, as Tambiah (1968) has argued. Whereas acts and substances represent substantially that which is of the here and now, the words of liturgy can connect the here and now to the past, or even to the beginning of time, and to the future, or even to time's end. In their very invariance the words of liturgy implicitly assimilate the current event into an ancient or ageless category of events, something that speechless gesture, mortal substance, or expendable objects alone cannot. Because of their symbolic quality, this is to say, invariant words easily escape from the here and now and thus can represent felicitously the canonical, which is never confined to the here and now. Objects like the cross can have symbolic value, it is true, and thus make reference to that which is present in neither time nor space, but such objects must be assigned symbolic value by words, and words are ultimately necessary to representations of the canonical.

The informative virtues of the physical and verbal aspects of liturgy thus seem to complement or even complete each other. But terms like "complement" or even "complete" do not express adequately the intimacy of the relationship between liturgical words and acts. By drawing himself into a posture to which canonical words give symbolic value, the performer incarnates a symbol. He gives substance to the symbol as that symbol gives him form. The canonical and the indexical come together in the *substance* of the *formal* posture or gesture.

* * *

In including within itself both word and substance, ritual may contain within itself a paradigm of creation. Many myths of creation, as Bateson (1972: xxiii ff.) has recently emphasized, do not take creation to be, simply, or even at all, the production of matter *ex nihilo,* but of giving form to inchoate matter already in existence. Creation, this is to say, is conceived as the informing of substance and the substantiation of form, a union of form and substance. Form—the ordering principle or agent—is often explicitly associated with word. The Mamandabari men, who appear in the myths of the Walbiri people of Central Australia, emerge from the yet featureless earth. First, they give themselves being by singing their own names, and then they walk across the land singing its places and species into being (Meggitt 1965). The Wawilak sisters of the Murngin people of Arnhem Land also created places and species by naming them (Warner 1937: 150ff.). In Genesis the world was formed out of waste by the utterances of God, and earth was transformed into man by the breath of God. Breath and word are surely connected. The second Adam was, of course, the Word become Flesh.

Creation, then, in some myths at least, is conceived as the primordial union of two primitive and irreducible categories, form and substance, and in ritual there seems to be a reunion of this primordial union. What better way to represent form than by the invariant words of a liturgical order, or substance than by drawing the body into a ritual posture or using some object or substance sacramentally? A similar theory concerning the sacraments was first propounded by William of Auxerre in the thirteenth century. "The sensible act or thing used in a sacrament was likened to formless matter, being indeterminate in use and adaptable to many purposes; it was determined to a spiritual significance by the use of words, which then played the part of the metaphysical *forma essentialis*" (Lacey 1918: 907). But as substance is formless without word, so form alone could not exist in this world of matter and energy independent of substance. Consequently, all Catholic sacraments require their proper *materia* as well as their proper invocation, and so do those of the Orthodox church. It should be noted that when William of Auxerre sought to account for the fact that the sacraments included both word and matter the term "sacrament" was used much more generally than it has been since the Council of Trent, which stipulated just seven sacraments "properly so-called." His proposal, that is, was advanced as a more or less general theory of Catholic ritual.

* * *

To observe that ritual in including both verbal and physical components may in some sense represent—re-present—a primordial union of form and substance does not account for why it is that men should take this union to be problematic, much less for why form should so often be associated with words. The distinction does not arise directly from experience, for, after all, no one has ever experienced either matterless form or formless matter. Nature is precisely as full of one as of the other. And yet, although no one has experienced chaos, everyone has experienced what he takes to be disorder. Moreover, although the natural world is full of form, the forms of the conventions pressing upon humans are not obviously given by the forms of nature. It is conventional, not natural form, that is problematic. If the distinction between form and substance is to be made at all the association of form with words may be obvious, for conventional forms must ultimately be specified in words. This is to say that conventional forms are, in a sense, naturally associated with words.

Bateson (1972: xxv) has cautiously suggested that the distinction between form and substance may be implicit in the subject-predicate relationship in ordinary language. Almost all subjects can be predicated in a number of ways and almost all predicates can apply to a number of subjects. The subject-predicate relationship forces upon the mind alternatives, including alternative orders and disorders, and in making them conceivable it makes at least some of them possible. The very characteristics of language that provide the basis for man's astounding adaptive flexibility also give birth to confusion, and threaten with chaos and babel the orders that groups of men do establish. Thus, if there are going to be any words at all it may be necessary to establish *The Word*. The Word is implicit in the invariant words of liturgical orders, of course, and in cosmogonic myths Word is established by the assertion that *it* has established the natural world. In the primordial union of form and substance expressed in myth and of which ritual may be a representation, the natural order is apparently formed by, and thus absorbed into, a conventional order. But the point of the exercise is not so much, I think, to make nature conventional as the reverse. By accounting for the palpable world of trees and beasts and places the conventional is transformed into the apparently natural and, in becoming natural partakes of the regularity, necessity, and solidity of natural objects and processes that apparently present themselves directly to the senses. To conventionalize the natural is at the same time to naturalize the conventional. In the ritual union of form and substance there is a reunion of convention with the nature from which words have alienated, but never freed it.

X

Word and words are components of language, and liturgical orders like language have regular structures that may be in some respects analogous to grammars. Both ritual and language are modes of communication, and it is not surprising that some anthropologists should take ritual to be a kind of language. This identification or analogy can be illuminating but, as those who propose it themselves hasten to point out (e.g., Leach 1966), it is very rough, for liturgy and language differ in interesting ways, some of which it is well to make explicit here.

One important difference is implied in the opposition of Word to words. All natural languages consist of words and sets of rules for combining them into meaningful utterances. While these rules restrict how things may be said they do not themselves restrict what things may be said, and it is possible in any language to say whatever there is vocabulary available to say. In contrast, to the degree that a liturgical order is invariant there are obviously restrictions being placed upon what it can communicate. In the extreme case what it can communicate is reduced to unity. Both language and liturgy may make use of the same words, often with the same designata, but the ways in which they may be related to each other semantically in the utterances of ordinary language are not formally specified in language, whereas they are in liturgy. As Maurice Bloch (1973) has put it, "the features of juncture" are fixed in liturgy, but open in language. Therefore, ordinary language easily accommodates argument, nuance, gradation, and modification, but liturgical language does not. A liturgy does not argue, but it may assert. The flexibility of ordinary discourse is such that it can be responsive to the ever-changing present, and when a speaker's utterances do not take account of changes in what is being said to him we take it to be a sign of pathology: he is obtuse, fanatical, insane or possibly deaf. The rigidity of liturgical discourse, in contrast, is such that it can represent whatever is conceived to be never-changing, and changes in it may be taken to be pathological: erroneous, unorthodox, inefficacious, unhallowed, heretical, or blasphemous. In short, natural languages are open *codes;* liturgies, although they must use the words of language, are more or less constricting *orders.* It may be suggested that the very act of confining words that may also appear in the free and loose usage of ordinary discourse to the places assigned to them in liturgy emphasizes that liturgies are restrictive orders standing against the possibility of unrestricted disorder.

* * *

While some words may have places in both ordinary and liturgical language, there are important differences between liturgical signs, even when they are words, and the words of ordinary discourse. As Victor Turner (1967, 1973) especially has emphasized, liturgical symbols are likely to be "multivocalic," that is, they have a number of significata and, as both he and Joseph Campbell (1959: passim) have argued, these significata are likely to have a bipolar distribution. "At one pole of meaning . . . significata tend to refer to the moral and social orders . . . at the other, the sensory . . . , are concentrated references . . . that may be

204 | ECOLOGY, MEANING, AND RELIGION

expected to stimulate desires and feelings" (Turner 1973: 1100), particularly references to organic structures, substances, and processes. It is
perhaps important in this regard that liturgical signs are often substantial,
and at once iconic and indexical as well as symbolic. In contrast, the
words of ordinary language also do frequently have more than one
meaning but an important difference distinguishes the way in which they
usually signify from symbolization in ritual. In everyday discourse the
context usually tells us to which of a word's several significata it presently
refers. If it fails to eliminate all but one of the possibilities we say that the
utterance is ambiguous, and under most circumstances take ambiguity to
be a fault. Ordinary discursive language is linear: one meaning follows
another.

In contrast, the signification of liturgy has a simultaneous dimension.
A ritual sign may refer to all of its significata at once, and it does not
derive its meanings from each of them separately so much as it derives its
meaning from the *union* of these several significata. This is to say that
that which is noise in ordinary language is meaning in liturgy. Of course
the meaning that may derive from a concatenation of significata among
which might well be included organic and psychic, as well as social,
environmental, and spiritual references, may finally be so abstract, complex, and emotionally charged as to be ineffable.

Paul Tillich long ago distinguished what he called symbols (by which
he meant liturgical signs particularly) from other elements of communication in noting that they "participate in that to which they point"
(1957). A vague notion of identification if not indexicality may be
implicit in this suggestion. Beattie implied the iconicity, or something
like it, of liturgical components in arguing that the relationship between
what *he* (in agreement with many others) called symbols and their significata is not merely arbitrary. They are joined by an "underlying
rationale" or appropriateness: the serpent biting its tail symbolizes eternity, the large-headed and inscrutable owl wisdom, whiteness purity and
virtue (1964: 69ff.). Firth follows a usage that has considerable currency
when he says that symbols have "a complex series of associations, often
of an emotional kind, and [are] difficult (some would say impossible) to
describe in terms other than partial representation" (1973: 75). These
and other understandings of the symbol and symbolization obviously
differ radically from the concept of symbols as, simply, signs only conventionally related to that which they signify.

John Skorupski (1976: 119ff.) has recently pointed out that designators are of two types, those that name or denote, and those that represent. Thus "Fido" names or denotes Fido, it does not represent him; on
the other hand, a serpent biting its tail represents eternity—it does not
name or denote it; equally whiteness represents purity rather than

naming or denoting it. The term "symbol" has been used to refer to both denotative and representational designators, and since the distinction between denotation and representation has seldom been made explicit some confusion has been engendered.

Skorupski would reserve "symbol" for representational designators, excluding from its coverage those that simply denote or name. His justification for this usage lies in the importance of representations in ritual action:

Thus the symbol substitutes for the thing symbolised. We are sometimes said to think in words—certainly we communicate with each other in words. *In* words *about* things. . . . The symbol is itself made the object of thought. It stands for, or *re-presents,* the thing symbolised. In other words, it makes it present to the senses, and is treated for the purposes of symbolic action as being what is symbolised. On this picture the logic of a symbolic action is clear: it represents or enacts an action, event or state of affairs in which the thing represented by the symbol plays a part analogous to that which the symbol plays in the symbolic action itself. [1976: 123]

This account suggests additional grounds for the substantial nature of liturgical signs. It accords comfortably with both the contagious and sympathetic principles of "magical" efficacy, and it is also compatible with a performative theory of ritual efficacy.

Skorupski's distinction between denotative and representational designators is important and useful but it seems to me that nothing is to be gained and something is to be lost by reserving "symbol" for representational designators exclusively. More important, to call signs that represent "symbols" and those that denote by another term may be to distinguish them too radically. On the other hand, to distinguish in a rough way between representational symbols and denotative symbols is to recognize their similarities as well as their differences. It also encourages recognition of certain aspects of the relationship of representation to denotation. First, representation is contingent upon denotation. The Worm Ourobouros could not represent eternity until denotative words had pointed to eternity; similarly, white could not represent purity or virtue until a number of denotative operations had taken place. Second, representational symbols may be fused out of associations of simpler significations, including denotative symbols, in liturgical performance. That is, in the liturgical sign, which is multivocalic and bipolar, which may be at once iconic, indexical, and denotative, and which is embodied in something substantial—a cross, a flag, a posture—there seems to be union of a concatenated mass of simple significations into a single but complex representation. Once such a representation is brought into being it may be "treated . . . as *being* what is symbolised." When that which is symbolized is abstract or ineffable but the symbol itself is substantial it is the symbol that provides reality to the symbolized. Moreover, it is easier to operate upon substantial representations than insubstantial significations. The distinction between denotation and representation is not absolute, and in liturgies denotations, joined with icons and indices, are transformed into representations. We may recall here Bateson's observation (1972: 183) that "in the dim area where art, magic and religion overlap" there is sometimes "an attempt to deny the difference between map and territory" characteristic of denotative symbols and to return to a more innocent mode of communication.

Two related points follow from the complexity of liturgical representation. First, although it is well-known that among some people liturgical orders are important in the regulation of social, political, or ecological relations, liturgical orders cannot be said to "reflect," "interpret," or "represent" them in any simple way. They are not simply social or psychic orders played out and mystified in public symbols. As we all know, some liturgies make no reference to existing social arrangements or if they do, at one and the same time, even in the self-same symbol, they may refer both to putative entities transcending the existing social orders and to the private processes of individuals. In their wholeness (a wholeness implicit in the term "order" as organization) liturgical orders are not simply representations of the social, physical, psychic, or imagined. They represent, that is, re-present, themselves (see Babcock-Abrahams 1973).

We note here another way in which liturgical representations differ from ordinary language. The distinctions of language cut the world into bits—into categories, classes, oppositions, and contrasts. It is in the nature of language to search out all differences and to turn them into distinctions which then provide bases for boundaries and barriers. It is, on the other hand, in the nature of liturgical orders to unite, or reunite, the psychic, social, natural, and cosmic orders which language and the exigencies of life pull apart. It is of importance in this regard that representations in ritual are often multi-modal, employing at one and the same time words, music, noise, odors, objects, and substances.

Liturgical orders bind together disparate entities and processes, and it is this binding together rather than what is bound together that is peculiar to them. Liturgical orders are meta-orders, or orders of orders, and if we were to characterize in a phrase their relationship to what lies outside of them we might say that they mend ever again worlds forever breaking apart under the blows of usage and the slashing distinctions of language.

XI

There is, of course, considerable range in the canonical content of liturgical representations. Not all liturgies give equal weight to all possible classes. The Mass, for instance, seems to be largely taken up with cosmic and spiritual references and it also includes profound body symbolism, but other rituals give more prominent place to representations, either mystified, implicit or explicit, of aspects of contemporary social life. Rules concerning social behavior are enunciated in some, and others incorporate conventional procedures for achieving conventional effects—transforming princes into kings, war into peace, dances into commitments. Sometimes a full range of messages are encoded in a single ritual. Among the Maring of New Guinea, for example, the ritual that establishes truces in accordance with conventional procedures also establishes deceased ancestors as sentient and powerful beings. In contrast, the Mass and Jewish sabbath services hardly refer to the existing social order. They do, however, establish the existence of cosmic entities upon which other rituals more directly concerned with social particulars are contingent. If a king is to be crowned in the name of God in a coronation ritual, or if men are to swear in the name of God in a courtroom, it is necessary for the existence of that God to have already been established. This may be done, in fact is perhaps best done, in rituals removed from crownings of courtrooms.

We have seen in previous sections that liturgical orders have both sequential and simultaneous dimensions. As acts and utterances follow each other, so meanings which are chordlike in their signification follow each other. Now we see that liturgy also has a hierarchal dimension which may be manifested either in single rituals or in related rituals, some contingent upon others. There are surely important differences in the hierarchical development of liturgical orders, and it may be that such differences correspond to differences among societies in the degree to which they are stratified or ranked. It is generally if not always the case, however, that the "ultimate" or "absolute" components of liturgical orders are the cosmic or spiritual entities to which they make references, while the contingent elements are their social referents and the liturgical performances associated with them. There could be no divine kingship without divinity; coronations in Catholic countries are contingent upon the Mass, which establishes as a social fact the divinity of the God in whose name, or through whose grace, men are transformed into kings. The hierarchy of contingency seems, obviously, to be hierarchy of authority and efficacy as well. Moreover, since the sacred, which I have not yet defined, is generally understood to have its purest expression in representations of spiritual or cosmic entities in the ultimate or absolute components of liturgical orders, liturgy's hierarchical dimension orders relations of sanctity as well as of authority, efficacy, and contingency. Indeed, these aspects of liturgy's hierarchical structure are virtually indistinguishable.

I have spoken of liturgical orders as "more or less" invariant, meaning to recognize by this language not only the sloppiness intrinsic to practice but also that some aspects of liturgy are more variable than others. It is of importance that as a rule the spiritual aspects of liturgy—both significata and representations—are less variable and more durable than those concerned with contemporary social arrangements. The liturgy of the Mass has persisted for close to two millennia, during which it has changed but slowly. The creeds recited in the Mass are in their present form very ancient. In contrast, certain contingent rituals concerned with social effects, such as homage and fealty, have virtually dropped out of use altogether. Although other aspects of their liturgies vary considerably, possibly reflecting differences in their social conditions and historical circumstances, the rituals of the Ashkenazic Jews of northern Europe, the Sephardic of the Mediterranean, the Falacha of Ethiopia (Leslau 1951: 124), the Beni of India (Stritzower 1971: 14), and the Karaites of the Crimea (Idelson 1932: 310) all retain the dedication of faith called the *Shema* in a central position. It is important to note that the self-same spiritual representations are likely to be the most invariant of ritual's elements not only in the sense of most enduring but also in the sense that they are those expressed with greatest punctilio. Relations of relative invariance, ideally at least, correspond to the hierarchical ordering of contingency, authority, efficacy, and sanctity.

XII

Invariance, as I stated at the beginning, is characteristic of all rituals, both human and nonhuman, and it may be that both the sacred and the supernatural arose out of the union of words with the invariance of the speechless rituals of the beasts from whom we are descended. Be this as it may, both the sacred and the supernatural are, I believe, implied by liturgy's invariance. Before developing this point more must be said about the sacred.

Elsewhere (1971a, 1971b) I have argued that we take liturgies to be religious if they include postulates of a certain sort. The Shema, "Hear, O Israel, the Lord our God, the Lord is One," is an example. So is "Deceased Ancestors persist as sentient Beings," which is implicit in the rituals in which Maring men pledge their military support to their hosts. Such sentences have peculiar qualities. Having no material reference they are neither verifiable nor falsifiable, and yet they are regarded as unquestionable. I take *sanctity to be the quality of unquestionabless imputed by a congregation to postulates in their nature neither verifiable nor falsifiable.* This is to say that sanctity is ultimately a quality of discourse and not of the objects with which that discourse is concerned. It is of interest in this regard, however, that the objects with which sacred discourse is concerned are often themselves elements of discourse: instances of the Creative Word. The distinction between sacred discourse and the objects of sacred discourse may thus be masked or, to put it differently, sacred discourse and its objects may be conflated.

Let us turn now to the relationship of sanctity to invariance. It was Anthony F. C. Wallace (1966: 234) who first pointed out that in terms of information theory ritual is a peculiar form of communication. Information is formally defined as that which reduces uncertainty, the minimal unit being the "bit," the amount of information required to eliminate the uncertainty between two equally likely alternatives. It is, roughly, the answer to a yes-no question. We touched upon this matter in discussing indexical messages, all of which, because they depend upon the possibility of variation, do contain information in the technical sense. But, Wallace observed, to the extent that a liturgy is invariant it contains no information because it eliminates no uncertainty. He further argued, however, that meaning and information are not the same thing, and that the meaning of this informationlessness is *certainty*. To put this a little differently, that which is stated in the invariant canon is thereby represented as certain because invariance implies certainty. Certainty and unquestionabless are closely related, and *one* of the grounds of the unquestionableness of these postulates which we may call "ultimately sacred," is the certainty of their expression. It is not, however, the only ground.

Certainty is a property of information or messages. It is one thing to say that a message is certain and another to say that it goes unquestioned. Whether or not a statement will be challenged does not rest only or finally upon the properties of the statement itself, but upon the disposition toward it of the persons to whom it is presented. We have already seen, however, that to participate in a ritual is to accept that which it encodes. This acceptance is entailed by participation in an invariant order that the participants themselves did not encode. Liturgical invariance, at the same time that it invests what it encodes with certainty, secures the acceptance of its performers.

This account distinguishes the sacred from the divine or supernatural, but it may be that the invariance of sacred utterances may imply the objects of these utterances. Bloch's recent (1973) arguments suggest that the notion of the supernatural as well as the idea of the sacred may emerge out of the invariance of liturgical performance. The words spoken by a performer are not his words. They are extraordinary and often immemorial words, and as such they imply extraordinary speakers who first uttered them in antiquity, or perhaps beyond antiquity, at the beginning of time. Gods and spirits as well as social contract and morality may be intrinsic to the structure of liturgical order.

While sanctity has its apparent source in ultimate sacred postulates which, being expressions concerning Gods and the like, are typically without material significata, it flows to other sentences which do include material terms and which are directly concerned with the operation of society: "Henry is by Grace of God King." "It is more blessed to give than to receive." "Thou shalt not bear false witness." "I swear in the name of God to tell the truth." Thus it is that association with ultimate sacred propositions certifies the correctness and naturalness of conventions, the legitimacy of authorities, the truthfulness of testimony and the reliability of commissives. To return to a question raised much earlier: that Maring men will honor the pledges to give military support that they undertake and display by dancing is certified by association with an ultimate sacred postulate.

It is important to observe here that the greater invariance of the sacred or spiritual than the social components of liturgical orders provides them with a certainty beyond the certainties of social orders currently existing. As the social content of canon is more or less enduring, providing an order within which the states represented in indexical messages may fluctuate, so the even less variable, more enduring references to gods and spirits provide an apparently eternal meta-order within which social orders themselves may be transformed. The adaptive implications of the greater invariance of the nonmaterial than the material are important, but are discussed elsewhere (see the essay "Adaptive Structure and its Disorders" in this volume). Here I would like to suggest that although the concept of the sacred and the notion of the divine would be literally unthinkable without language it may also be that language and social orders founded upon language could not have emerged without the support of sanctity. Earlier we noted one of the problems inherent in language—its extraordinary talent for deceit, and later another—the innate ability of language users to comprehend the arbitrary nature of the conventions to which they are subordinated and their ability, also intrinsic to language, to conceive of alternatives. Lie and alternative, inherent in language, it is interesting to note, are taken by Buber (1952) to be the ground of all evil. At the very least they pose problems to any society whose structure is founded upon language, which is to say all human societies. I have therefore argued that if there are to be words at all it is necessary to establish *The Word,* and that The Word is established by the invariance of liturgy. It may be at least suggested, furthermore, that it emerged phylogenetically as some expressions drawn from the burgeoning language of earlier hominids were absorbed into, and subordinated to, the invariance of already existing nonverbal rituals which seem to be common in the animal world.

We may now note that liturgy ameliorates some of the problems intrinsic to symbolic communication, particularly lying, by moving in two opposite directions. On the one hand, as we observed in an early section of this paper, it eschews symbolization in favor of indexicality in at least some of its representations of the here and now. On the other hand it sanctifies references to that which is not confined in the here and now. Like the lies to which they are a partial antidote, ultimate sacred postulates are made possible by denotative symbols, for denotative symbols free signs from that which they signify.

To summarize, truthfulness, reliability, correctness, naturalness, and legitimacy are vested in conventions and conventional acts by their association with ultimate sacred postulates. The notions of truthfulness, reliability, correctness, naturalness, and legitimacy are closely related to that of unquestionabless, which I have identified with the sacred. Unquestionableness in turn is closely related to certainty and acceptance, certainty and acceptance to invariance. The invariance of ritual, which antedates the development of language, is the foundation of convention, for through it conventions are not only enunciated, accepted, invested with morality, and naturalized, but also sanctified. Indeed, the concept of the sacred itself emerges out of liturgical invariance.

XIII

Yet, as important as liturgical invariance may be, surely language and the human way of life must be founded upon more than a trick in information theory. So far I have spoken only of the sacred, which is in language and which faces language and the public orders built upon language. But the sacred is only one component or aspect of a more inclusive phenomenon which I call the Holy. The other aspect of the Holy, which, following Rudolph Otto (1926), may be called the "numinous," is its nondiscursive, ineffable, or emotional aspect—what is called "religious experience" (James 1903) in the broadest sense. We know that this, as well as the sacred, is invoked in at least some rituals. "Communitas" (Turner 1969) or "effervescence" (Durkheim 1961 [1915]) is one of its manifestations. Scholars differ with respect to the nature of religious experience. Some would apply the term to any emotional state taken by the individual to be a response to what is construed to be a divine object. Others, like Rudolph Otto (1926), would take it to be a general undifferentiated "ur-emotion" encompassing love, fear, dependence, fascination, unworthiness, majesty, connection. Witnesses agree that it is powerful, indescribable, and utterly convincing.

I do not mean to make too much of this, but Erikson (1966) suggests that the numinous emotion has its ontogenetic basis in the relationship of the preverbal infant to its mother. The child's experience of its mother has characteristics similar to those that Otto attributes to the worshiper's experience of his God: she is mysterious, tremendous, overpowering, loving, and frightening. It is learning to trust her upon whom he depends utterly that makes subsequent language learning and, for that matter, continuing socialization possible. This trust is learned in what Erikson calls "daily rituals of nurturance and greeting" (1966), stereotyped interactions between mother and child taking place dependably at regular intervals, or at times specified by the child's needs. Through the course of ontogeny the numinous emotions initially associated with mother are displaced to other objects. Of importance here is the bipolar reference of ritual symbols noted by Turner (1973) and Campbell (1959: 461ff.). At one and the same time they point to cosmic and social conceptions on the one hand and psychic and physiological experience on the other. Through the mediation of such representations the conceptual is given the power of the experiential and the experiential the guidance of the conceptual. Again, we note a relationship here between conceptual form and experiential substance.

Erikson's ontogenetic suggestion has phylogenetic implications. If ontogeny has a phylogeny and if the mother-child relationship among humans is but a variant of the primate or even mammalian pattern, it may be that the basis of the numinous is archaic, antedating humanity, and it may further be that religion came into being when the emerging, discursive, conventional sacred was lashed to the primordial, non-discursive, mammalian emotional processes that in their later form we call "numinous."

Be the ontogenetic and phylogenetic bases of numinous experience as they may, such experience is often invoked in ritual. In an earlier section I emphasized the digital aspects of liturgical orders, but noted that the binary nature of ritual occurrence, that makes it possible for rituals to distinguish before from after with perfect clarity, obliterates neither ritual's analogic virtues nor its affective power. Between the before and the after marked by the occurrence of ritual, there is a "liminal period" (Van Gennep 1909). To recall Reeves remarks about digital machines, it is a time when variables, in ritual the states of performers, do not have their unambiguous before or after values, but are, rather, changing. It is a time out of ordinary time and is marked as such by the prominent place given to representations that connect the moment to the eternal, and thereby disconnect it from the everyday and ordinary.

In some rituals the contrast with the everyday is radical and the canons of reality which guide everyday behavior seem inappropriate and are discarded. During such ritually marked times out of time, emotions—often very strong and persuasive—are generated, and these emotions may obliterate the boundary that liturgical performance itself establishes between public acts and private states. In the fervor of religious emotion the private states of the performers sometimes come into accord with their public performances. As William James put it, their acceptance is "enthusiastic." The performer "runs out to accept the divine decrees" (1903: 289). Bateson (1972), following Huxley, agrees with James in referring to such states of psychic reunion by the term "grace."

This self-unification must be encouraged, in some cases at least, by performing an invariant liturgy, but conformity to such an order is not simply to unite or reunite alienated or warring parts of the self. It is to participate in—that is, to become part of—something larger than what is ordinarily experienced as the self. It is of interest that the experience of which I speak need not be, indeed, is perhaps not often, individual. In the union or reunion of their private and public selves the performers may achieve a corporate state of communitas (Turner 1969), an "effervescent" state (Durkheim 1961) in which the sense of individual self that ordinary consciousness imposes upon men becomes less sharp, or is even lost in the sense of participation in the larger whole that the performance makes palpable. It is, perhaps, important in this regard that the coordination of persons in ritual performances is often much tighter than usual (Radcliffe-Brown 1964: chapter 2). Indeed, the levels of coherence (see "Ecology, Adaptation, and the Ills of Functionalism" or "Adaptive Structure and Its Disorders" for discussions of coherence) often achieved in ritual is more typical of organisms than of social groups. It is important that unison is a common feature of ritual, and it may be made comprehensive by engaging several sense modalities and modes of expression simultaneously.

In sum, I earlier argued that liturgy's invariance gives rise to the sacred, meaning by the term "sacred" to designate only the discursive aspect of a more encompassing category which may be called the Holy. The sacred, the ultimate constituents of which are in language, is that aspect of the Holy which faces language, reason, the public order, and their problems. But the Holy also has a nondiscursive, affective and experiential aspect which we may, following Otto, call "the numinous." As the sacred may emerge out of the invariance of liturgical orders, so may the numinous be invoked by ritual's unison.

*　　*　　*

The canons of liturgy, in which are encoded both postulates concerning that which is ultimately sacred and sentences concerning temporal social orders may, then, receive in the rituals in which they are enunciated the support of numinous emotions. Numinous communitas, perhaps substantiated in acts of unison, may add a dimension—or a magnitude—to the orderliness of the sacred canonical. But unison is not all that is to be found at ritual's heart, nor is the relationship between canonical order and numinous emotion always complementary.

At the heart of some rituals there is not always heightened order but hilarity, confusion, aggression, and chaos, expressed in clowning, transvestism, attacks upon initiates, self-mortification, sexual license, blasphemy, and otherwise indecorous actions. Such behavior may challenge, tacitly or explicitly, the very canons that ordain it, and Abrahams (1973) suggests that the "vitality" of ritual springs from the confrontations of order and disorder for which it provides an arena. This is to say that liturgical orders may include not only canons of order but their antitheses as well. As Abrahams puts it "there is a simultaneous proclamation of the order of the world as seen by the group and its (almost) absolute denial (1973: 15).

The orders of liturgy do generally manage to contain, and even to sublimate, the emotions that they themselves generate, and they surely may be vitalized or invigorated by confrontations with their anti-orders. But these confrontations may be more than invigorating. They may be limiting and corrective as well. The denials of order in ritual are seldom if ever absolute, and while they may be denials of this world's order, liturgical orders are usually concerned with more than the order of the world of here and now. They also proclaim an order that transcends time, an ultimate or absolute order of which the temporal order is merely a contingent part. It is the temporal, and not the ultimate, aspects of order that are most open to challenge, and that are most likely to be challenged by what appears to be anti-order. And it is the temporal and contingent nature of conventions that is exposed by ridiculing and violating them. In being exposed for what they are, they are prevented from themselves becoming ultimate. The king who is ordained by God is told—and so is everyone else—that he is no more than a man when he is demeaned in the name of God. Liturgy's challenges to the temporal are in the service of the ultimate, for they keep the conventions of time and place in their places by demonstrating that they are not ultimately sacred, but only sanctified by the ultimately sacred. They are also thereby in the service of evolution, for they make it easier to discard temporal conventions when times and places change.

XIV

The union in ritual of the numinous, a product of emotion, with the sacred, a product of language, suggests possible grounds for the notion of the divine going somewhat beyond Bloch's ingenious but perhaps too simple suggestion. Because the notion of the divine is a human universal we must search for its ground in a universal experience or condition.

I would hesitantly suggest that the notion of the divine has at least four features. First, while divine objects may be incarnated, the quality of the divine itself is not material in any ordinary sense. Second, the divine exists, or, rather, has being. It is not deemed to be, simply, a law, like the laws of thermodynamics, or an abstraction, like truth, but a being, like Zeus. Third, it is powerful, or efficacious. It has the ability to cause effects. Finally, it is something like alive. It possesses something like vitality. To use Rudolph Otto's term, it is "urgent."

I would hesitantly suggest that the first three of these qualities are supplied by fundamental linguistic processes as they are expressed in ritual's utterances, the last by the emotions generated in ritual.

First, the existence of the nonmaterial is made conceptually possible by the symbolic relationship between sign and signified. Whereas concept is intrinsic to the symbolic relationship, material reference is not intrinsic to concept. If the sign is not bound to the signified there is nothing to hold the signified to materiality at all, and it can easily escape into the abstract, imaginary, or otherwise purely conceptual.

The existence of the conceptual may be made conceivable by the fundamental linguistic process of predication. To say that "X is an aspect of Y" is to endow Y with the attribute X. The copula "is" in this sentence has, simply, a logical function, which is to invest Y with X, but this logical function has an existential implication. Moreover, this implication may be unavoidable. To say that "X is an aspect of Y" might be to say, or to *seem* to say, that both X and Y in some sense exist. Yet the existence entailed by predication may be no more than conceptual existence, like the way in which honor or the axioms of geometry exist. But Gods are beings. The problem is, then, to transform the conceptual— that which exists merely as concept—into that which seems to have being.

The conception of the nonmaterial as efficacious, i.e., as capable of causing effects, may contribute to such a transformation, for humans generally realize that effects are not directly caused by concepts alone (any more than, let us say, houses are built by plans alone). The efficacy of the nonmaterial, this is to say, implies the being of the nonmaterial. The notion of the efficacy of divine beings, in turn, might well be founded upon the performativeness and meta-performativeness of language as expressed in ritual. The very invariance of ritual proposes, as Bloch has suggested, an agent to whom the efficacy of performativeness intrinsic to ritual's language can be attributed.

Divine beings by the account so far offered remain nothing more than inductions from mystified performativeness. This, however, seems neither satisfactory nor correct, for we know that people are often convinced of the existence of divine beings in the absence of effects from which they could induce, however correctly or incorrectly, such beliefs.

We must consider not only the capacities of the propositions and performatives that language may present to the worshiper but also the worshiper's experience of those utterances and acts, and the relationship between their qualities and his experience. A mediating or connecting term may be noted. At least in languages in which it is an independent lexical element, and perhaps in all language, the verb "to be" may give rise to the notion of being independent of instances of being. It is of interest in this respect that the most sacred name of God in Hebrew, the tetragrammaton, is said to be a form of the verb "to be" (Brandon 1970: 655). Tillich (1957, etc.) refers to God as "The Ground-of-All-Being" and "Being-Itself." It is of further interest here that the profoundly altered states of consciousness characteristic of religious experience are sometimes described as states of "pure being," the word for trance in Java is "being" (Geertz 1965: 32), and Bushmen refer to the states they achieve in trance dancing as "really being" (Katz 1974).

The predication of that which is represented in an ultimate sacred proposition may become conflated in ritual with the numinous state of "pure being" of the performer. Numinous experiences, even those that are much less intense than may be suggested by references to Javanese and Bushman trance, are widely described as ones in which the presence of the divine being is "experienced." Sometimes, indeed, with loss of distinction, the worshiper senses that he is participating in, or becoming one with, the divine being. I would suggest that divine objects, which are represented by ultimate sacred postulates, are predicated as living, or even supplied the predicate of being, by the numinous experiences of worshipers. The vitality that the worshiper feels in the divine object is his own projected upon what he takes to be other or "encompassing." Ritual, then, is possibly the furnace within which the image of God is forged out of the power of language and of emotion.

XV

Earlier I spoke of the acceptance of convention entailed by participation in liturgy. I insisted that ritual acceptance is a public act and that it is not necessarily associated with an inward state conforming to it. Acceptance does not entail belief but, I proposed, it is sufficient to establish the obligations upon which human societies stand. I would now suggest that formal acceptance in the absence of something more profound may be fragile and that the numinous, when it is experienced, supports acceptance with conviction or belief. Those who have reached those profound states called mystical report a loss of distinction, an experience of unification with what they take to be the divine object and perhaps the cosmos. The experience, they say, is ultimately meaningful, but being devoid of distinction is devoid of reference. It points to nothing but itself. Ultimate meaning is not referential but is, rather, a state of being or even of pure, seemingly unpredicated being. I cannot discuss the validity of the illuminations vouchsafed in those states in which meaning and being become one, but will only note that to say such meaning is convincing is inadequate, for, being directly experienced, it simply *is*. As such it is undeniable, and so, indeed, may be numinous experiences falling short of the mystical.

It is of interest that sacred propositions and numinous experiences are the inverse of each other. Ultimate sacred postulates are discursive but their significata are not material. Numinous experiences are immediately material (they are actual physical and psychic states) but they are not discursive. Ultimate sacred postulates are unfalsifiable; numinous experiences are undeniable. In ritual's union ultimate sacred propositions thus seem to partake of the immediately known and undeniable quality of the numinous. That this is logically unsound should not trouble us for, although it may make problems for logicians, it does not trouble the faithful. In the union of the sacred and the numinous the most abstract and distant of conceptions are bound to the most immediate and substantial of experiences. We are confronted, finally, with a remarkable spectacle. The unfalsifiable supported by the undeniable yields the unquestionable, which transforms the dubious, the arbitrary, and the conventional into the correct, the necessary, and the natural. This structure is, I would suggest, the foundation upon which the human way of life stands, and it is realized in ritual. At the heart of ritual—its "atom," so to speak—is the relationship of performers to their own performances of invariant sequences of acts and utterances which they did not encode. Virtually everything I have argued is implied or entailed by that form.

REFERENCES CITED

Abrahams, Roger
    1973   Ritual for fun and profit. Paper prepared for Burg-Wartenstein Conference-59 on Ritual and Reconciliation.
Austin, J. L.
    1962   *How to do things with words*. Oxford University Press.

(Austin, J. L.)
  1970   Performative utterance. In *Philosophical papers,* 2d ed., ed. J. O. Urm-
         son and G. J. Warneck. Oxford.
Babcock-Abrahams, Barbara
  1973   The carnivalization of the novel and the high spirituality of dressing
         up. Paper prepared for Burg-Wartenstein Conference-59 on Ritual
         and Reconciliation.
Bateson, Gregory
  1972   *Steps to an ecology of mind.* New York: Ballantine Books.
Beattie, John
  1964   *Other cultures.* London: Routledge & Kegan Paul.
Bloch, Maurice
  1973   Symbols, song, and dance, and features of articulation. *European
         Journal of Sociology* 15:55–81.
Brandon, S. G. F.
  1970   *A dictionary of comparative religion.* New York: Charles Scribner's
         Sons.
Brown, W. Norman
  1972   Duty as truth in ancient India. *Proceedings of the American Philosophical
         Society* 116:252–268.
Buber, Martin
  1952   *The eclipse of God.* New York: Harper & Bros.
Campbell, Joseph
  1959   *The masks of God.* Vol. 1, *Primitive mythology.* New York: Viking.
Duchesne-Guillemin, Jacques
  1966   *Symbols and values in Zoroastrianism.* New York: Harper & Row.
Durkheim, Emile
  1961   *The elementary forms of the religious life.* Joseph Ward Swan, translator.
         New York: Collier.
Eliade, Mircea
  1959   *The sacred and the profane: the nature of religion.* New York: Harcourt
         Brace Jovanovich.
Erikson, Eric
  1966   The ritualization of ontogeny. In *A discussion of ritualisation of be-
         haviour in animals and man,* Julian Huxley, organizer. London: Philo-
         sophical Transactions of the Royal Society of London, Series B, Bio-
         logical Sciences, vol. 251, no. 772.
Finnegan, Ruth
  1969   How to do things with words: performative utterances among the
         Limba of Sierra Leone. *Man* 4:537–551.
Firth, Raymond
  1940   *The work of the gods in Tikopia.* London.
  1973   *Symbols, public and private.* London: George Allen & Unwin.
Fortes, Meyer
  1966   Religious premises and logical technique in divinatory ritual. In *A dis-
         cussion of ritualisatin of behaviour in animals and man,* Julian Huxley,
         organizer. London: Philosophical Transactions of the Royal Society
         of London, Series B, Biological Sciences, vol. 251, no. 772.
Freud, Sigmund
  1907   Obsessive actions and religious practice. *Zeitschrift für Religions-
         psychologie* 1:4–12.

Geertz, Clifford
  1965   Religion as a cultural system. In *Anthropological approaches to religion,*
         ed. Michael Banton. ASA Monograph no. 3. London: Tavistock.
Gluckman, Max
  1954   Rituals of rebellion in South-east Africa. The Frazer Lecture, 1950.
         Manchester University Press.
Goffman, Ervin
  1956   The nature of deference and demeanor. *American Anthropologist* 58:
         473-503.
Goldman, Stanford
  1960   Further consideration of the cybernetic aspects of homeostasis. In
         Self-organising systems, ed. M. C. Yovitz and Scott Cameron. New
         York: Pergamon Press.
Goody, Jack
  1961   Religion and ritual: the definitional problem. *British Journal of Soci-
         ology* 12:142-164.
Idelson, A. Z.
  1932   *Jewish liturgy and its development.* New York: Schocken paperbacks
         (1967)
James, William
  1903   *The varieties of religious experience.* New York: Collier Books (1961).
Katz, Richard
  1964   Education for transcendence: lessons from the !Kung Zhu/Twasi.
         Journal of Transcultural Psychology 2:136-155.
La Fontaine
  1972   *The interpretation of ritual: essays in honor of A. A. Richards.* London:
         Tavistock.
Lacey, T.
  1918   Sacraments, Christian, Western. In *Encyclopedia of religion and ethics,*
         ed. James Hastings, vol. 10, pp. 903-908.
Leach, E. R.
  1954   *The political systems of Highland Burma.* Boston: Beacon Press.
  1966   Ritualisation in man in relation to conceptual and social develop-
         ment. In *A discussion of ritualisation of behaviour in animals and man,*
         Julian Huxley, organizer. London: Philosophical Transactions of the
         Royal Society of London, Series B, Biological Sciences, vol. 251, no.
         772.
  1972   The influence of cultural context on non-verbal communication in
         man. In *Non-verbal communication,* ed. R. A. Hinde. Cambridge:
         Cambridge University Press.
Leslau, T.
  1951   *Falasha anthology: the black Jews of Ethiopia.* New York: Schocken.
Levy, Robert
  1973   *The Tahitians: mind and experience in the Society Islands.* Chicago:
         University of Chicago Press.
Lyons, John
  1970   Human language. In *Non-verbal communication,* ed. R. A. Hinde.
         Cambridge: Cambridge University Press.
Meggitt, M. J.
  1965   *Gadjari among the Walbiri aborigines of Central Australia.* Oceania
         monographs.

O'Doherty, F.
  1973a Ritual as a second order language. Paper prepared for Burg-Warten-
      stein Conference-59 on Ritual and Reconciliation.
  1973b Nature, grace, and faith. ms.
Oliver, D.
  1955 *A Solomon Island society.* Cambridge, Mass.: Harvard University Press.
Ortiz, A.
  1969 *The Tewa world.* Chicago: University of Chicago Press.
Otto, Rudolph
  1926 The idea of the holy. London: Oxford University Press. J. W. Harvey,
      translator.
Peirce, Charles
  1960 *Collected papers of Charles Sanders Peirce,* Vol. 2, *Elements of logic,* ed.
      Charles Hartshorne and Paul Weiss. Cambridge, Mass.: Harvard Uni-
      versity Press.
Radcliffe-Brown, A. R.
  1964 *The Andaman Islanders.*
Rappaport, Roy A.
  1968 *Pigs for the ancestors.* New Haven: Yale University Press.
  1969 Sanctity and adaptation. Paper prepared for Wenner-Gren Confer-
      ence on the Moral and Aesthetic Structure of Adaptation. Reprinted
      in *Io* 7(1970):46–71.
  1971a Ritual, sanctity, and cybernetics. *American Anthropologist* 73:59–76.
  1971b The sacred in human evolution. *Annual Review of Ecology and Sys-
      tematics* 2:23–44.
Reeves, C. M.
  1972 *The logical design of digital circuits.* New York.
de Rougement, Denis
  1944 *La part du diable.* New York: Brentan.
Searle, J. R.
  1969 *Speech acts.* Cambridge: Cambridge University Press.
Skorupski, J.
  1976 *Symbol and theory: a philosophical study of theories of religion in social
      anthropology.* Cambridge: Cambridge University Press.
Stritzower, Schifira
  1971 *The Children of Israel: the Beni Israel of Bombay.* Oxford: Basil Black-
      well.
Tambiah, S. J.
  1957 The magical power of words. *Man* 3:175–208.
Tillich, P.
  1957 *The dynamics of faith.* New York: Harper.
Turner, Victor
  1967 *The forest of symbols.* Ithaca, N.Y.: Cornell University Press.
  1969 *The ritual process.* Chicago: Aldine.
  1973 Symbols in African ritual. *Science* 179–1100–1105.
Van Gennep, A.
  1909 *The rites of passage.* M. Vizedom and G. F. Caffee, translators, with
      introduction by Solon Kimball. Chicago: Phoenix Books, University
      of Chicago Press, 1960.
Wallace, Anthony F. C.
  1966 *Religion: an anthropological view.* New York: Random House.

Warner, W. F.
  1937   *A black civilization.* New York: Harper & Bros.
Wilden, A.
  1972   *Systems and structure.* London: Tavistock.
Young, Michael
  1971   *Fighting with food.* Cambridge: Cambridge University Press.

Sanctity and Lies

in Evolution

I shall be concerned in this essay with the place of the holy in adaptive processes and, further, with the disordering of the holy in the course of evolution. I shall examine the holy and its constituents, the sacred and the numinous, in light of problems of language, namely those of false-hood, and shall, therefore, also explore the evolutionary significance of lies. In the course of the essay I shall attempt to identify, in addition to the ordinary lie, a number of forms bearing a family resemblance to it. I shall call them vedic lies, lies of oppression, diabolical lies, and idolatry, and I shall consider their roles in degrading the sacred, deluding the numinous, and breaking the holy. At the end I shall discuss the mal-adaptive consequences of such desecration.

I

In another essay, "The Obvious Aspects of Ritual," I have argued that the sacred, the numinous, the holy, and perhaps even the divine, are products of ritual, but I have observed that they always escape from ritual's confines. Sanctity, I proposed, emerges out of canonical invari-ance and its performance, first investing certain sentences expressed in ritual but flowing from those "ultimate sacred postulates" to others that are directly implicated in the affairs of society. Having escaped from

An earlier version of this essay, "Liturgies and Lies," was published in the *International Yearbook for the Sociology of Knowledge and Religion* 10:75–104, 1976. In the revision much that would have repeated arguments presented more fully in "The Obvious Aspects of Ritual" was excised and other discussions were expanded to increase their clarity.

ritual, sanctity, sometimes with the support of the numinous, becomes a partial antidote to certain problems intrinsic to the very virtues of language. These were noted in "The Obvious Aspects of Ritual," but may be treated at greater length here.

The first of these problems is that of the lie. There is a family of forms that may be designated "lie," but at the beginning I shall consider only ordinary lies. I use the term "ordinary lie" to refer to the willful transmission of information thought or known by senders to be false. Lying is often associated with deceit, but deceit seems to be more general in scope. The term "deceit" implies, I think, an intention to mislead to the disadvantage of those who are misled. Both terms imply intention, but the defining intention of lie is related to the signal transmitted, that of deceit to the effect upon, or more specifically to the response of, the receiver. It may be that lies are usually deceitful and that deceit often employs lies, but some lies, like telling a dying man that he will be well, may not be deceitful, and deceitful acts may be other than lies in a strict sense. The horse that the Greeks left for the Trojans was not a lie, but it was the central element in what seems a rather implausible deceit. There are problems with these simple definitions, or rather characterizations, of lie and deceit, but they are sufficient for our purpose.

Lying seems largely a human problem, but deceit may be more widespread. At least there are phenomena of considerable importance throughout the animal world that do share characteristics with deceitfulness: mimicry, bluff, camouflage, broken-wing behavior, playing possum. But intentionality is lacking from some of these phenomena, and besides, even the intention to mislead may not be sufficient to identify deceitfulness. There are contexts in which it is acceptable to mislead. No reasonable person would consider a feint in boxing, or a trap in chess, to be deceitful. The notion of deceit may suppose the existence of a relationship of trust which deceit then violates, and it may be significant that aside from bluffing, the sorts of instances that I have noted among animals are generally employed by members of one species to mislead members of others with whom they do not share a communication code and with whom they certainly don't stand in a relationship of trust. We may, nevertheless, be confident that even if deceit is more widespread than lying, and even if lying is not always deceitful, lying expands the possibilities for deceit enormously.

The contention that lying is largely a human problem is not novel. Hobbes (1930: 31ff., 164ff.) said as much, and so in this century has Buber (1952: 7). More recently, Hockett and Altmann (1968) have added the ability to prevaricate to Hockett's earlier list of the "design features" of human language. Thorpe, an ethnologist, in a discussion of Hockett and Altmann, observes that this ability is "highly characteristic of the human species and is hardly found at all in animals" (1972: 33). Thorpe's qualification should be noted, for there do seem to be some well-attested cases of animals lying or doing something very much like it. A nondomesticated adolescent male chimpanzee called Figans by the researchers at the Gombe research station in Tanzania was observed to do something that might well qualify. It was the practice of the ethologists to leave bananas in a certain clearing to attract the animals for observation. Expectably, high-ranking adult males dominated the assemblages and appropriated most of the fruit for themselves. Now when chimpanzees have been at rest, if one gets up and leaves briskly others are likely to follow him, perhaps because he is assumed to have seen or heard something. On a number of occasions Figans led the group away from the feeding area in such a manner, coming back quietly and alone a short while later to gorge himself in solitude. Van Lawick-Goodall states that "quite obviously he was doing it deliberately" (1971: 96). Margaritha Thurndahl (personal communication), who watched Figans on other occasions, suggests that his guile was even more elaborate. He would act as if he had heard something and dash off vocalizing, stimulating others to vocalize as well, returning then under the cover of the general commotion.

We can admire Figans's ingenuity, but our very admiration is a recognition of how awkward and difficult is lying that relies upon gross physical action, and how few must be the occasions in which it is possible. It is not surprising that even for apes for whom lying is evidently possible it is probably uncommon. But for many, if not indeed most, other species, lying may not occur because of a certain familiar feature of animal signaling recently characterized by J. C. Marshall, a linguist, as follows:

The most striking differences between animal signs and language behaviour are to be found, then, in the rigid, stereotyped nature of the former and in the fact that they are under the control of independently specifiable external stimuli and internal motivational states. [1970: 234]

In other words, given a particular state of affairs, internal or external, a particular signal will be transmitted because the signal is related to the event in roughly the same way that a nimbus on the horizon is related to forthcoming rain. The rustling of the peacock's fan, this is to say, is as intrinsic to his sexual arousal as his tumescence. It is a perceptible aspect of an event indicating to the observer the occurrence of other nonperceptible aspects of the same event. It is a simple *sign* (in Peirce's terms "index," 1960: 143ff.), of that event. In contrast, linguistic signals are not intrinsic, but only conventionally related, to their significata.

They are, to follow both Peirce and a usage widespread in American anthropology, *symbolic*.

The advantages of symbolic communication are so enormous that some anthropologists (White 1949: 22ff.) have claimed that its emergence in evolution can be compared in importance and novelty only to the appearance of life. Symbolic signals can be transmitted in the absence of their referents, and therefore discourse can escape from the here and now into the past, the future, the distant, and the hypothetical. The scope of thought and action is increased by magnitudes and dimensions by the use of the symbol, but the problem with which we are concerned is intrinsic to its very virtues. When a signal can be transmitted in the absence of its referent, or when, conversely, an event can occur without ineluctably signaling itself, lying becomes possible. It may be noted that the criterion of intentionality is implicit here. When communication is symbolic, it is no longer "under the control of external stimuli and internal state," no longer under the control of that which it signifies. It is, rather, subject to a higher-order control to which choices are available, and choice implies intention.

It is no doubt the case that Marshall (as others before him have done) overdraws the distinction between the communication of animals and of men if "animal signs" are taken to be transmitted only by animals and "symbolic communication" only by humans. Men continue to communicate through "animal signs" (Bateson 1972a: 177ff.), and there seems to be some symbol use by animals other than man, even some animals not taught symbols by men, and, as we have noted, some instances of what might be lying have been observed among them. The point is that lies are the bastard offspring of symbols. While there may be some use of symbols by nonhuman animals, the *reliance* of humans upon symbols surpasses by magnitudes any *rudimentary use* of symbols by other species, and therefore lying is essentially a human problem.

I take this problem to be fundamental. The survival of any population of animals depends upon social interactions characterized by some minimum degree of orderliness, but orderliness depends upon reliable communication. If the recipients of messages are not willing to accept the messages they receive as sufficiently reliable to inform their actions, their responses are likely to tend towards randomness, becoming increasingly less predictable, leading to yet more random responses, reducing orderliness yet further. When the communication system can accommodate lies it becomes a problem to assure the recipients of messages that the information they receive is sufficiently reliable to act upon (see Waddington 1961).

Not all symbolically encoded messages are problematic, or course. Those communicating necessary truths or well-known and immutable facts or empirical laws may not present difficulties. The message that 1 + 1 = 2 does not trouble a normal receiver. Given the meanings assigned to the terms it would be self-contradictory to deny this statement. Similarly, the assertion that the application of sufficient heat to ice produces liquid water is not likely to excite doubt. But most socially important information is not of these kinds. A law concerning heat, water, melting points, boiling points, and so on does not tell what the temperature of a distant lake is at this time, or whether the fish are now biting. That 1 + 1 = 2 does not tell us how many men are coming to help us or how many dollars remain in the treasury. The information upon which humans must act is seldom concerned directly with the general laws in accordance with which systems—psychological, biological, social, ecological, physical—operate, but rather with the contemporary or future states of those systems. Frequently it is not feasible for the receiver to verify such information transmitted to him; often, indeed, there is no possible way for him to do so. For instance, among the Maring, a people among whom I lived for a while in New Guinea, men communicate their pledge to give military assistance to groups of which they are not members by dancing at those groups' religious festivals (Rappaport 1968). There is no way for their hosts to verify or validate the sincerity or steadfastness of their pledges. How then can they rely upon them?

II

With symbolic communication there emerges not only the possibility of lying, but also of sanctification. Sanctity seems to emerge out of ritual, or at least it is continually re-established in religious ritual, but ritual is more widespread than religious belief. Indeed, the term "ritual" has been used to refer to formally similar conduct observed not only among members of other species but even of other phyla. Among the obvious shared characteristics of all that is called ritual are stereotypy, material non-instrumentality, performance, and, possibly, emotional force. It is also generally accepted that among both men and animals ritual is a mode of communication.

In all ritual, both animal and human, there is transmitted what Lyons (1972: 71ff.), following Abercrombie (1967) and Laver (1968), calls "indexical information," that is, information concerning the current physiological, psychological, or social state of the transmitter. This is probably all that is transmitted in most or all animal rituals. For instance, when one baboon presents his rump to another he is communicating his submission; when the other mounts he is communicating his dominance. Nothing else seems to be communicated, which is to say that the message content of the ritual is exhausted by the indexical messages transmitted in the ritual. But some human rituals are different. Although all human rituals have an indexical component, and although this component is always of great importance—a matter to which we shall return—the message content of some human rituals is not exhausted by the indexical messages transmitted in them. Additional messages are embodied in the canon, the fixed sequence of formal acts and utterances not encoded by the performers but merely transmitted by them. The originators or encoders are likely to be taken to be creators, or ancestors, or spirits, or ancient heroes.

The messages encoded in liturgies vary, but in some of them rather curious postulates, typically without material referents, are likely to be found. Included here are such sentences as the *Shema* of the Jews and those included in the Christian creeds. In the rituals in which Maring men pledge their future military support there are addresses to ancestors, and it is reasonable to posit as an analogous postulate "Deceased ancestors persist as sentient and powerful beings."

Such postulates, being without material referents, are not in their nature falsifiable, nor can they be verified, and yet they are taken to be unquestionable. I take sanctity to be the quality of unquestionableness imputed by the faithful to such unfalsifiable postulates. That the unquestionableness of ultimate sacred postulates is a consequence of the invariance of the canons in which they are expressed has been argued at length in "The Obvious Aspects of Ritual" and need not be discussed further here. This use of the term "sacred" is, of course, more restricted than is usual. I use it to refer to one aspect of a more inclusive category, "the holy," that includes not only the discursive sacred, but also the nondiscursive or emotional aspect of religious phenomena, which I call the "numinous." In my usage, "sanctity" is that part of the holy that can be expressed in language and that, as it were, faces conscious reason and discourse. Indeed, it accords with this usage to say that sanctity is a characteristic or quality of discourse rather than of the objects, real or putative, with which the discourse is concerned.

While sanctity may have its source, so to speak, in "ultimate sacred postulates," it flows to other sentences which, unlike them, do include references to material objects and activities, sentences directly concerned with the affairs of society. In literate societies theological exposition may sometimes be the vehicle for transporting sanctity from ultimate sacred postulates to sentences including material terms. But ritual association, which does not depend upon writing, is surely more ancient and remains more widespread, and it is also more persuasive and binding (see "The Obvious Aspects of Ritual"). The message "We shall help you in warfare" transmitted by Maring men by dancing at the festivals of their friends, seemingly partakes of the truthfulness that is a property of the ultimate sacred postulates with which it is associated. To sanctify messages is to certify them. This function of sanctity remains important in the swearing of oaths.

I am not arguing that sanctity eliminates falsehood, although it may decrease its prevalence. I do argue that sanctification increases the willingness of recipients of symbolically encoded messages to accept the messages they receive as sufficiently reliable to act upon. The problem of falsehood is not merely that of falsehood itself, nor even of its direct effects, as devastating as they may be, but of the corrosive distrust bred by falsehood's mere possibility. To the extent that the recipients of messages accept them as trustworthy, their actions will tend to be nonrandom and therefore predictable. Moreover, the regularity of their responses may bring about the states of affairs that they assume. To put it a little differently, the validity of some messages is a function of their acceptance (Bateson 1951: 212ff.), and their acceptance is a function of their sanctification. As far as informing behavior is concerned, sanctified truth is a third member of the set that also includes the necessary truth of logic and the empirical truth of experience.

I am also not arguing that all the messages of any society have ever been directly sanctified in ritual. I am proposing that the sanctification of strategic messages must have been important in the evolution of mankind, and whereas the sacred would be literally unthinkable without symbols, so the emergence of symbolic communication might not have been possible without the sacred, because, among other things, of the subversive possibilities inherent in the capacity to lie.

Like lies, the ultimate sacred postulates from which sanctity flows are made possible by symbolic communication, by freeing the signal from that which it signifies. Thus, the quality of language out of which the problem of falsehood arose also proposed its solution through a move of astonishing—yet inevitable—simplicity and profundity. Whereas lies are made possible by the freeing of signals from material significata, ultimate sacred postulates are made possible by the freeing of significata from material embodiment altogether. It may be noted, in passing, that if lying is the intentional transmission of information thought or known by the transmitter to be false, then ultimate sacred postulates, which in their nature are unfalsifiable, cannot be lies in an ordinary sense. They can, however, be faulty in ways related to lying. We shall return to them later.

III

The emergence of sanctity may be an example of the evolutionary principle that Hockett and Ascher (1964: 137) have called "Romer's Rule," which proposes that the initial effect of an evolutionary change is conservative in that it makes it possible for a previously existing way of life to persist in the face of changed conditions. For example, in the passage that inspired Hockett and Ascher, the zoologist Alfred Romer (1954: vol. 1, 43 ff.) argued that through the enlargement of their fins and other relatively minor organizational modifications of certain of their organs, the lobe-finned fish, who were ancestral to the amphibia, became able to migrate overland from one drying-up body of water to another, and thus were able to maintain their general aquatic way of life in the face of the intermittent dessication presumed to have characterized the Devonian period. Similarly, sanctity may have permitted the persistence of some previously existing mode of social organization, or even the survival of the associations of organisms termed "societies," in the face of the threat posed to orderly social life by an increasing ability to lie.

The certification of questionable information is only one of sanctity's offices. All sorts of sentences may be sanctified, including directives specifying particular rules, such as "thou shalt not kill," and homilies like "it is more blessed to give than to receive," and they may also include sentences certifying authorities, like "Elizabeth is by grace of God queen." Sanctification may, finally, be extended to, or invest, all of the sentences through which society is regulated. These are likely to include those in terms of which thought and attitude are organized: the truisms of child-rearing and kinship obligation, and all of the mythic discourse in which pangolins unite (Douglas 1966: 170ff.), snakes corrupt, and cassowaries are related to your brother-in-law (Bulmer 1967)—all of the myth and classification in terms of which the world is ordered.

This is a matter of great importance given another evolutionary trend that was surely associated with the emergence of language. I refer to the decrease in the degree to which behavior and patterns for behavior are genetically specified. The replacement of genetic determination by cultural stipulation of patterns of behavior has permitted men to enter and eventually to dominate the great range of environments the world presents to them. But intrinsic to increasing flexibility is the concomitant problem that men are no longer genetically constrained to abide by the conventions of the societies in which they do happen to live. Sanctity in the absence of genetic specification of behavior stabilizes the conventions of particular societies by certifying directives, authorities who may issue directives, and all of the mythic discourse that connects the present to the beginning, establishing for men particular meanings from among the great range of meanings available to their genetically unbounded imaginations.

To put this a little differently, the second problem intrinsic to the powers of language is alternative. With an increasing range of cultural orders becoming genetically possible for any human organism, the adaptive capacities of the species are enhanced and its adaptive processes accelerated. But possibilities for disorder are also magnified. If cultural orders are built upon words, there is not only the possibility of false words, but of many words, not only of lie, but of babel, of overwhelming alternative. The conception of alternative orders is an inevitable concomitant of lexicon and syntax. If it is possible to say "Christ is God and Jove is not," it is possible to say or imagine "Jove is God and Christ is not." If it is possible to say "Monarchy is good and democracy is not," it is possible to say or imagine the converse. The conception of alternative may be the first step toward the disruption of the existent if not toward the realization of the alternative, and any conventional order must protect itself against the disordering powers of the linguistically informed imagination. If there are any words it thus may be necessary to establish *The Word.* Once again Romer's Rule may be cited. Although the initial effect of an innovation is conservative its subsequent effects might not be. As the terrestrial vertebrates emerged out of the genetic changes initially making it possible for the lobe-finned fish to maintain an aquatic way of life, so sanctity, once emerged, provided a principle upon which the great range of novel human social organizations made possible by language could rest.

Lie and alternative, in sum, are two fundamental problems—perhaps *the* two fundamental problems—besetting language. It is of interest that Buber (1952) takes them to be the two grounds of evil. I have argued, however, that sanctity—also a precipitate of language, but of language subordinated to propriety-generating canonical invariance—ameliorates those evils by certifying the truthfulness of putatively factual information and the correctness of convention.

Truthfulness and correctness are, of course, related notions. It is of interest here that, according to some scholars, in the Zoroastrianism of the ancient Persian empire (Duchesne-Guillemin 1966: 76ff.) as well as in Vedic India (Brown 1972: 252ff.) the term *rta* meant both truth and order and the word *anrta* may have been used for both lie and violation of correct order. We may note a second member of the family of lies. Whereas an ordinary lie is of the class of incorrect statements, statements that do not correspond to the states of affairs they purport to describe or report, what we may call *vedic lies* are incorrect states of affairs, states of affairs, that is, that do not conform to the specifications they purport, or are supposed, to meet.

IV

Ultimate sacred postulates, which are often expressed only in ritual, may sanctify sentences concerning ethics, authorities, categories of thought, the maxims of socialization and the rules of social interaction, economic organization and ecological relations—sentences, this is to say, having directly to do with the regulation of society. To put this into terms proposed by Victor Turner (1969), ultimate sacred postulates, perhaps supported by "communitas,"* the "destructured" and often numinous state of society prevailing in ritual, may sanctify what he means by "structure," the differentiated, rational organization through which societies conduct their day-to-day affairs and meet their material needs.

That sanctity supports social order is one of anthropology's most ancient truisms. That it may increase the adaptiveness of social systems is not, for flexibility is central to adaptiveness, and to maintain the predominance of some conventions against the challenge of alternatives seems hardly to be to maintain flexibility. The ability to modify or replace conventions is central to human adaptiveness, and the suggestion that that which constrains change preserves such an ability seems, at first, to be virtually paradoxical. Flexibility, however, is not mere versatility but, rather, a product of versatility and orderliness. The innumerable possibilities inherent in words and their combination are not all eliminated by the unquestionable Word enunciated in ritual's apparently invariant canon but are reduced, constrained, and ordered by it. The conventions through which societies are regulated, it should be emphasized, are *sanctified,* but they themselves are not *sacred.* The ultimately sacred, and thus absolutely unquestionable, is, in an orderly adaptive system, confined to certain postulates expressed in the most invariant portions of liturgies. A feature typical of ultimate sacred postulates is of great significance here. I refer to their material and social vacuity. In "The Obvious Aspects of Ritual" I observed that this feature places them beyond falsification. Now it may be suggested that this self-same characteristic is of importance to the flexibility of adaptive systems as wholes.

I have discussed the nature of these systems in "Adaptive Structure and Its Disorders" and can be brief here. Such systems, including social systems, do not have special goals or outputs, their properly adaptive goal being nothing more specific than to persist, which is to say to continue to be able to transform themselves in response to the vicissitudes of history and environment. As Lawrence Slobodkin (1968) has put it, such systems are "players of the existential game," a game in which there are no payoffs having value external to the game because the "player" can't "leave the table," a game in which, therefore, the only reward for successful play is to be allowed to continue to play. Since the conditions and even the rules of play are likely to change, flexibility—the capacity for orderly self-transformation—is advantageous, rigid

---

*I am using the term in a slightly more restricted sense than does Turner.

commitment to particular modes of play—particular conventions or institutions—is disadvantageous, or even lethal. Now ultimate sacred postulates, which contain no material terms, do not in themselves specify particular material goals or institutions. They can, therefore, not only sanctify any institution while being bound to none but can also sanctify changes in institutions. Continuity can be maintained while allowing change to take place, for the association of particular institutions or conventions with ultimate sacred postulates is a matter of interpretation, and that which must be interpreted can always be reinterpreted without being challenged. So, gods may remain unchanged while the conventions they sanctify are transformed through reinterpretation in response to changing conditions. Usage is not sufficient to establish conventions but the conventions established in liturgy may be modified, through reinterpretation, in response to changing usage arising out of changed historical conditions. It may be suggested here that reinterpretation is facilitated by the cryptic as well as the nonmaterial nature of ultimate sacred postulates. It is important, if a proposition is to be taken to be unquestionably true, that no one understand it, and it is not surprising that ultimate sacred postulates are often "mysteries."*

This brief account suggests an encompassing corrective operation through which regulatory structures that have become oppressive or maladaptive are divested of their sanctity. Material and social conditions are in some considerable degree a function of the operation of regulatory structures which, in turn, are sanctified by postulates the ultimate sacred status of which is contingent upon their formal or numinous acceptance by congregations of the very persons whose lives they order. If material and social conditions remain oppressive or unsatisfactory, the willingness or ability of congregations to sanctify the structures responsible for their misery will, sooner or later, be adversely affected and, if conditions do not improve, those structures, or those manning them, will sooner or later be stripped of sanctity.

The phrase "sooner or later" is important here. The withdrawal of sanctification is likely to be a more or less direct function of understanding, and the operations of some societies may be so mystified or so complex that the sources of distress are grasped only slowly. Moreover, even when the nature of the difficulties becomes more or less apparent people are often willing to put up with a good deal in the name of God. It is probably well that they are, for unhappy conditions are likely to be as reversible as they are ineluctable, and fortitude is often a better response

---

*A *Catholic Dictionary* defines a "mystery properly so called" as a "truth which, though it is not *against* reason, so far transcends it that no created intelligence could ever discover it, and which, even when it is revealed, is impenetrable by any created intelligence" (Attwater 1961: 336).

to them than deliberate corrective action. Premature structural responses to adversity may cause long-run difficulties as they alleviate short-run stresses (see "Adaptive Structure and Its Disorders"). The restraint and fortitude that sanctification encourages may provide time for less profound, more easily reversible corrective responses to operate first, sanctified structural changes following only if less radical corrective measures fail. In short, sanctity maintains order in adaptive response sequences.

This simplified account of sanctification and desanctification describes a cybernetic structure, for those who are subordinate to sanctified regulatory hierarchies are those who invest them with, and may divest them of, sanctity. Therefore, if authorities wish to maintain their sanctity they must keep the operations of the regulatory structures they administer in reasonable working order. If they do not they may find themselves deprived of sanctity, either passively as people withdraw from participation in rituals supporting existing hierarchies (possibly because they no longer experience numinous emotions while performing them) or actively by being deposed through sanctified procedures (e.g., Frazer 1963: 308ff.) or, possibly, through the instigation of prophets who challenge their connection to the sources of sanctity, or even declare new ultimate sacred postulates.

This ultimate corrective operation inheres in systems as wholes. It is interesting in this regard that the etymology of the word "holy" is shared with the words "whole" and "health." In this light the use of the term "holy" for the larger category that includes both the discursive sacred and the nondiscursive numinous seems to me to be especially appropriate. The sacred and the numinous, the rational and the affective, the everyday formal structure of society and its occasional ritual or festive state of communitas, form wholes through the mobilization of which the ambitions of separate men may be subordinated to common interest while at the same time the operations of society are continually reviewed and tempered by the needs of those composing it. Wholeness, holiness, and adaptiveness are closely related if not, indeed, one and the same.

V

It may be that liturgical order, sacred understanding, and the sanctification of convention together constituted an evolutionary response to the increasing possibilities for lie and alternative that developed as concomitants of symbolic communication and that continue to threaten the social orders built upon symbolic communication. Can it not be argued, however, that liturgical operations and the sacred and supernatural entities at once conceived through them and rationalized by them are as false as the lies for which they are antidotes?

It is obvious, first, that ultimate sacred postulates cannot be lies in any simple sense because, as we have already noted, to the extent that their terms are nonmaterial, they are nonfalsifiable. Moreover, even if they could be shown to be in some sense false, there may not be on the part of those transmitting them any intention to transmit false information. More important, it is possible to argue that ultimate sacred postulates, which are without material referents, are members of the class of statements the validity of which is a function of their acceptance (Bateson 1951), and the same may be said of the regulatory sentences they sanctify. The process of naturalization that occurs in some liturgies is likewise straightforward, and the states of affairs that come into being through liturgical actions are, finally, as much of nature as those that come out of tectonic activity. "Brute" and "institutional" facts (Searle 1969: 50ff.) are inseparable in nature.

Other possible flaws which are not encompassed by any narrow definition of lie but which are, nevertheless, related to lie may be intrinsic to liturgical orders, and to the conceptions emerging out of them of forces or sentient beings transcending mortality and society, or even space and time. I note first, mainly to disagree with it, the charge that religious conceptions are inherently deceitful simply because they are illusory. In the next section we shall turn to more substantial difficulties that may beset liturgy and sanctity.

It is well known that Freud (1927) took religious conceptions to be illusions, and for much the same reason that Durkheim took all religion to be in some sense true, Marx (1842, 1844) took it to be false (Skorupski 1976: 32ff.). Durkheim, who rested his case largely upon Australian aboriginal material, took such conceptions to be symbolic representations of society, veils of mystification being perhaps necessary because men are likely to find the necessity of the apparently natural, and the authority of the naturalizing supernaturals, to be more compelling than mere rational conventions as bases for living in some degree of concord with other men and nature. Marx, in contrast, who was concerned largely with state societies, took religious conceptions not to be more or less useful or necessary mystifications but deceptions facilitating the manipulation of the many by the few.

Freud and Marx were in considerable agreement in seeing religious conceptions not only to be illusions, but because illusory deplorable, for illusion denies to man the illuminations which his unclouded reason could provide him, and prevents him from establishing social orders founded upon reason. But the twentieth century has perhaps taught us that the faith of the nineteenth in reason may have been too sanguine.

I think we know now that conscious reason has not been an imprisoned angel that would save us if only it were freed from its bondage to the irrational. To the extent that it has been possible to free reason it has been freed, perhaps as never before, in the time of our fathers, our grandfathers, and ourselves, and it has discovered evolution and relativity and the double helix. It has also spawned monsters of such power that they threaten the existence of the species that reasoned them into being. But we do not need history to tell us that noble conceptions are not alone in being born of conscious reason. It is in consciousness that men scheme and conspire against their fellows, and if reason is not always downright treacherous, it is often narrowly self-serving. Indeed, the word "rational" in economics, the discipline that probably more than any other guides the affairs of modern societies, has come to refer to a class of activities that pits men against their fellows and that must be, in some sense, antisocial: the application of scarce means to differentially graded ends to maximize the position of the actor vis-à-vis others. If rationality in the economic sense is what conscious reason can come to it may be suggested that reason alone could not provide a secure and sound basis for social life even if it could be freed from the nonrational. Fortunately it can't be, for the nonrational is not only the home of rage and fear, but also of art, poetry, and whatever it is that people mean by the word "love." Moreover, the understandings that eventually lead to formal theories concerning space, time, matter and energy are as likely to be grasped initially by the left hand of the nonrational as by the right hand of conscious reason (Bruner 1970).

Conscious reason is incomplete, and so are its unaided understandings. The common sense of conscious reason, which has its loci in individual organisms, proposes a sense of separation. Consciousness separates humans from each other, each in solitude behind his own eyes, each imprisoned by his own skin, each enclosed alone between the dates of birth and death. The common sense of separation endorses the common sense of self-sufficiency and autonomy, notions that are sanctified virtually to the point of apotheosis in Western capitalist society. But of course they are illusions. Although humans are metabolically separate from one another, and although consciousness is individual, humans are not self-sufficient and their autonomy is relative and slight. They are parts of larger systems upon which their continued existence is contingent. But the wholeness, if not indeed the very existence, of those systems, may be beyond the grasp of their ordinary consciousness. Although conscious reason is incomplete, the mode of understanding encouraged by liturgy may make up for some of its deficiencies. Participation in rituals may enlarge the awareness of those participating in them, providing them with understandings of perfectly natural aspects of the social and physical world that may elude unaided reason.

Gregory Bateson's recent (1972: 448ff.) discussion of mind casts light on those aspects of nature that may be grasped by ritual's insight. Bateson suggests that the minimum unit of idea is a "difference which makes a difference," a *bit* in information theory. The elementary cybernetic circuits around which such units of information flow are the simplest units of mind. Mind, that is to say, is immanent in cybernetic systems. While it is surely the case that some such circuits are contained entire within individual consciousness, the mind of the individual is more comprehensive than his consciousness alone, as Freud long ago showed us. We also know directly from experience that our information-processing circuits include more than our brains, because in response to some messages we experience changes in our visceral states, and these changes enter into the computations that produce our total reactions to the information received. We further imply here that the information circuits that are significant to us include not only more than our brains but more than the selves our skins bound. We are dependent upon circuits that include portions of environments; some of them include many individuals, often individuals of a number of species. Whereas animals are, as a rule, quite separate from each other as far as metabolism is concerned, they are less autonomous with respect to information processing. This is to say that matter-energy processing systems and information processing systems are not coextensive. But the adequate functioning, indeed the very survival, of metabolically autonomous individuals as well as societies is contingent upon supra-individual information processing circuitry immanent in social and ecological systems, and disruptions of such circuits are likely to lead to results not formally dissimilar from the effects of brain lesions or neuroses. In the absence of reliable information, total systems or their parts cease to be self-correcting. The doctrine of I-Thou which Buber (1970) proposes as an ethical dictum is in fact an adaptive imperative, and it does not denigrate Tillich's concept of the "Ground of Being" or "Being Itself" (McKelway 1964: 123ff.) to suggest that the structure of information processing in nature accords with it. Bateson has recognized these similarities:

. . . there is a larger Mind of which the individual mind is only a subsystem. This larger Mind is comparable to God and is perhaps what some people mean by "God" but it is still immanent in the total interconnected social system and planetary ecology. [1972b: 461]

Conscious reason may of course provide us with knowledge about the structure and function of ecological and social systems and present to us reasonable arguments for complying with their imperatives. But such knowledge and reasons are likely to be overcome by what economists call "rationality." To ask conscious reason to lead unaided the separate individuals in which it resides to favor the long-term interests of eco-systems and societies over their own immediate interests may be to ask too much of it. Sustained compliance with the imperatives of larger systems not only may require more than ordinary reason, but may have to be maintained in defiance of a consciousness that *in its nature* informs men of their separateness. It may, indeed, require that the common sense of separation be transcended and replaced from time to time by an extraordinary sense of participation, of being joined together with enti-ties, from which one is separated by the evidence of the senses and by competitive rationality, into wholes—societies and ecosystems—that are natural, but not in their nature directly perceptible.

To perform a liturgical order is to participate in it, act as part of it; and where the ritual is public, it is to join with others in this participation. In many rituals strong emotions are engendered and consciousness altered. Not infrequently there is a feeling of "loss of self"—that is, a loss of the sense of separation—and a feeling of union with the other members of the congregation and even more embracing entities. It is obviously important that singing, dancing, and speaking in unison are common features of public rituals. To sing or dance in concert or in unison with others, to move as they move and speak as they speak is, literally, to act as part of a larger entity, to participate in it; and as the radical separation of the everyday self dissolves in the communitas (Turner 1969) of par-ticipation—as it sometimes does—the larger entity becomes palpable. Such extraordinary or even mystical experiences seem to be profoundly satisfying but, more important here, they also may provide deeper and more compelling understandings of perfectly natural and extremely im-portant aspects of the physical and social world than can be provided by reason alone. In sum, liturgical order does not always hide the world from conscious reason behind a veil of supernatural illusions. Rather, it may pierce the veil of illusions behind which unaided reason hides the world from comprehensive human understanding.

VI

But admiration for liturgy and sanctity must, at the end, be tempered, for they are both subject to real and malignant disorders of their own.

First, it is obvious that if liturgical orders "naturalize" some conven-tions they must stipulate, at least tacitly, that others are unnatural. As a consequence, the conventions of other cultural groups are likely to be thought not to be simply different from those of one's own, nor even merely immoral, but abominable. Those practicing them may, consequently, be taken to be other than, or less than, human, and treated accordingly. To use Erik Erikson's (1966) term, cultural groups become pseudo-species. Sanctity and liturgy may magnify minor cultural differences into seemingly major natural differences. They may not only envenom enmities for which they themselves were not initially responsible, but are themselves capable of setting men against each other.

Less obvious difficulties may beset the structure of sanctification. If adaptive systems are to remain flexible the degree of sanctity accorded to directives should be inversely correlated with their material specificity. A problem that may be intrinsic to sanctification becomes apparent here, for dissonance may develop between sanctity and specificity. Highly specific directives may become oversanctified. A case in point might be birth control prohibition in Catholicism. To an outsider it would seem that birth control devices could be made acceptable through reinterpretation without challenge to dogma. But highly specific low-order directives concerning them are being accorded a degree of sanctity greater than their specificity warrants, a degree of sanctity approaching that of ultimate sacred postulates, or dogma, and the church seems to be suffering widespread defection as a result.

Oversanctification of the specific, a disorder akin to mistakes in logical typing (see Bateson 1972c) and one that stifles social change, is a possibility intrinsic to sanctification. It may be, however, that it becomes especially likely, and thus especially serious, in state-organized societies, for in such societies specialized clergies, often in possession of powerful means of coercion, may be in positions allowing them to adjudicate questions of orthodoxy.

But oversanctification of the specific may develop for reasons other than an inflexible orthodoxy's confusion of specific rules with general principles. I have argued in "Adaptive Structure and Its Disorders" that as the subsystems of societies become increasingly differentiated and differentially powerful, the more powerful are ever more able to elevate their own special goals and interests to positions of predominance in the systems of which they are only components. As their special goals and interests are elevated they are invested with the sanctity of the more general postulates they replace or define. If, as President Coolidge said, "The business of America is business," and if America is "One Nation under God," as the pledge of allegiance stipulates, then business and all that is related to it—profit, private enterprise, high consumption— become conflated with "life, liberty, and the pursuit of happiness." The theologian Paul Tillich (1957: 11ff.) characterized the "absolutizing of the relative and the relativizing of the absolute," which identifies the ultimate with the material and with the status quo, as "idolatry," and he took it to be evil. I will only add that to accord a higher degree of sanctity to propositions or goals than their specificity warrants is to narrow the range of conditions under which the society can persist. Evil and mal-adaptiveness, it may be suggested, intersect in what Tillich called "idol-atry," and I include idolatry in the family of falsehoods.

If we can take to be "adaptively true" postulates the acceptance of which enhances chances of persistence, we can, I think, take idolatrous postulates to be adaptively false, for the apotheosizing of the material, it is ironic to observe, defeats the material goal of survival. I take idolatrous postulates to be false, be it noticed, regardless of the degree of accep-tance accorded them. This is to say that consent and consensus are not in themselves sufficient to establish all conventional truths. The only ulti-mate sacred postulates that can be adaptively true are those that, having no material terms, do not irrevocably commit the societies accepting them to particular institutions or conventions. "The lie," said Martin Buber, "is from time and will be swallowed up by time; the truth, the divine truth, is from eternity and in eternity, and in devotion to the truth . . . partakes of eternity" (1952: 13f.).

The very quality of nonidolatrous ultimate sacred postulates that seems to render them rationally illusory, that they are neither verifiable nor falsifiable, makes them adaptively true. Nevertheless, the possibility of idolatry, which bears a family resemblance to lie, is intrinsic to sanctity. Its likelihood, however, is perhaps increased with increasing social dif-ferentiation and technological development, both of which tend to in-crease disparities in the distribution of power among the subsystems of societies. Social differentiation and technological advance, both aspects of cultural evolution, place at the disposal of authorities coercive instru-ments at once increasingly powerful and decreasingly available to their subjects. The possession of such means of coercion diminishes the dependence of the authority upon his sanctity. As he become increas-ingly powerful he can stand more upon power (a function of men, resources, and organization; see Bierstadt 1950: 730 ff.) and less upon sanctity.

This is not to say that powerful authorities necessarily dispense with sanctity. It is to say that as power accumulates the relationship between sanctity and authority is likely to be inverted. Whereas in the techno-logically simple society the authority is contingent upon its sanctity, in the technically advanced society sanctity may be degraded to the status of authority's instrument.

An aspect of this degradation may be a change in the basis of the unquestionable status of ultimate sacred postulates. Whereas they once rested upon the uncoerced acceptance of the faithful, perhaps supported by numinous experiences, they later come to rest upon force—heretics are burned, infidels put to the sword. When acceptance is coerced it becomes a lie, but it is not the lie of he who accepts. It is the lie of the coercer. We may refer to these lies as "lies of oppression." In lies of oppression the coercer is not only the liar but also the ultimate victim of his own lie, for if, as I have argued, both acceptance and its waning inform the regulation of society, then for an authority to coerce acceptance is for it itself to distort the information by which it is guided. Power threatens truth and threatens the cybernetics of adaptive systems, for adaptation relies upon information concerning current conditions that is in some degree accurate. This is to suggest that oppression is not only inhumane but maladaptive and, finally, self-defeating.

I do not argue that with degradation of sanctity by power religious experiences no longer occur, nor that acceptance is never freely given. But, invoked in the churches of state-organized societies by visions of ultimate or other-worldly salvation, they may be disconnected, so to speak, from corrective effect upon the here and now. They no longer form part of an encompassing adaptive structure. Indeed, to the extent that the experience of ritual participation alleviates the anxieties of the faithful without alleviating the causes of their anxieties it bears formal resemblance to neurosis, as Freud (1907) claimed, and to opiates, as Marx (1844) claimed, and rituals are parts of deceits if they lead the faithful into bondage while promising salvation. Sanctity, itself the foundation of truth and correctness, and the numinous supporting it, when subordinated to the powerful and material become false, for they falsify consciousness. But the cost is great even for those who are not deluded. For them ritual becomes empty and meaningless, indeed the very term "ritual" comes to denote empty form (Douglas 1970: 19). The act of ritual acceptance, once more profound than belief, becomes a proverbial form of hypocrisy. But in refusing to participate hypocritically no less than in hypocritical participation, the conscious minds of men and women become divorced from those deep and hidden portions of themselves to which ritual participation introduced and bound them. The self becomes fragmented and some of the fragments may be lost. The consciousness that remains is likely to remain trapped in its radical separation. For those not deluded there is alienation.

So the sacred and the numinous may get detached from each other and from their cybernetic or corrective functions. Given the association I have made between wholeness and holiness it is not inappropriate to say that they become unholy. As holiness stands to wholeness, adaptiveness, and survival, so does unholiness stand to fragmentation, maladaptation, and annihilation. It is of interest that in the Kabbalah of Isaac Luria (Scholem 1969: 110ff.) the origin of evil is not ascribed to the appearance of any particular substance or being, but to the fragmentation of a primordial unity. The disruption of the cybernetics of holiness is such a fragmentation. We may recall once again the Vedic and Zoroastrian notion of lie as violation of sacred order, but now the order itself becomes disorderly, disrupting ecosystems, oppressing men and women, leading societies into decline. Many years ago de Rougemont (1944) made a distinction between ordinary lies and what he called "diabolical lies," in recognition of the putative proclivity of "The Father of Lies" for appearing as his own opposite. Diabolical lies are not simply false transmissions but lies that tamper with the very canons of truth. I think it not wrong to assign to this category assertions of sanctity for discourse the unquestionable status of which rests ultimately upon force, which is subject rather than superior to the authorities it sanctifies, which misleads ritual acceptance and numinous experience away from corrective effect upon the here and now, which encourages fragmentation and maladaptation while promising wholeness and heaven.

Diabolical lies are not new to this world, as Buber's (1952: 7 ff.) analysis of the 12th Psalm informs us. The psalmist, according to Buber,

no longer suffers merely from liars but from a generation of the lie, . . . the lie in this generation has reached the highest level of perfection as an ingeniously controlled means of supremacy . . . [removing] completely . . . the basis of men's common life . . . those the psalmist has in mind speak "delusion" . . . they breed "delusion" in their hearers, they spin illusions for them. . . . Instead of completing their fellow-men's experience and insight with the help of their own, as required by men's common thinking and knowing, they introduce falsified material into his knowledge of the world and of life, and thus falsify the relations of his soul to his being. . . . In order that the lie may bear the stamp of truth, the liars as it were manufacture a special heart, an apparatus which functions with the greatest appearance of naturalness, from which lies well up to the "smooth lips" like spontaneous utterances of experience and insight . . . all this is the work of the mighty in order to render tractable by deceits those whom they have oppressed. [pp. 8–10]

Diabolical lies, like lies of oppression and idolatrous lies, are the products of power, and if they are not new to this world, new and increasing possibilities for diabolical lying are offered by the increasing ability of ever smaller groups of men and ever more specialized institutions to control the flow of ever greater volumes of information more comprehensively and the disposition of increasing concentrations of energy more totally. This ability has been enhanced by advances in technology, which is to say that it is correlated with what seems to have been the central factor in cultural evolution.

It thus may be that humanity's fall is one with its evolution: as its evolution has been founded upon its possession of words, so may its possession by words have sealed its fate. Of words are inevitably born not only ordinary lies and vedic lies, which may be benign, but also lies of oppression, idolatrous lies, diabolical lies, and no doubt other forms, that join together into the encompassing and world-dissolving generation of the lie that seems to vex our times even more than the times of the psalmist. Be this as it may, ancient divines understood as well as we do, or better, the paradoxes of the human condition, and there is an early medieval Jewish legend of creation (Scholem 1969: 179ff.) that also seems to identify the fall with the word. Before He breathed sense into the earth that was to be man, God put his seal upon His creation's forehead. The three letters *aleph, mem,* and *tov,* of which the seal was composed, encompass all speech, for they are the first, middle, and last letters of the alphabet. But in the mystical tradition of which this legend is a part, words themselves are creative and even identified with God himself (ibid.: 167ff.). Thus, the three letters in encompassing all language encompass all things: they are the beginning, end, and continuity. They also spell the word *emet,* which means "truth." When the sense that God had breathed into him led man, as it inevitably did, into lie, and vedic lie—violation of the order protected by the primordial prohibition against making distinctions—God erased from his forehead the letter *aleph,* which, signifying the beginning of all things, was associated most closely and unambiguously with Himself. This left on man's forehead the word *met,* meaning "death."

But in attending to ancient words we should remember that when they were expelled from Eden ("bliss"), the Hebrew name that man bestowed upon the woman who was to be "the mother of all the living" was Chawwā, meaning "life." It is not only human death that the fall invents, but also human life, a mode of existence characterized by discourse, and by the reason and choice discourse makes possible. For human life to persist it was necessary for the one commandment that had for a while preserved Eden to be replaced by the 613 derived from the Torah, for, being founded upon words for whose lies there is no sure cure, the conditions of human life are tenuous. But if discursive reason and speech are unique on this earth to human life, human life remains more than reason and speech, and the generation of the lie is continuously challenged by the living—by prophets, mystics, youth, revolutionaries, and reformers—who, in their search for wholeness, restore holiness ever again to the breaking world by re-establishing the adaptive connection of the timeless sacred and the immediate numinous to the continuing here and now.

REFERENCES CITED

Abercrombie, D.
  1967   *Elements of general phonetics.* Edinburgh: Edinburgh University Press.

Attwater, Donald, ed.
1961   A Catholic Dictionary (The Catholic Encyclopaedic Dictionary), 3d. ed.
        New York: Macmillan
Bateson, Gregory
1951   Conventions of communication: where validity depends upon belief.
        In Communication: the social matrix of psychiatry, ed. J. Ruesch and G.
        Bateson, pp. 217-227. New York: Norton.
1972a   A theory of play and fantasy. In Steps to an ecology of mind, pp. 177-
        193. New York: Ballantine.
1972b   Form, substance, and difference. In Steps to an ecology of mind, pp.
        448-468. New York: Ballantine.
1972c   The logical categories of learning and communication. In Steps to an
        ecology of mind. New York: Ballantine.
Bierstadt, Richard
1950   An analysis of social power. American Sociological Review 15:730-738.
Brown, Norman W.
1972   Duty as truth in ancient India. Proceedings of the American Philosophical
        Society 116(3):252-268.
Bruner, James
1970   On knowing: essays for the left hand. New York: Atheneum. (Harvard
        University Press, 1962).
Buber, Martin
1952   Good and evil: two interpretations. New York: Charles Scribner's Sons.
Bulmer, Ralph
1967   Why is the cassowary not a bird? Man, N.S. 2:5-25.
Douglas, Mary
1966   Purity and danger. New York: Praeger.
1970   Natural symbols. Harmondsworth: Penguin.
Duchesne-Guillemin, Jacques
1966   Symbols and values in Zoroastrianism: their survival and renewal. New
        York: Harper & Row.
Durkheim, Emile
1961   The elementary forms of the religious life. Joseph Ward Swain, trans-
        lator. New York: Collier. (First published 1912).
Erikson, E.
1966   The ritualization of ontogeny. In A discussion of ritualisation of be-
        haviour in animals and man, ed. J. S. Huxley, pp. 249-272; Philo-
        sophical Transactions of the Royal Society of London, Series B,
        Biological Sciences 772, vol. 251.
Frazer, Sir James
1963   The golden bough: a study in magic and religion. One volume, abridged
        edition. New York: Macmillan. (First published 1922).
Freud, Sigmund
1907   Obsessive actions and religious practices. Zeitschrift für Religions-
        psychologie 1:4-12. (Translated 1959 in the standard edition of The
        complete psychological works of Sigmund Freud, ed. J. Strachey, vol. 9.
        London: Hogarth.)
1927   The future of an illusion. (Translated by W. D. Robson-Scott, revised
        and newly edited by James Strachey, 1964. First published as Die
        Zukunft einer Illusion, Vienna.)

Hobbes, Thomas
   1930   *Hobbes: selections.* Ed. Frederick J. E. Woodbridge. New York: Charles Scribner's Sons.
Hockett, C. F., and S. Altman
   1968   A note on design features. In *Animal communication,* ed. T. A. Sebeok, pp. 61–72. Bloomington: Indiana University Press.
Hockett, C. F., and R. Ascher
   1964   The human revolution. *Current Anthropology* 5:135–168.
Laver, J. D. M.
   1968   Voice quality and indexical information. *British Journal Disorder Comm.* 37:43–54.
Lyons, J.
   1972   Human language. In *Non-verbal communication,* ed. R. A. Hinde, pp. 49–85. Cambridge: Cambridge University Press.
Marshall, J. C.
   1970   The biology of communication in man and animals. In *New horizons in linguistics,* ed. J. Lyons. Harmondsworth: Penguin.
Marx, Karl
   1842   Religion and authority. In *Karl Marx: the essential writings,* ed. Frederic L. Bender. New York: Harper, 1972. (First published 1842 in July number of *Rheinische Zeitung* as "On the leading article in no. 179 of the Kölnische Zeitung: religion, free press, and philosophy.")
   1844   Contribution to the critique of Hegel's philosophy of right: introduction. In *Karl Marx and Friedrich Engels on religion.* New York: Schocken, 1964. (First published 1844.)
McKelway, Alexander
   1964   *The systematic theology of Paul Tillich—a review and analysis.* New York: Delta Book, Dell Publishing Co.
Peirce, Charles
   1960   *Collected papers of Charles Sanders Peirce.* Vol. 2, *Elements of logic,* ed. Charles Hartshorne and Paul Weiss. Cambridge, Mass.: Harvard University Press.
Rappaport, Roy A.
   1968   *Pigs for the ancestors.* New Haven: Yale University Press.
Romer, A. S.
   1954   *Man and the vertebrates.* Baltimore: Penguin. (First published 1933)
de Rougemont, Denis
   1944   *La part du diable.* New York: Brentano's.
Scholem, Gershom
   1969   *On the Kabbalah and its symbolism.* New York: Schocken.
Searle, J. R.
   1969   *Speech acts: an essay in the philosophy of language.* Cambridge: Cambridge University Press.
Skorupski, John
   1976   *Symbol and theory: a philosophical study of theories of religion in social anthropology.* Cambridge: Cambridge University Press.
Slobodkin, L. B.
   1968   Toward a predictive theory of evolution. In R. Lewontin, ed., *Population, biology, and evolution.* Syracuse, N.Y.: Syracuse University Press.

Thorpe, W. M.
  1968   The comparison of vocal communication in animal and man. In *Non-verbal communication*, ed. R. A. Hinde, pp. 27-48. Cambridge: Cambridge University Press.
Tillich, Paul
  1951   *Systematic Theology.* Vol. 1. Chicago: University of Chicago Press.
  1957   *Dynamics of Faith.* New York: Hayner.
Turner, Victor
  1969   *The ritual process.* Chicago: Aldine.
Van Lawick-Goodall, J.
  1971   *In the shadow of man.* London: Collins.
Waddington
  1961   *The ethical animal.* New York: Atheneum.
White, Leslie
  1949   *The science of culture.* New York: Farrar Strauss.

Index

McKay, Bonnie, 53f., 150
McFarlane, W., 35
McKelway, Alexander, 237
Maladaptation, 100, 145–173
  correction of, 169f.
  defined, 160f.
  and evolution, 100, 165–170
  forms of
    cybernetic disorders, 161
    escalation, 162, 167
    hierarchical maldistribution of
      organization, 162
    hypercoherence, 162, 167
    idolatry, 165
    overcentralization, 162
    over-response, 161
    oversegregation, 162, 167
    overspecification, 162
    premature override, 162
    premature response, 161
  and oppression, 241
  structural nature of, 161
  substantive consequences of, 163f., 166f.
Management. *See* Regulation
Mangaia, 14f.
Mangareva, 8, 10, 15, 21
Manioc, 30, 102
Maoris, 9
Margalef, Ramon, 55
Maring, 27–42, 43, 51, 69–73, 75, 90, 101–126, 181–183, 185, 227
Marquesas, 15, 17
Marshall Islands, 2
Marshall, J. C., 225f.
Marshall, J. T., Jr., 8
Marx, Karl, 44f., 79, 168, 235, 241
Materialism
  cultural, 44
  vulgar, 43, 44ff.
Maude, Harry, 5, 7, 8
Mauritius, 11
Meaning, 83–85. *See also*
  Meaningfulness; Understanding
  and Being, 127f., 157, 217
  control of, 133
  costs of, 85
  destruction of, 129
  disordering of, 133, 142
  disparities between meaning and need, 141, 159
  false meanings, 141, 160. *See also* Lie
  hierarchies of, 90, 126ff., 142, 156–160
  and icons, 128
  and indices, 128
  and instrumentality, 85
  and money, 130f., 142, 167
  and natural law, 139–143
  non-discursive, 157
  orders of
    low order, 84, 126f., 156
      dissolution of, 131
      and distinction, 126
      and information, 127
    high order, 84, 127, 129
      demeaning of, 130ff.
      and metaphor, 127
      and similarity, 127
    highest order, 127, 129, 157
      in adaptive structure, 157
      degradation of, 130f.
      and identity, 127
  and power, 132–135
  structure of, 126ff., 142
    and adaptive structure, 142f.
    anomalies in, 165
    and subordination, 135
    and symbols, 128
Meaningfulness, 102, 127f.
  of cognized models, 102, 126–131
  and identity, 127, 157
  and liturgical order, 124, 126
  locus in individuals, 159
  and material processes, 85, 131, 140–143
Meggitt, M. J., 134, 151, 201
Melanesia, 11, 23
Merrill, E., 8
Messer, Ellen, 133
Metaphor, 127
  material, 136f.
  and predication, 136f.
Micronesia, 9
Miller, James, 151
Mind, 237f.
Moala, 10
Models
  analytic, 50f.
  "for" and "of," 139
Money, 130f., 142
  and ecological degradation, 167
  and meaning, 130f., 142, 167
Monod, J., 81